Recent Titles in
Contributions in Drama and Theatre Studies

Radical Stages: Alternative History in Modern British Drama
D. Keith Peacock

A Search for a Postmodern Theater: Interviews with Contemporary Playwrights
John L. DiGaetani

The Age of *Hair*: Evolution and Impact of Broadway's First Rock Musical
Barbara Lee Horn

The Gymnasium of the Imagination: A Collection of Children's Plays in English, 1780-1860
Jonathan Levy

Every Week, A Broadway Revue: The Tamiment Playhouse, 1921-1960
Martha Schmoyer LoMonaco

The Simple Stage: Origins of the Minimalist *Mise-en-Scène* in the American Theater
Arthur Feinsod

Richard's Himself Again: A Stage History of *Richard III*
Scott Colley

Eugene O'Neill in China: An International Centenary Celebration
Haiping Liu and Lowell Swortzell, editors

Toward an Aesthetics of the Puppet: Puppetry as a Theatrical Art
Steve Tillis

George Sand's *Gabriel*
Gay Manifold

Confronting Tennessee Williams's *A Streetcar Named Desire*: Essays in Critical Pluralism
Philip C. Kolin, editor

Challenging the Hierarchy

Collective Theatre in the United States

Mark S. Weinberg

Contributions in Drama and Theatre Studies,
Number 48

GP

Greenwood Press
Westport, Connecticut • London

Library of Congress Cataloging-in-Publication Data

Weinberg, Mark S.
Challenging the hierarchy : collective theatre in the United States / Mark S. Weinberg.
p. cm.—(Contributions in drama and theatre studies, ISSN 0163-3821 ; no. 48)
Includes bibliographical references (p.) and index.
ISBN 0-313-27219-0 (alk. paper)
1. Theater—United States—History—20th century. 2. Collective behavior. 3. Creation (Literary, artistic, etc.) I. Title. II. Series.
PN2266.5.W45 1992
792'.0973'0904—dc20 92-10068

British Library Cataloguing in Publication Data is available.

Library of Congress Catalog Card Number: 92-10068
ISBN: 0-313-27219-0
ISSN: 0163-3821

First published in 1992

Greenwood Press, 88 Post Road West, Westport, CT 06881
An imprint of Greenwood Publishing Group, Inc.

Printed in the United States of America

The paper used in this book complies with the Permanent Paper Standard issued by the National Information Standards Organization (Z39.48-1984).

10 9 8 7 6 5 4 3 2 1

Copyright Acknowledgments

The author and publisher gratefully acknowledge permission to use the following extracts from:

The unpublished manuscripts of *Dakota Roads: The Story of a Prairie Family*, *Dusting Off the Thirties*, and *Welcome Home*; unpublished letters and reports and publicly distributed publicity packets and fliers; and personal interviews is reprinted courtesy of Joe E. Nelson.

Letter to the Actors Equity Association dated August 30, 1979 is reprinted courtesy of D. Scott Glasser.

Split Britches, *Beauty and the Beast*, *Upwardly Mobile Home*, and *Little Women: The Tragedy* created by Split Britches are reprinted courtesy of Deborah Margolin, Peggy Shaw, and Lois Weaver.

The unpublished manuscripts of *Implication*, *A Buck Apiece*, and *Shadows Beyond the Benefit of a Doubt*; unpublished letters and "artistic statements" and publicly distributed publicity packets and fliers; and personal interviews are reprinted courtesy of Bob Feldman, Deborah Langerman, and Jeff Glassman.

"The Living Story." *Theaterwork* 2.2 (January/February 1982): 21; "Popular Theatre and Political Content." *Theaterwork* 1.1 (November/December 1980): 12; "Playmaking with the Dakota Theatre Caravan." *Theaterwork* 2.3 (March/April 1982): 7 & 16; "Some Theoretical Questions of People's Theatre." *Theaterwork* 3.2 (January/February 1983): 9; and "A Progressive Critique of the Theory of Richard Schechner." *Theaterwork* 4.2 (May/June 1981): 16 & 18 are reprinted courtesy of Douglas Paterson.

Stage Left by Jay Williams. Copyright 1974. Reprinted with permission from Macmillan Publishing Company and Harriet Wasserman.

"Technique as a Message." *Theaterwork* 2.4 (May/June 1982): 27 & 28; "Theatre as a Political Tool." *Theaterwork* 1.5 (July/August 1981); 30; "Toward a Hopeless Theatre." *Theaterwork* 3.5 (July/August 1983): 30 & 44 are reprinted courtesy of Deborah Langerman.

Letter to Arnau dated July 3, 1978 is reprinted courtesy of Jeff Glassman.

Letter to the author dated February 26, 1986 is reprinted courtesy of Candice Walworth.

Unpublished interview with Peggy Shaw and Lois Weaver is reprinted courtesy of Rhonda Blair.

Necessary Theatre: Six Plays About the Chicano Experience, edited by Jorge Huerta and *La Victima* by El Teatro de la Esperanza are reprinted courtesy of Arte Publico Press.

The TENAZ Manifesto is reprinted courtesy of Jorge Peña.

Contents

Preface

In 1963, Julian Beck, a founding member of the collectively organized Living Theatre, asked, "How can we make a theatre worthy of its spectators?" As I examined my own answers to that question, I began to realize that there were, for me, two more important issues: How can we make a theatre worthy of those who do *not* yet come to see our work, and how can we make theatre worthy of theatre makers themselves?

The questions continued to disturb me, even after my education as a director had, I believed, taught me how to develop a performance text and critics in newspapers told me that my productions did have worth. There was something missing; fruitful sharing of creative energy was often lacking in the student, community, and even professional groups with which I worked. The only times I consistently felt the communal vision that I sought to instill in casts and production teams was during meetings of the collective that managed the food cooperative in my neighborhood.

A fortuitous encounter with the Provisional Theatre of Los Angeles; later experiments with a group of adventurous students at Marycrest College in Davenport, Iowa; and finally, a three-year stint as a member of the Other Theatre Company in Madison, Wisconsin, led me to believe that the collective process could generate the polyvocal and supportive center I desired, could provide the "how's" I sought, and could produce fine theatre as well.

While I do not feel that any one mode of theatrical production can provide completely adequate answers for everyone, I do feel that there is much to be said for and about collective creation that has not been said. I hope that by examining collectives, elaborating an ideological and theoretical basis for collectivization, and documenting the strengths and weaknesses of methods already tried, this book can point a way for theatre makers seeking change, provide a sense of place for newly formed collectives, and assist former members of those theatres no longer in existence to retain a sense of their legacy.

I came to the research for this book, then, partially as an advocate, partially as an investigator, partially as an advisor, and partially as a participant. I think the collective approach provides support for the creative artist that rarely exists in any other environment and provides a model structure for the revitalization of accessible and representative theatre for the majority of peoples and their cultures in the United States. Aware of these biases, and of my political views, I have attempted to remain balanced in my assessment of the work of collective theatres as a whole, and of the four companies I examined specifically: El Teatro de la Esperanza, the Dakota Theatre Caravan, the United Mime Workers, and Split Britches; on the whole, however, the book is, unashamedly, an endorsement of their processes and their productions.

Each of the members of these companies went to great effort to assist me in the research necessary to produce this study. They gave me unrestricted access to their archives; opened their rehearsals, meetings, and even homes to me; and devoted many hours to interviews and explanations. They asked in return only honesty in my assessments of their work, maintaining the positive and creative attitudes that are the mainstays of their organizations. Without their cooperation, this book could not have been written. I thank them.

I wish to thank also the University of Minnesota Graduate School, the McMillan Foundation, and the University of Wisconsin Centers for grants that enabled me to complete my research and the many friends and colleagues with whom I debated issues and from whom I received both formal and informal advice, including Rhonda Blair, Assunta Kent, Bruce McConachie, Barry Opper, Phillip Zarrilli, and the past members of the Other Theatre Company.

Finally, I want to thank my family for their love, support, patience, and prodding. Many of their sacrifices inform the pages of this work.

Challenging the Hierarchy

Introduction

> Theatre is the place where the life of a society is shown in public to that society, where that society's assumptions are tested, its values are scrutinized, its myths are validated and its traumas become emblems of its reality. Theatre is not about the reaction of *one sensibility* to events external to itself, as poetry tends to be; or the *private* consumption of fantasy or a mediated slice of social reality, as most novels tend to be. It is a public event, and it is about matters of public concern....It is a place of recognition, of evaluation, of judgement. It shows the interaction of human beings and social forces. How could it remove itself from the other acts of recognition, evaluation, and judgement known as politics?
>
> John McGrath, *A Good Night Out* (83)

In every age, changes in society have led to an awakening of the theatre. One need only to look at the movement from feudalism to capitalism and the parallel change in the theatre, a change that culminated in the rise of realistic domestic tragedy as the representative form of the new social order, to see this in relatively modern times. Most recently, there has been a great deal of activity on the political left that has focused on what many see as the exploitative nature of current social and economic policy. There has been expressed in a variety of ways a desire to return control of society to those who have suffered most from cultural and economic hegemony—to "the people." There has been a parallel rise in people's art and, most prominently, in people's theatre.

This current movement, however, has been responsible for greater modification to the *organization of the theatre-making unit* than ever before. Prior to this, changes in the theatre as workplace have been centered around a dominant figure. The progression has been from the supremacy of the actor to that of the playwright to that of the director. The current change does not merely place a new individual at the top of the hierarchy; it attempts to dismantle this traditional structure completely and replace it with a democratic and nonhierarchical organization—with a *collective.*

Contemporary collectives, born out of the turmoil in the arts and in the streets in the sixties, have remained antiestablishment in almost every way. They have used a process that denies many assumptions of commercial, regional, and even so-called alternative theatres to create productions that challenge many assumptions about the society those theatres represent. They have sought new audiences to whom to tell new stories in new ways, and their success merits documentation.

This study will provide a general theory of the process of collective creation and explore its application and results in the theatre. The first chapter defines collective structure and examines collective process, bringing to bear the methods of small group analysis in the development of a theory of collective theatre making. Chapter 2 briefly traces the history of collectives, indicating the place of collective and people's theatre in the continuum of cultural tradition in the United States. With this as a basis, detailed case studies of four theatres—El Teatro de la Esperanza, the Dakota Theatre Caravan, the United Mime Workers, and Split Britches—will be presented to illustrate some of the ways in which the process has manifested itself in various companies and to provide detailed descriptions of exemplary methods and their results. Concern will be given to the political nature of the organization of collective theatre companies and of their processes, to the art and politics of their plays, and to the relationship of process to production.

El Teatro de la Esperanza, the most long-lived of the companies, concentrates on issues of concern to Chicano communities. It has used its carefully structured collective process to produce documentary drama, melodrama, adaptations, collaborations, children's theatre, and music shows. The theatre continued to operate collectively for over two decades, even though all the founding members had left the company. The Dakota Theatre Caravan (which is no longer functioning) created its productions during residencies in small towns in South Dakota, touring that state (and then others) with its affirmations of the culture of rural America and gently nudging its audiences toward political awareness.

The United Mime Workers began as a traditional mime troupe but, working in an idiosyncratic style, challenged their audiences by presenting alternatives to the systems that defined the work-a-day world, composing new possibilities and surprising realities. Split Britches concentrates on the elaboration of images on stage, presenting layers of development in performances that combine narrative, vaudeville, and personal history. Often focussing on feminist or lesbio-centered issues, the company is challenging the very basis of traditional American theatre through startling and hilarious performances.

Differing greatly in style, focus, and specifics of methodology, these companies represent a variety of approaches to collective theatre making. The final chapter points to similarities in the processes described above and notes the strengths and weaknesses of collectivization. The recent history of collective theatres is outlined to form the basis for an analysis of the current situation, while some speculation on the theoretical and practical values of recent trends in collective creation for the theatre and society of the future bring to a close this examination of one method of challenging the hierarchy and the ideology it represents.

1

The Collective Process

> To supply a productive apparatus without—to the utmost extent possible—changing it would still be a highly censurable course, even if the material with which it is supplied seemed to be of a revolutionary nature....Only by transcending the specialization in the process of production that, in the bourgeois view, constitutes its order, can one make this production politically useful; and the barriers imposed by specialization must be breached jointly by the productive forces that they were set up to divide.
>
> Walter Benjamin, *The Author as Producer*

Often throughout the twentieth century, modes of presentation venturing beyond the restrictions imposed by commercial considerations were developed by particularly forward-thinking directors. Their experiments with the art form were, and still are, valid and viable explorations. In some periods (e.g., the thirties and again in the sixties), however, many theatre companies began to search for less esoteric forms than the ones experimental theatres were creating and to form bonds *with*, even while they shocked, their audiences. These groups were organized along a variety of lines, each of which was designed to increase the contribution of everyone involved, of every worker in the workplace of the theatre. The structure that has come to be most representative of the ultimate goals of the people's theatre, and that has produced some of its most exciting work, is *collective creation*—the creation of a production by a group that shares power and responsibility as fully as possible.

The generation of the sixties led this movement as part of its theatricalization of political life and its use of theatre as a weapon in its political struggles. The work continues today in numerous collectives, producing theatre for a variety of audiences who do not normally attend mainstream theatre because they find it irrelevant, inaccessible, and unaffordable. These theatres are generating performances out of the needs and desires of their communities and their members, and yet are often to be found on the cutting edge of both political and theatrical movements.

Little study has been done in this area, although there are two disciplines in which appropriate investigation might be undertaken. The literature of the theatre almost ignores people's and collective theatres. The groups themselves are too busy and too poor to devote time or effort to the task. *Theatre in America*, a report for the national theatre conference done in the political heyday of 1968, did not even mention political theatres, let alone collectives (Gard, Balch, & Temkin). Theodore Shank's more recent *American Alternative Theater* did devote a chapter to "Theatre of Social Change," but is basically descriptive, so it makes only brief mention of organizational patterns.

Sociologists, in the literature of small group analysis, avoid, as well, the question of collectivization and never mention cultural work of any sort as a group task. The assumption of most scholars is still that art is the province of the creative individual genius in spite of the fact that the history of noncommercial theatre in the United States since the sixties is more accurately the history of groups than of individuals.

THE STUDY OF COLLECTIVES

One of the greatest difficulties in studying the collective process is that very few groups, even those that call themselves collective, have bothered to define the word, and those that have have defined it almost exclusively in political terms. The reason for this is that the decision to operate as a collective, especially for people's theatres, is almost always in response to perceived inequities in society or in the workplace, and is therefore political. For these groups collective organization is the means to duplicate in work the egalitarian democracy that they seek in society. The political nature of collective organization is their primary concern.

In addition, each group seems, on the surface, to be organized in a unique manner. It is possible, though, to define the collective process from the standpoint of small group analysis as being more than idiosyncratic. Experts in the field, however, have not made this attempt because, it seems to me, there is an underlying assumption that collectively organized *task* groups cannot function. Why has such a conclusion been reached, and why has it been accepted not only by business, but by the arts and their funding sources as well?

First of all, many scholars in our society operate under the misconception that the range of possibilities for organization can be adequately defined in terms provided by psychology, particularly Sigmund Freud and the behaviorists, or by capitalist economics. This accounts for the ascendancy in the recent past of the Exchange Theory of small group dynamics, which defines interaction between individuals in small groups in terms of profit and loss, but rarely considers the holistic nature of the group as system. It is this set of essentially political assumptions against which collective organization is a revolt in the first place.

Misinformation is also the result of the ambiance in which the collective movement grew during the sixties. There was confusion between the communal and the collective at this time, as well as many attempts to establish groups with nebulous goals and with organizations that were described in terms of *familial* rather than *functional* reference. The concern of many individuals at the time was to replace repressive hierarchies with free-flowing, patternless, *primary* groups, whose significance was more emotional than purposeful. Theatre collectives, as well as those that run a wide variety of business and service organizations, are seen by their members as *task* groups, characterized by clarity of definition and specificity of purpose.

The mystique of the protective family, however, still remains in the minds of analysts, critics, and even some members of the collectives themselves. El Teatro Campesino, which was originally a collectively organized and highly influential Chicano theatre company, survived its early years because it was "a tight group. Because it function[ed] as a family, the frustrations [were] frequently offset by the genuine feelings the members [had] for one another and the strong sense of purpose they all share[d]" (B. Diamond 57). In a study of the working methods of several people's theatres, Robert Jenkins noted that "because these groups perceive of themselves as families, an individual's departure can be traumatic and acquiring a replacement is extraordinarily difficult" (330).

This last observation not only helps to account for the failure of many collectives to survive the departure of their founding members, but also points to another reason why the structural patterns of collectivism have not been studied. The social order and structures that develop in any group are relatively static and prescriptive, but the informal patterns and processes of interaction often mitigate between the defined working mode and the actual creative activity. There is no need for analysts to search for new patterns if they assume a familial structure, and therefore, concentration has been on peculiarities of familial process and not on regularized patterns. This focus is reinforced by the anti-establishment stance of most collectives—a stance that makes each of them seem to be an entity that is detached from the influence of outside or traditional patterns of operation and knowable only as a unique venture.

Finally, collective theatres, in particular, have until recently, not had the opportunity to study themselves because of their relative isolation and their financial needs, both of which force groups to spend nearly all their time mounting productions or seeking funds to maintain their existence. From 1982 through 1985, however, *Theaterwork Magazine* ran a series on group creative processes in which several theatre groups described their working methods. In addition, there has been a growing body of theoretical writing on the revitalization of people's theatre in the past decade: writing that includes discussions of organization and creative approach. New ventures such as the Theater, Performance and Social Change program at the New College of California, as well as the inclusion of a Theatre and Social Change focus group in the Association for Theatre in Higher Education (ATHE), indicate continuing interest.

ANALYSIS OF SMALL GROUP PROCESS

How, then, can one define the structure of groups that are specifically organized to *prevent* the formation of static and often repressive, but easily describable, hierarchies? Is it possible to create a theory of interaction on which such a description can be based? Can the processes of collective creation be discussed in terms of conformance to or deviation from a general pattern; or is each collective the result of a unique combination of individual personalities who cannot establish a methodology that can be communicated and perpetuated? That is, are collectives merely the province of youthful exuberants who outgrow their "idealistic misconceptions," or do they provide a model for future work? In spite of what seems to be the desire of the theatrical and political establishment to believe the former hypothesis, a number of groups are proving the latter to be the case.

In order to define and examine the recognizable patterns in collective creation, though, it is necessary to review the assumptions of those who analyze small groups, develop a vocabulary for describing collective dynamics, and create a model by which to compare hierarchical and collective operations.

The Collective Dynamic

The theoretical orientations of those who study small group dynamics can be classed in two very broad categories: those who concentrate on the group as system and those who concentrate on the individual dealings between members of the group (Ridgeway).[1] The latter view focuses on the Exchange Theory, which assumes that individuals are motivated to maximize personal profits (i.e., to maximize rewards and minimize costs by seeking rewarding experiences and avoiding painful ones). It seems to me that this combination of capitalist economics and behaviorist psychology, while accurate in describing certain types of interaction, is reductionist, concentrating on the individual's needs without any consideration for the life of the group and the effects of its system on the actions and attitudes of group members.

On the other hand, the theorists who study small groups as holistic entities or social systems, while varying greatly in specific approach, agree that the key to understanding groups is to focus on the functioning networks, the interdependencies, and the dynamics that allow a group to function both socially and productively. While the tendency of this theory is to reify social systems and ignore personality influences, it is clear that this is the approach that must be taken if we wish to acknowledge the fact that collectives can and do exist and achieve substantial accomplishments.

Both groups of theorists agree that there are certain patterns and structures that all groups exhibit. In no case, however, does either faction talk about a small group developing the communicative and problem-solving potential that I will call the *center* and that seems to be the key to understanding the operation of collectives.

If we begin with a very general definition of a collective as a "worker--managed, worker-controlled project which attempts to function non-hierarchically and tries to make group decisions by consensus" (Boston Vocations for Social Change 3), we can immediately see the danger of "ultrademocracy [which is] as much a poison as tyranny within a group" (Opper, "Provisional"). Obviously, some structure must be developed to ensure that the group can focus attention more often than not on its chosen task.

This is true for any task group. The difference is that collectives maintain a different sense of social order: "a more or less common conception of identity and purpose and a shared set of expectations and evaluations that the group members hold for each other. The system of common beliefs is called the social order of the group...[and] is analogous in many ways to the concept of culture in society" (Crosbie, "Introduction" 6-7). The beliefs include: *values*, assumptions ranking individual behaviors in terms of importance to the group; *norms*, "rules" specifying a range of acceptable behaviors; and *roles*, expectations for actions in different positions in the group structure. These beliefs are based on the group's perceptions of the external society and its own place within it. The social order is the foundation for the behavior of group members and, while it precedes the formation of group structure, it is often difficult to define.[2]

The Collective Structure

It is obvious that the culture of any society elicits certain types of behavior and exerts pressure toward a limited range of structural patterns. In the United States today, the expectation is that every group will develop a recognizable hierarchy, "a pattern of power and deference relations among the members [of a group that is] characterized by a series of ranks occupied by members who share different degrees of power and prestige" (Ridgeway 202). This hierarchy will, in turn, support a range of dominant and submissive behaviors with a variety of positional rights that include decision making and distribution of rewards. The major difference between collectives and other groups is not that collectives do not recognize certain hierarchical structures, but that they are organized to avoid them whenever possible and use them only to support the goals of equalization of influence and ability. The key is that certain structures restrict, while collective organization is intended to maximize, access to power. The culture of the collective thereby reflects the sought-after pattern in the broader society.

The structure of any group that is most apparent to an outsider is the *leadership structure*: the distribution of decision-making rights and compliance obligations (Marak 174). The assumption of leadership by one or more individuals results in a certain normative expectation: that a particular member will make decisions in certain areas and every other member (follower) will comply with that decision regardless of the alternatives he or she might have chosen if given the opportunity. While this does not necessarily restrict the input of other members as advisors, it does regulate the use of power. As is obvious, leadership structure in a collective (or what frequently appears to be a lack of leadership) is based on a far more democratic conception of the workings of society than that of traditionally structured task groups.

There are other structures besides leadership that analysts examine while studying small group interaction. The first, the *sociometric structure*, describes the pattern of emotional relations between individual members in a group. While there is no difference between the ways in which personal relationships develop in or out of collectives, more channels are open in collectives due to the similarity of attitudes among the members and the diminution of status or class importance.

However, since so many emotional contacts can be made in a collective structure, the group's cohesiveness is more vulnerable to disruptions due to interpersonal situations. For this reason, most collectives are far more sensitive to sociometric interactions than are other task groups, and many have established specific structures for handling emotional difficulties.

Status structure, the patterning of prestige relations in a group, can also be examined, and it is considered most significant by some theorists. The causes of status stratification include external characteristics (education, sex, age, titles, etc.), first impressions, and early performance. Higher-status members are given greater opportunity to act in most groups and are more often deferred to by lower-status members. In addition, the majority of communication in stratified groups is either vertical, from lower to higher, or between members of the highest status plateau (Hare).

Collectives attempt to avoid this stratification in several ways, including elaborate processes for admittance to the group and a conscious deemphasis of external characteristics such as sex, age, and race. Collectives also try to reduce the mystified elitism of "professional specialization" by creating structures that allow for, and in fact demand, the expression of individual ability and training.

This does not mean that collectives deny skill.

"Skills are a concrete reality. To deny this reality is to oppress both the person with skills and everyone else...But to rush into glorifying expertise is to invite disaster. The fact is that our experiences have given each of us valuable skills. Our goal in collectives is to demystify these skills by learning them from each other" (Boston Vocations for Social Change 28). In this way, collectives work to avoid both mediocrity and status stratification.

The last structure that must be considered is the *communication structure*, which is, to me, the most significant and the most useful for clarifying collective organization. The nature of small group communications has been studied in a number of ways. Not only has the direction of communications vis-à-vis status been given scrutiny, but so has the content between status levels.[3] Researchers have noted that those in lower status positions are removed from full participation and that their insights are rarely given a full testing—a weakness avoided by collectives.

The most important research has been conducted on patterns of communication. In a seminal experiment, A. Bavelas tested a number of communication patterns to determine their effect on problem-solving effectiveness. As expected, it was found that the primary source of difference in problem-solving speed was degree of centrality, which, for the most central member (who rapidly became acknowledged as the leader), is a measurement of the availability of direct access to all necessary information. The more centralized the communication network, the quicker and more accurate was the problem solving.

There were, however, a number of negative aspects to centrality. Peripheral members became increasingly dissatisfied with the limits placed on their participation and their degree of dependence on the leader. Most importantly, follow-up experiments revealed that "centrality is *negatively* related to problem-solving efficiency when the group is confronted with complex problems."[4] In addition, a centralized pattern caused a great loss of productive potential because "both occurrence and utilization of insight will be found to drop rapidly as centrality is more and more highly localized" (Bavelas 511). In other words, centrality adversely affects creativity and represses individual contribution: a charge, ironically, that has been leveled by outsiders at collective patterning. Yet it is the assumption in almost all arenas that group communication must be the sum of the communications between individuals who are so organized.

In a collective, task-specific messages between individuals are supplementary to communication with the whole or with what I have called the *center*, which is at once a repository of ideas, information, images, and responses, and a source of new combinations and perceptions. It is the metaphorical locus of action and reaction, the developing group response free of reference to or ownership by individual contributors of any one part. Through it, each member has the potential for equal access to all information and, because leadership and status structures are deemphasized, equal power to use his or her individual strengths on that information in the development of solutions to creative problems. In other words, unless there are particular disruptions, the communication structure in a collective not only opens all individual channels, but also creates *a new means of group interaction and a new source for ideas.*

This is very different than brainstorming, which is an artificial process used by committees to generate a less restricted flow of ideas. Brainstorming often results in such a chaotic exchange that, in the sorting-out process, one or more individuals usually emerges as a leader. After this happens, a pattern rapidly stabilizes and the number of open channels decreases.

In a collective, however, open-channel communication remains possible because communication with the center supports it. Every member thereby retains equal access to the whole (i.e., every member is "central," has a maximum of flexibility, and is independent to use the information to create solutions. In addition, the mix of ideas in the central pool begins to generate new ideas "from the center of the group."[5]

The concept of the center is at the core of the collective process. It is a natural part of the ebb and flow of interaction: an interaction that is allowed because the barriers to it are removed by the openness and by the political consciousness of the collective organization. It accounts for the apparently paradoxical statements by the members of a number of collectives that they feel more independent and more powerful in a structure that demands a very high level of cooperation if it is to succeed.

The basic structure of a collectively organized small group may be described, then, as a system in which as many barriers as possible to total participation by all members are removed. In the "model" collective, since rewards are distributed equally or by need, there is no pressure to modify the system to create equity. Since status level within the group is minimized, there is no pressure to modify the system to open interaction between levels. Since ability is respected, shared, and given full play, there is no need for an individual to hoard information to gain power. Finally, since communication is open, everyone has equal access to information and, ultimately, to power.

This is not to say that collectives are trouble-free. In the final chapter I will examine a number of problems that have caused the dissolution of companies and that prevent any group from conforming absolutely to the paradigmatic description of collective process described in the next section.

THE COLLECTIVE PROCESS

Because there is no need to establish a great number of normative restrictions to maintain a stratified structure, there is time for each group to concentrate on process, on the dynamics of interaction and creative problem solving.[6] It is for this reason that collectives form unusual working methods that allow them to make the maximum use of their open structures and of the abilities of each member to discover unique and progressive responses to a wide variety of tasks and pressures. It is, in addition, this dynamic that often leads to the development of new modes of representation that reflect the collective apparatus in the performance event.

It seems, however, as if a group that fosters such independence will fly apart at the seams unless it creates a structure for decision making—and yet, it is often such a structure that mitigates against individuality and the expression of minority viewpoints. The traditional views of hierarchical efficiency or professional competence steer some groups to defer to either the leader or the expert. Other groups (and some collectives use this approach) rely more on *participatory democracy*, allowing all people who will share in the results of the decision to have access to the process. In these cases, the final authority is the majority, which then either relies on all group members to conform, threatens sanctions for deviation, or gives power to a leader to make certain that the functions necessary for fulfilling the decision are carried out. A difficulty in this process is that if a majority becomes apparent early, the minority will have a tendency to withhold its objections. In addition, there is no room in such a process for someone to step outside of the decision to demand change.

A method of decision making frequently used by collectives to avoid the problems mentioned above is consensus: decisions are made only when agreement is unanimous, and the strenuous objections of even a single member are sufficient to demand the reevaluation of any decision. This requires that every member of the group express her or his doubts and objections and encourages full participation by ensuring that everyone will be heard. Consensus does not rule out compromise, nor does it make decision making impossible, although it frequently makes it more difficult. What it does do is focus concern away from individual or subgroup gain to the needs of the whole. The goal of this process is to find solutions that are not only acceptable to everyone, but also best for the individuals, the group, and the product or production.

There are several positive side effects of a reliance on this consensus. For one, because every member of the group has agreed to a certain action, every member can usually be relied on to put his or her full energy into its completion. Second, each member of the group is made personally responsible for the decision, so it is likely that each will have given careful consideration to the problem before agreeing to a solution. This promotes more careful analysis, making each group member more critical and thereby decreasing the phenomenon called *groupthink*—the tendency to concur with an idea and to defend it from the basis of group coherence and a sense of self-importance rather than a critical perspective.

Another consideration, but one that affects production style and can have its own drawbacks in terms of performance possibilities, is that consensus is usually possible only in relatively small groups. However, because finances are such a problem for people's theatres, it would be impossible for a large theatre group to support itself in any case. In addition, small groups can be more intimate and can provide a more immediately accessible support system for its members.

These factors contribute to the third effect, the *decrease* of self-serving behavior in decision making. This may seem paradoxical when one considers that each individual is given such a great amount of power, but the structure does encourage each person to consider his or her actions in relation to the group. This can easily be explained if one considers that the consensus making process maximizes the sense of individual importance and empowerment and thereby minimizes the need for selfish behavior as a means of gaining or maintaining self-respect. It asserts the supportive bond of the individual with the community of decision makers.

Such a process also returns control of the means of decision making—the means of the process of artistic production—to the workers who develop the performance piece. This radical transformation of the techniques of artistic production reflects, in the change of social relations between the theatre makers, a hoped for change in society or, at a minimum, a new relation between artist-as-maker and audience. In Walter Benjamin's terms, the collective process promotes the recognition of "artist as producer," thereby overcoming "the contradiction which limits artistic forces potentially available to everyone to the private property of a few" (Eagleton 61-62). Not only does such a view invite experimentation with a variety of forms that embody both the ideology and process of a group, but it also keeps those forms "open" to audiences. Most collectives, in recognition that their productions should not be "symmetrically complete...but like any product should be completed only in the act of being used" (Eagleton 70), include a variety of methods for making pre- and postperformance contact with their audiences.

In this way, the goals and processes of collective decision making reflect one concept of *popular*, a watchword of almost all people's and collective theatres. *Popular* is used by politically oriented theatres to mean promoting the people's interests regardless of what may be the theatre's limited appeal at the moment, as opposed to the definition of the word based on audience size. *Popular culture*, by this definition, integrates and incorporates a variety of specific cultures, simultaneously preserving and liberating the people attached to such a plurality of ideas. The result is neither "melting pot" nor conservative support for the hegemony of the dominant ideology, but rather a confederation of differences. The collective provides the paradigm for this process, and it is a political awareness of this paradigm that usually accounts for a group's decision to organize collectively.

However, there are processes that can disrupt even the most cohesive and politically savvy group, the most devastating (and widespread) of which is the attempt to wield personal power. Collectives are particularly susceptible to power struggles when they do not have a working method that allows for the fullest utilization of each individual's talent or resources. In these cases, individuals acting from the best of motives—the betterment of the product or, in theatre groups, of the production—feel that they must bully their way into control in order to use their particular expertise. One way that such struggles are avoided is the inclusion of an ongoing training process as a part of the collective procedure. Those with a special skills teach other members of the group to perform tasks, and then temporary leadership roles necessitated by the nature of the task can be rotated.

Another method is to collectivize certain aspects of the group's work and to divide the labor according to ability or desire the rest of the time. Responsibility is not delegated to individuals, however, until there is a clear vision of the product or process in the group consciousness. At that point, it can be safely assumed that every member of the company can actualize the vision from the center in her or his own area, medium, or moment. Once it is possible for the group to confidently defer to the judgment of members with particular skills for decisions on *how* to get a job done (e.g., publicity, staging a scene, spending money), then the group can return to the task of creative problem solving. All the groups studied in detail in the following chapters used a variation of this method.

In one sense, then, collective productivity is increased by giving control not to leaders, but to the task itself. The need for vertical and repressive hierarchies is reduced as the logic of the solution to the problem makes itself clearer. This clarity is most easily developed through the communication pattern that collective organization allows. This is particularly true in the theatre (an art collaborative at its core), where the task of play creation and production requires the coordination of a great number of artistic and technical decisions. It is even more important for theatres whose concern is social action because of their needs to balance specific political or social theories, community or constituency needs, and educational or action goals, with production values.

> Open, decentralized communication is best if the group task is ambiguous, technically complex, or requires innovation. It seems likely that socially complex tasks as well would require free-flowing discussion. To achieve open communication, the size of the status differences among the members of the group would have to be relatively small. Groups faced with a technically or socially complex task, then, would do better if they organized themselves democratically with a relatively flat status hierarchy (Ridgeway 295).

This describes the essence of collective organization—and there are few tasks more complex than the creation and performance of a play. A collective, then, is far more than an anarchic conglomeration of voices that dismisses the value and relevance of knowledge, skill, and training. It is far more than a committee, which replicates the hierarchical structure of the organization of which it is a part and has a particular charge that it must meet without being able to organize in a manner particular to the task or the members. It is far more than a support group for an individual, paternalistic genius who molds contributed pieces into his or her creative vision. It is intimate and supportive like a family, but committed far more to its task and to the broad social implications of its actions and organization than to the egos of its members.

This is not to say that collectives do not provide a supportive and protective atmosphere in which people can explore ideas and ideals, take great risks, and be vulnerable in the service of discovery. The principles of collective organization: nonexploitative structures, nonrestrictive norms, pluralistic leadership, equal access to information and power, equal respect and rewards, equal responsibility, and democratic decision making (i.e., the principles of *worker control*) lead to a process by which each group can create a particular working methodology that is likely to be responsive to the needs of its members and of the task and that maximizes both freedom and responsibility. Collective organization is, in these terms, an extension of the principles of creative problem solving and group interaction described by theorists, and yet it is "revolutionary" in its recognition of the relationship of techniques of performance creation to form and content and audience response, as well as in its desire to find ways of creating theatre experiences for its members and its audiences that will help liberate their theatre from the restrictive ideology of dominant (capitalist) modes of production and representation. It confronts the issue of ownership of means of production and of product and resolves the dilemma of the need for efficiency and stability, which is provided by centralization in opposition to the needs of the members of the group to feel involved in decision making, by creating a *center* of which everyone is a part.

It is, in many ways, difficult to describe what it feels like to participate in a collective because of this apparent contradiction. In artistic terms, the process, regardless of the specific methodology of a particular group, is improvisational: ideas are more freely expressed and responses more immediate than in limited communication networks; each person is the voice of the group at the moment when she or he is speaking, and each idea is the province of the center as soon as it is expressed. The sense is one of ensemble, of creative unit, and of freedom and expansion. Ed Bereal, a popular graphics artist and founder of Bodacious Buggerrilla, a guerilla theatre in the sixties, described the experience in terms organic and particularly "sixtyish:"

> A creative thing with one cat is one thing; a creative thing with 12 people being very creative and coming off each other is another, man. The one cat, like me a member of a group, can do heavier shit if I've got a group to run my shit on and then come back and write it down or whatever than if I'm out there cuttin' off my ear on the top of a hill someplace tryin' to say, you know, whatever it is you say on top of a hill after you cut off your ear....It's just as if each member of the group--say you're talking about 10 people, somebody just got 18 more arms, 18 more legs, 9 more heads (Weisman 72).

Others, like Julian Beck of the Living Theatre, have described this form of association as a "new tribalism" (53). Joan Holden of the San Francisco Mime Troupe compared collective work to a jazz band "that gives everybody something to wail on" (33), while Ivan Steiner, an exchange theorist, said that "the group is an active enterprise in which members reciprocally shape one another's action. Collective process transforms an assortment of people into a social system" (165).

TOWARD A THEORY OF COLLECTIVE THEATRE MAKING

It is, in fact, this concern with social systems that has provided much of the impetus for the formation of collectives in and out of theatre. In theatre there began in the sixties to be a growing dissatisfaction with the traditional domination of either the director or of commercial interests, as theatre makers began to see themselves as part of the larger society and of its political difficulties. Certainly not all politically concerned or otherwise alternative theatre was collectively created. "Awareness of the political character of the theatre does not always influence the process of theatrical production. The fact that the production will inevitably make political statements, and therefore perform political functions, is often ignored in the process of creating a work" (Vincenti 3). What is often considered the golden age of political theatre in the U.S., the 1930s and 1940s, rarely developed collectively organized theatre companies. Some of the most influential contemporary political theatres (e.g., John O'Neal's Free Southern Theatre and the current San Francisco Mime Troupe) do not function as collectives, but do produce high quality, socially responsible theatre work.

What began to happen in the sixties, however, is that theatre moved out of traditional performance spaces to reach nontheatre-going audiences: in other words, to reach "the people." As this alternative to relatively elitist theatre developed an alignment with the more general populace, and as it became concerned with developing an art that reflected the needs and concerns of its new audience, alternative companies created their own pressure to become exemplary, to live the lives they advocated and to adopt the changes they considered progressive. In other words, for many theatre people, the separation between their art and their politics was erased. This is not to say that they were no longer concerned with high quality art ("Bad art is bad politics" is almost axiomatic), but rather that theatre makers recognized themselves as cultural workers and the theatre as a workplace.

As one would expect, turning away from traditional associations led to radical changes in working methods and in product. As the number and variety of theatre groups responding to these changes increased, and as people's theatres began to create theatre for an ever-broader audience (audiences, really), a number of theories began to arise out of their developing practices, each of which had to provide answers to questions in three areas: *social and political analysis*; *decision making and control*; and the *actual theatre making process*.[7]

Questions of Social and Political Analysis

I must begin this exploration with the following caveats: Not all people's theatres are collectives; not all collectives are people's theatres; and not all people's theatres label themselves political. If we define people's theatre as theatre that: is aligned with audiences not normally attending the theatre (98% of all people); is involved in creating a bond with a specific community as defined by geography, occupation, class, sex, sexual preference, ethnicity, age, or race; and is devoted to performing plays that come out of the lives and concerns of that community, we see that there must be a political (or, at least, socially conscious) orientation to the work. We may call it theatre of social change, of progressive ideology, or even of the left (although this leads too frequently to red-baiting as a way of dismissing the work of any group that does not align itself with the dominant class), but whatever label we use, it is essential to remember that people's theatre attempts to make positive contact with an audience and to celebrate that audience's culture without denigrating it in any way. This is not to say that people's theatres are not critical; they realize that their audiences must be held at least partially accountable for their own oppression and need new perceptions that are liberating. It is to say, however, that people's theatres recognize the value of democratic pluralism and *communitas* (implying both community and communal identification), and promote empowerment through the revitalization of people's culture.

From this definition, we can see why it is only logical that many people's theatres would choose to organize themselves along lines that recognize the value of each individual, of her or his experience, and of her or his cultural heritage, while avoiding the supremacy of the individual over the group and its needs. The process of collective creation has as one of its premises respect for each member of the company, in the same way that people's theatre has as one of its premises respect for its audience.

In addition, the collective process is seen by many as a model along the lines of which capitalist, Christian, patriarchal, and white American society should be reorganized. Collective organization is a radical departure from the so-called norms of society—and many people feel that only a radical departure can have any real impact. The usual liberal attitude toward social ills is to define problems in terms of conformance to the declared goals of society in society's own terms. That is to say, there is really no questioning of the concepts on which the status quo is based. The real concern is

> exploring and improving the existing social conditions within the framework of the existing societal institutions....If the given form of society is and remains the ultimate frame of reference for theory and

> practice, there is nothing wrong with this sort of sociology and psychology....[However,] the rationality of this kind of social science appears in a different light if the given society, while remaining the frame of reference, becomes the object of a critical theory which aims at the very structure of this society, present in all particular facts and conditions and determining their place and their functions. Then their ideological and political character becomes apparent, and the elaboration of adequately cognitive concepts demands going beyond the fallacious concreteness of positivist empiricism (Marcuse, *One-Dimensional Man* 107).

In other words, the exploration of particulars within a context makes that context seem inevitable or makes contradictions within that context seem unavoidable. The political nature of people's theatres demands that the lives of their audiences be examined outside the structure so that the oppressiveness and inadequacies of the current social system can be explored *with the understanding that the system can be changed.* This concept is, in many ways, what Bertolt Brecht meant by *alienation*, or making the familiar strange. It is not surprising that most theatre collectives list the work of Brecht as a primary influence.

Collectivization provides a new context for explorations, a change in the structure of work that provides one focal point for a change in the structure of society. Similarly, this new context provides a means by which theatre makers can change their audience and their relation to it. Since mainstream theatre has such a small and elite audience, it is only logical that it usually represents the interests of that audience in forms that are acceptable to its members. If the theatre is to represent and appeal to a new audience, it must change its political orientation and find artistically viable popular forms (popular in terms of the culture that is from the general populace). This requires a new creative methodology that tends, by its very structure, to move away from serving the top of the power ladder.

It is necessary at this point to dispel two notions commonly accepted by those who are currently involved in establishment theatre. The first notion is that the only theatre that can be considered political is theatre that is self-consciously so (i.e., that is specifically programmatic and didactic). In 1975, Michael Kirby, in a special issue of *The Drama Review* asserted this belief in the hope that experimental theatre would be released from the pressure of the type of political criticism that judges a work of theatre solely by its political message or line. In the process, he defined didactic and pedantic theatre (theatre that usually does not make much of an impact) as political and excluded all other theatre work from that rubric (129–35). Instead, it is more accurate to understand the political and rhetorical nature of all culture and to realize that political stance is a valid, though partial, criteria for judging the quality and efficacity of any art form. It is helpful to remember that the instrumental music of dissident Mikos Theodorakis was banned by the right-wing government of Greece, in spite of the fact that notes on a staff do not have any programmatic thrust.

A second notion, and one that is far more self-serving and insidious, is that a greater percentage of the population would come to the theatre if it could be educated in the "perceptual strategies" that are already the province of "seasoned playgoers" (Davis 12–13). The assumption behind this idea is that the artist in the theatre is the culture maker and the people are the recipients of that culture. This is exactly the opposite of people's theatre, in which it is assumed that the theatre maker is a worker whose job it is to use his or her skill to create expressions in a particular medium of the audience's culture, while making the audience aware of the forces that shaped that culture. What is the basis for assuming that the audience does not know enough to enjoy the theatre? Is it not possible that mainstream theatre is, in reality, foreign to the needs, concerns, and knowledge of an audience that has been educated to themes that are more relevant to its own experience? What about the inaccessibility of the theatre due to place (the "cultural palaces" of the coasts), cost, time, and so forth, rather than the intellectual incapability of the audience? Even if the notion is correct (and I do not believe it is true for a majority of the people), why is it the people's job to accommodate themselves to the theatre and not vice versa?

An even more fruitful approach is to examine the theatre's relationship with its audience and that audience's society in terms of comodification, to recognize the power of audience response to performances in molding form and convention as much as the power of those performances to attract and "train" their audiences. "Play performance and audience response must be looked at together as mutually interactive elements of a single phenomenon....The result is what may be termed a theatrical formation, the mutual elaboration over time of historically-specific audience groups and theatre practitioners participating in certain shared patterns of action."[8] If this view is accepted, it is incumbent on people's theatres to enter into an open discourse with their audiences, one in which the response of the viewer is considered a locus of meaning and sense, rather than retaining supposedly absolute control of meaning in the hands of the theatre-maker.

The traditional response to such claims is that it is necessary to lower one's standards to appeal to, or even make contact with, a broad audience. While there is no doubt that some forms of performance seem to be more accessible than others, it is certainly not true that all those forms are "lower." In addition (and this debate has raged in people's and collective theatre circles), it is possible that there are "people's forms" that must be discovered or invented to accommodate or contain the ideology of the theatre of social change; and that these forms can supplement or supplant the bourgeois concept of art. I believe that as people's theatre becomes more experienced and sophisticated in the use of new techniques such as collective creation, it will develop a series of constantly changing forms designed to represent or elaborate a content that will be in flux as society changes in evolutionary or revolutionary fashion. One need only look at the theatre in Latin America: "Popular Theatre (*Teatro Popular*) historically has provided a perspective on class struggle. Realistic in approach, individually authored texts have traditionally been used; but more recently it has relied on the collective creation in Latin America. The traditional playwright is considered too distant from the people in *teatro popular*'s advocacy of social change" (Miller 4). Similarly, one can read Enrico Buenaventura's definition of realism as an *interpretation* of reality or witness the experimentation of Otrabanda, Theatre X, Split Britches, or the United Mime Workers in the United States to see the development of new, yet relevant and entertaining, forms from collective processes. Many believe that these modes of representation cannot be developed within the strictures imposed by hierarchical theatre organization.[9]

However, even successful popular theatres still need to examine some basic political and artistic questions concerning, according to Darko Suvin, "neither politics in performances nor performances in politics, but the possibility of an organizational mediation between politics and performances. What kind of organized ensembles can and should exist if theatre art is neither a platonic idea in timeless heavens nor a profit-oriented business in arithmetic time? How can a performing group be organized when a coherent tradition of performing for several years is necessary for *any* significant spectacle?" (Suvin 28) In our age, Suvin believes, there are only three possibilities for the organization of theatres. The first, commercial and monopolistic, "implies in sociological terms the ideological rule of the economically dominant class. In aesthetic terms it means the rule of the *ancien regime*: conservative individualism, inert illusionism, and the sentimental pieties of the more-or-less well-made play" (29). The second, national or municipal, can be relatively progressive until the inevitable conflict that arises when the bounds of the funding government's "bureaucratic taste" is crossed, as was clear in battles over National Endowment for the Arts (NEA) funding in the late 1980s and early 1990s.

The final possible organizational form is:

> self-management guaranteed by an economic and political democracy working upward from the community level....Only a socialized theatre, a system of associations of creative theatre workers, has a historical chance of achieving a coherent and significant body of theatre for our age...This follows of necessity if one accepts the strong argument for identifying the enjoyment specific to our age with a scenically-organized insight into, and understanding of, contemporary *possibilities*—latent as well as actual—for human relations. (Suvin 29)

In other words, long-term associations of theatre makers, as opposed to the commercially necessitated short rehearsal period, allow for the types of exploration Suvin sees as necessary to create significant theatre, and for positive forms of interaction with the community that the theatre serves—claims as significant for collectively organized people's theatres as they are for the socialized theatre that Suvin thought was most desirable.

One final political consideration has entered into the choice of collective organization. The isolation of individualism hinders the fullest use of each person's power as a member of a community, and deprives many, especially those in the theatre, of a sense of participation in the creation of culture and history. A collective has its own history, one that is knowable by all its members and is, therefore, a relevant factor in current decisions and future planning. In this way, the collective is a model for the reenfranchisement of marginalized groups and the revitalization of indigenous cultures, cultures and histories that are frequently the sources of insights into the causes of contemporary inequities. The importance of community and *communitas* to collective theatres cannot be over stated.

Questions of Decision Making and Control

The politics of collective organization naturally leads to the second area of questions: decision making and control. Prior to the rise of political theatres (what Philip Arnoult calls the "sixth theatre" as opposed to commercial, university, community, regional, and research or experimental theatres), essentially all theatre in the United States participated in the progression of the rise of the director as the "true" and controlling artist of the theatre. Much of the theatre revolt in the sixties was against the tyrannical director, yet much of it was under the tutelage of directors of a different sort, most of whom eventually had to leave the groups that they helped to form. Since

> the director's theatre is quintessentially a theatre of supremacy, a theatre where the key element is the control of others, it is a theatre that must be challenged by progressive theatre makers. There is clearly an important place in people's theatre work for the perspective a director can bring. But...the progressive theatre movement must be continuously critical of the director's tendency to become hierarchical, authoritarian, and imperial. We need a theatre that bridges our work to the life of the American people. This cannot be achieved where either the director or the theatre itself occupies an imperial, controlling position. (Paterson, "Critique" 18).

The need was to escape the tyrannical or even paternal control of the director without sacrificing form, which is the essence of art.

Many of the earliest experiments at self-direction resulted in ill-defined performances that were merely extensions of explorations made in rehearsal, unfinished performance statements about little more than the actor's sense of relief and freedom. Other groups rejected the entire premise of the theatre and gave decision making power to performers and spectators simultaneously. *Happenings* allowed chance and license to replace the form-giving director. The Living Theatre invited audiences to move naked with the company members out into the streets. Guerrilla and street theatres ignored concerns with structure to concentrate on the expression of a clear political message. Life itself (rallies and demonstrations, war shown on television, and costumed and festooned flower people) became theatrical. This period of anarchy was probably healthy, since it allowed the pendulum that had been held too long in one position to swing wildly, but those who felt that theatre was a distinct yet essential part of culture realized that some organizational pattern was necessary if decisions about form and structure, as well as the more mundane concerns about time and place of performance, were to be made.

The search for a viable structure led many progressive theatre makers, and other cultural workers, into collective organizations in which the power that had previously been assumed to be the director's and the playwright's was taken over by the whole company. The problem of *ultrademocracy* arose almost immediately. Everyone felt that they had to have the final say on everything, and everyone wanted to do everything all the time. The idea of hierarchy was rejected completely, and competency was ignored. Often, power struggles dominated the rehearsal periods and little was accomplished.

Learning from these lessons of the past, current collectives have devised a number of strategies to make decisions, but most have reserved consensus as the final power. For some, responsibility for certain tasks, and the accompanying decision-making power about how those tasks are to be accomplished, are given to different people on a regular rotation. All successful groups recognize that each task is of equal value to the creation and performance of a play and that no one is to be denigrated or valorized for a particular role in the process. This can only be accomplished if every facet of the process (even if a particular member of the company is given control of that area) is open to democratic review and criticism.

The most difficult part of the redefinition of the theatre-making decision process concerned the means for performing some of the functions that were previously the province of the director. Many groups used improvisational techniques that caused the roles of director and playwright to be redefined in such a way that "the processes of design, scripting, staging and other theatrical elements occur simultaneously and interact to a degree impossible in traditional rehearsals" (Jenkins 323). The director's position, then, was seen as one of an educated or critical audience, noting what worked and advising on changes. No longer was she or he seen as the author/composer of the production or the giver of the unifying concept.

Some groups just used whoever was not performing in a particular scene as an outside eye, while many groups developed rather idiosyncratic solutions. El Teatro de la Esperanza created a complex system of division of responsibility by scenes and an oversight committee (see Chapter 3). The Provisional Theatre had a primary director who usually sat out and acted as a critical audience and an internal director who worked as an actor with the other actors and advised from that point of view. The Provisional often brought in a collaborator to assist, and in a final collaboration, after an initial short run, it restaged each play to incorporate audience suggestions before mounting an extended run. The Other Theatre Company, after nightly improvisations and discussions, had a designated playwright script from, or in response to, that work and reimprovised from that basis the next night. When all scenes were scripted, a designated director did the final staging, usually by advising each actor on modes of appropriate exploration. In almost every case, the director is also a performer; a situation that has its difficulties, but also facilitates complete sharing of knowledge, power, and support. Each system is designed to create a working method that promotes freedom through access to information and power.[10]

Questions of Process and Product

The final area of concern for collective theatres is artistic. A collective does not choose a script and then cast according to the play's needs. It must make its artistic decisions "from scratch" without the form-giving tyranny of a traditional playwright or director, regardless of how comfortable it might be to temporarily regress into the position of *ubermarionette*.[11]

The first question that the collective usually asks is, "What should we write and perform about?" The question is not merely a political one. Its answer must take into account the community to which the theatre is attached, the artistic growth of the group, and the needs of the individual artists in it. Any theatre that does not experiment with developmental change is doomed, as is any stagnant community, to find its voice growing weaker. Many theatre people who became disenchanted with earlier political theatre that relied on, and was limited by, agitprop still see no vitality in the theatre of social change. To others, it seems as if the importance of the art of the theatre is denied by considering the importance of political statement.

The collective, however, provides an arena for artistic growth that actually can make use of more resources for artistic development than either commercial, regional, or even university theatres, whose concerns are outside those of their communities and broader societies. The intention of collectivization is to find an organization and process that can actualize in theatre art the culture of the people. It is

> *not* to banalize the artistic production. Performances by such theatre groups need not be thematically limited to neighborhood problems. The vision is *not* a re-constructed agit-prop theatre form. Rather it is a call for a revitalization of the group theatre—to return its function, context and source of inspiration. It is to the new group theatre movement's advantage to anchor itself again in society, to draw information and energy from the broader population, its hopes and realities. We signal the end of art created in an artist's vacuum—the sinking of the island

> of artist societies, where actors perform for actors and critics, where each performance takes place in a context of "theatre" history, without ever affecting "human" history. We wish to give the theatre-artist a deeper, more beautiful multi-toned voice, rooted in the rhythms of daily life. (Torch 5–6)

Obviously, one can only believe that the daily life of the audience can offer the stuff of theatre if one respects one's self as participant in the life of that audience.

A related artistic question is that of the place of the playwright in the creation of the performance or the script. One of the major weaknesses of early collective creation was the writing. *Condensed significance*, in which every line said exactly what it meant, was the norm. Improvisational techniques that allow for full participation by the group in performance creation do not rely on the spoken word. Inspired interaction between actors does not usually consist of emotionally charged language that is speakable from the stage and understandable by a general audience.

The concern about dominance by a particular individual prevented collective theatres from using playwrights effectively. What was discovered, however, was that after decisions had been made collectively, the unifying hand or voice of one who scripted the work gave coherence to, and allowed for the inclusion of the subtext in, the written text. What is essential, though, is that the playwright share with the actors in the creative process that precedes writing; otherwise it will be impossible for the group to trust that the playwright understands the vision from the center. Playwrights can, however, "finish" the discoveries made in process into communicative pieces.

This discovery helped signal the movement of politically concerned collectives away from experimental theatre groups, which had a tendency to exhibit for audiences the creative act with less concern for the creative product. According to many, this innovation in process can be attributed to Joseph Chaikin's leadership of the Open Theatre, the partially collectivized theatre company that produced talented playwrights and actors who still are active in the people's theatre movement.[12] It also raised the level of collective creations by a quantum leap, even though the dominant concern of collectives for the performance text still led to scripts produced exclusively for the group that developed the play and that do not include information that would give the reader a sense of the fullness of the performance.

A third question beside topic and text concerns style and form. The debate is essentially over the concept of *popular*. On one side are the theatres that seem to believe that *popular* can be defined in terms of those forms that have received the broadest acceptance by audiences over the years. They argue that in order for their political message to reach an audience, it must be couched in accessible (i.e., familiar) forms. They argue, as well, for a resurgence of older forms that used clearly defined roles to explain political concepts. The Play Group's use of musical forms, Dell'Arte's comic creations, and the San Francisco Mime Troupe's melodramas all provide examples of exciting and entertaining productions with strong political messages and traditional forms.

On the other side of the debate are the collectives that believe that existing forms are inadequate. They argue that form shapes meaning and that the use of existing forms in the theatre prevents the inclusion of new concepts and even the use of new working methods. Existing theatre forms are, they maintain, the creation of a theatre that is exploitative itself and that represents an exploitative minority. In simple terms, ruling-class forms cannot contain working-class messages. The most frequently used forms in establishment theatre, they maintain, are basically narrative, realistic, and illusionary. However, this "realism" is neither accurate nor innovative: it is essentially conservative and should be rejected.

> It is the nature of literary realism to deny its own aesthetic nature, to pose as a truthful account of social life. But realism is non-mimetic. Roland Barthes has argued that it is the essential middleclass form precisely because it functions by turning bourgeois culture into nature ("Life"), thus fulfilling the requirements of bourgeois ideology. This process has nothing to do with reportage, but rather concerns mobilizing the stereotypes of social discourse for the purpose of making them appear universal. Middle-class audiences go to the theatre to see realistic plays not because they want real life on the stage (this is exactly what they do not want), but because they want their own ideology inscribed in art. (Hirsch 90)

Traditionally accepted nonrealistic forms, like the opera and the musical comedy, can also be rejected because they romanticize endeavors at social change or trivialize attempts at a democratic assertion of people's culture by making everything that is not in a shopping mall seem quaint and antique (i.e., irrelevant). Even socially conscious playwrights (like Arthur Miller who writes basically realistic plays) end up romanticizing their heroes who, tragically, go to their deaths choosing to uphold their personal *morality* regardless of the consequences. Tragedy and comedy must also be rejected in their traditionally defined forms. In traditionally structured tragedy, the dignity of humankind is affirmed through the individual who faces indomitable forces or who errs because his or (very rarely) her personal sense of power leads him or her to misperceive the "proper order of nature." In traditionally structured comedy, the source of ridicule is deviation from the status quo, and a reestablishment of the proper social order provides the happy resolution. Both tragedy and comedy dehistoricize society by asserting that the order of things is inevitable and immutable. They are essentially antiprogressive and need to be reanalyzed by collectives, that affirm the interdependency of all parts of a society and the fluidity and mutability of social structure.[13]

Some people assert another reason why collectives need to develop new forms: so many of the traditional structures are centered around individual heroic protagonists. For one thing, the collective process asserts the value of every participant and is opposed by its very nature to the idolization of an individual. In addition, the political analysis that most collectives use is in some way related to the concept of class struggle—a struggle of groups, and not individuals. To present a hero theory of history, which is justified by asserting the need for conventional theatre forms, contradicts the basic tenets of collectivism. The rejection of heroes has been countered by "discussion of the classical Lukacsian idea of the protagonist who incarnates the clash of antagonistic social forces. [However, many maintain that hero creation implies] a tendency to envision social problems as the problems of an extraordinary individual, usually male" (Yarbro-Bejarano, "Image" 20). Recently, some feminist theorists have asserted that narrative itself "reifies the dominant ideology" by asserting an essentially seamless flow of events and their direct connection with gender defined "human nature" and prevents the representation of women and other disenfranchised groups as subjects on the stage.[14]

Finally, it seems to many people that new forms indicate new possibilities and generate new reactions from audiences. There have been countless productions during which insights have been gained by audience members because an innovative presentation led them to a new appreciation of causal relationships. We need a theatre, people's theatre makers assert, that reflects the real lives of the people: lives that are profoundly political and not concerned exclusively with money and sex in high society. The theatre we have now is inadequate to this task.

People's theatre companies that have succeeded in using existing forms to create political insight have almost always done so by rediscovering the *roots* of the form and not by repeating its commercially successful manifestation. In fact, a part of the people's theatre movement that has been most influential recently has been concerned with rediscovering the stories and culture of the people and returning to them those stories on stage. Experimental theatre has recognized the need to return to the roots of people's lives, but has often mistakenly sought those roots in rituals that are, in modern life, disconnected and without vitality. Collective theatres, by promoting long-term research into and open sharing of the communal past of their members and their communities, are often able to rediscover indigenous forms and to use them to express the culture of the people. In this way, even the "old" forms are made new.[15] The question of the relationship of collective process to forms and modes of representation is discussed in more theoretical terms in the final chapter.

It is often difficult for actors to learn appropriate methods for playing these plays, and so actor training and development is a constant concern for collectives. Most collectives, while honoring the Stanislavskian call for honesty, find Brecht's call for a "definite gest of showing" (often accompanied by the externalization of emotion "into a gesture;" Brecht 136–40) to be more conducive to political expression than the Method's psychological focus. Each character in political theatre must reveal his or her social role in order to support the entire play's analysis of social causality. Actors, then, must learn to *create* characters (remember that the actor is not "developing" characters as in traditional theatre) who clearly express the nature of the situations around them.

In addition, each actor also serves as a representative of the culture she or he is expressing: the culture of the audience. However, the actor must maintain artistic integrity, and compromise neither political nor artistic standards. The collective offers a protective environment in which the actor can take risks that may lead to the discovery of effective (both in political and aesthetic terms) means of performance.

Many collectives, therefore, have built actor training into their work schedules. For some this is merely a warm-up and stretching period; for others, it is a time during which group members teach each other new techniques or develop new performance strategies. Still others invite outside teachers, often from other collectives, to train them, while some collectives just use the critique time during and after rehearsals to advise and train. Most of the techniques are modifications of those used in mainstream theatres and universities, although in recent years, Latin American *teatros* and Augusto Boal's workshops have introduced groups in the United States to performance strategies used in places where revolution is much closer at hand.

The final aesthetic question is one of criticism and evaluation. It is sometimes quite difficult for one member of a group to criticize another without creating interpersonal friction. The only real solution is to concentrate the criticism on the idea or its realization and not on the maker. Collectives have done remarkably well in this area because of their supportive structure. The real difficulty is in developing standards for the evaluation of performance.

There are three sides to this debate. One group believes that the only real standard for judging the value of political theatre is political effectiveness. This group maintains that a political theatre must define its social goals and determine whether its play was successful by how much it accomplished toward furthering those goals. However, this is almost impossible for theatres with a broad social agenda. Members of this group also believe that clarity of expression can be substituted for quality as the sine qua non.

The second group of collectives is more concerned with the political situation in their own arena than with the broader society. This group's greatest contribution has been expanding the bounds of the art of the theatre and testing new approaches to that art. To them, theatrical viability or innovation is the standard, though it should not be reached at the expense of the company's political goals. To them, the search for narrative clarity or easy accessibility can actually prevent both political and aesthetic viability. "It is not enough simply to organize an argument in theatrical terms. You are no longer simply dressing a piece of agitation with theatrical devices, you are trying to stretch the possibilities of theatre itself. And yet the central issue must emerge plainly, the analysis show itself clearly, or you simply end up with a slice of life...[which is] uninformative and inconclusive" (McGrath Theory 50). Members of this group often believe that the critical standards used to judge mainstream theatre are directly applicable to political work, a belief that has been challenged, often successfully, by those who point to the ideological assumptions embedded in mainstream critical standards.

The third faction presents a compromise. Its adherents feel that the standards need to be different for different types of producing groups. For example, a group of employees that presents plays to explain issues to fellow union members and successfully lobbies for a strike should not be subject to the same critical criteria by which a long-lived professional producing group is judged. The first type of theatre group would be deserving of praise regardless of its level of attainment in terms of "art." The second type should be subject to scrutiny by theatre makers, critics, and audiences alike, regardless of its political punch or how well it has integrated its members into the creative process. The assumption for these groups is that one cannot use the arts to promote social action without providing an entertaining and challenging experience for the audience—and audiences will only be fully entertained by high-quality theatre.

THE COLLECTIVE PARADIGM

While it is possible to present a description of a theoretically "perfect" collective process, to do so would seem to set up an ideal with which to compare specific theatres to determine their success. Instead, the following chapters on individual theatres will examine demonstrably successful processes from which it will be possible to generalize later. Let it suffice at this point to say that, in the simplest terms, collective theatre making is the sharing of work by theatre artists in such a way as to maximize access to information and the freedom of each individual to use ideas from the *center* in every aspect of the creation, and to minimize the differences in power and status between individuals in the troupe. This provides a road to artistic development and a model for social change.

Collectivization is often seen, more specifically, as a particular organizational response to the political and artistic domination and exploitation that are inherent in contemporary society and the theatre of its ruling and middle classes. Moreover, although there are as many working methods as there are groups, the basic process of each is quite similar.

NOTES

1. Cecelia Ridgeway, in her book *The Dynamics of Small Groups*, and Paul V. Crosbie, in the Introduction to *Interaction in Small Groups*, are the only authors to give any attention to collectives, which they call "leaderless groups."

2. Crosbie, "Introduction" 7. The definitions of values, norms, and roles were gleaned from various places in this book as well.

3. R. F. Bales' Interaction Process Analysis chart, first presented in 1950 in "A Set of Categories for the Analysis of Small Group Interaction" (p. 258), has been the basis for analysis in many experiments. It is very general and provides a measure of individual actions and reactions without an adequate way to measure the response of the group as a whole.

4. Crosbie, introductory comment, pp.266–67. See also M. E. Shaw, "Some Effects of Unequal Distribution of Information upon Group Performance in Various Communication Nets," and "Some Effects of Problem Complexity upon Problem Solution Efficiency in Different Communication Nets."

5. This phrase was a favorite of the Provisional Theatre, and it is after hearing it from them that the model of the collective communication network began to crystalize for me.

6. Collectives, in fact, fulfill the "requirements" for creative problem solving better than any other organizational pattern. See Richard L. Hoffman, "Conditions for Creative Problem Solving," for a fuller discussion of this technique.

7. These questions were articulated in this manner by Douglas Paterson in "Some Theoretical Questions of People's Theatre," a relatively early call for research and analysis in this area.

8. McConachie 232. See also Terry Eagleton, *Marxism and Literary Criticism* (pp. 20–36), and Anne Übersfeld, "The Pleasure of the Spectator," for other ways of examining the role of audience in the development of modes of theatre.

9. An anecdote about the Provisional Theatre of Los Angeles, a now disbanded but very long-lived collective theatre, illustrates the difficulty of the search for people's forms. After the Provisional Theatre had established itself through its antiwar pieces, the members decided to do a play with a more general social significance. The resulting *America Piece* was a fine theatrical work and received much praise from theatre people. It did not, however, appeal to a

general audience. Their next play, *Voice of the People*, generated much excitement among audiences, but its didactic structure and overt political message drew poor critical notices and jeopardized the theatre's National Endowment for the Humanities funding. The style of their next play, *Inching through the Everglades*, attempted to use the theatricality of *America Piece* while clearly exploring the issues enunciated in *Voice*. For the Provisional, the work responded to various forces, but remained, in form and content, people's art.

10. Another question about decision making concerns the power of the sources of funds. Many companies at first tried to avoid taking foundation or governmental monies, but the financial burdens became too great. After a short time, concerns about the impact of productions on their funding sources at least partially trapped some groups in the very system they were hoping to change.

11. The ubermarionette is an egoless, mindless superpuppet capable of carrying out all performance demands made by the theatre master-artist. Ironically, the term was coined by Edward Gordon Craig in *On the Art of the Theatre* (1905) in an attack on the destructive hierarchy of the various elements of the theatre.

12. See R. G. Davis, *The San Francisco Mime Troupe: The First 10 Years*, and Arthur Sainer, *Radical Theatre Notebook*.

13. For a rejection of tragedy on grounds of desired audience emotional response see Augusto Boal, *Theatre of the Oppressed*.

14. See, for example, Janelle Reinelt, "The Politics of Form: Realism, Melodrama and Pam Gems' *Camille*."

15. See, for example, the Dell'Arte Players use of Commedia or some of Bread and Puppet's fine work. The clearest support for the position that traditional forms can be mined for new ways of making political people's theatre is provided by John McGrath, whose work with the 7:84 Theatre Company in England and Scotland is the basis for "The Theory and Practice of Political Theatre," and *A Good Night Out*, and Split Britches, whose use of vaudeville raises questions about the very basis of theatrical representation and the ideology it supports.

2

Collective Theatre: Precedents and Histories

Why is remaining on the sidelines more artistic than jumping into the fight? A left-wing artist who is jealous of his independence risks crossing into that 'exempt' status for which artists trade away a noble role in history.

Joan Holden, "The Melodrama is the Message"

The detailed studies of individual theatres that are contained in Chapters 3 through 6 reveal how this basic process can manifest itself in a variety of methods and approaches. Each collective has developed a working method over the years that has served not only its audiences, but its members as well. Each method is well enough defined that it has been teachable to new members, thereby enabling these theatres to overcome the most difficult problem in collective theatre: that of replacing members who leave and of finding new blood to revitalize the group.[1]

All four groups have received critical acclaim both in and out of people's theatre circles and each continued to produce ever more complex, yet effective, productions throughout its history. They represent a range of creative approaches, a variety of performing styles, and a number of different focal concerns.

These theatres, and many others like them, however, are neither isolated combinations of rare genius nor unique endeavors into performance creation. Nor are they a complete break from the tradition of theatre in America. Rather, they are a re-connection to the continuum of people's culture, of which indigenous theatre has always been a part, and to the reaction of that culture to exploitation, elitism, and cultural imperialism. People's theatres, especially those that are collectively organized, are also in the tradition of positive change through rejection of a limited and limiting status quo: traditions, conditions, and conventions in the theatre that inhibit the inclusion of both form and content that are significant to, or representative of, the lives of the nontheatregoing population. "Alternative theatre sprang not from its own head but from the unfulfilled expectations of elite and commercial theatre and the inordinate boredom of middle-class life; not merely to entertain, rather to educate, not merely to educate, to be an example...not merely to create an opposition, rather to change to a reproduction of self for more than the privileged" (Davis 13). Finally, they are an elaboration of the interactive nature of the development of theatre in general in terms of the relationships of theatre to both its makers and its audience.

EUROPEAN PRECEDENTS

The desire for a theatre that is an integral part of the lives of the masses is not new. Some trace the direct articulation of the concept of people's theatre to Romain Rolland's *The Theatre of the People* (1903), in which the author called for the establishment of local performing groups that would remain parts of, and do plays meaningful to, their communities.[2]

Actually, the movement toward decentralized and self-governing theatres had begun in France more than three decades earlier. In 1871 the Paris Commune debated the creation of many small, socialist (what we might now call collective) theatre associations that would remain in their local areas to perform plays for what would amount, when they were considered in the aggregate, to a mass popular audience. The debate was frankly political, although aesthetic concerns were voiced.[3]

It was not until Fermin Gemier's attempts to bring theatre to all audiences in prewar France that the more modern people's theatre movement began. His Théâtre Ambulant toured the country from 1911 through 1913, presenting performances at affordable prices to nonurban, nontheatregoing audiences. He became influential enough to pressure the government to create a national touring company in 1920. The Théâtre Nationale Popular still brings theatre to the people of France, and under the direction of Roger Planchon has had an impact on theatre around the world.

This is not, however, the people's theatre that contemporary collectives seek to create. Merely bringing traditional theatre to the masses, they would maintain, is not making popular theatre in any real sense. It is just a continuation of the cultural hegemony of class oriented art, regardless of the motives of the practitioners.

Somewhat closer to the American concept of people's theatre was Walter Gropius's *Bauhaus*, which was established in Weimar in 1919. Gropius was interested in the communal expression of culture. He realized that culture was not something manufactured by artistes who were separate from (i.e., above) the people, but rather that it was an expression of the lives of the people. His *Bauhaus* became an art object in itself, making art functional, the functional artistic, and everything accessible to the general public (Brockett 512–14).

Gropius was more consciously political than either Gemier in France or Max Reinhardt in Germany, whose prewar work indicated a desire for a truly accessible theatre. He developed a relationship with Erwin Piscator whose tracts on political theatre were influential into the sixties. In an interesting twist, one of Piscator's American students was Judith Malina who, with Julian Beck, founded the Living Theatre collective, which was influential, during its exile from the United States in radicalizing the European theatre in the late sixties.

There was, as well, a tradition of people's theatre in America, which was most clearly visible in early twentieth century pageants such as those mounted by Percy MacKaye and in the active story-telling traditions in Appalachia and elsewhere. However, this theatre was overshadowed by touring stars and commercial concerns. It is not surprising, then, that during the flourishing of people's theatre in the United States between the wars, the major impetus would come not from established theatre circles, but from broader social concerns and movements, particularly the plight of the American worker and the revolution in Russia.

As was Bolshevism, the revolutionary (or at least socially concerned) theatre in America was a response to cultural imperialism and economic exploitation. There had been ripples of social consciousness in plays at the beginning of the century (such as Shaw's *Mrs. Warren's Profession* in 1905, and international productions of Henrik Ibsen's work), but these were dismissed by critics in the United States as indecent. "The critic, William Winter, said in 1913 of one pernicious radical:

> Granting to Ibsen and his followers the highest and best motives, they have altogether mistaken the province of the theatre in choosing it as the medium for the expression of social views . . . which once adopted, would disrupt society. . . . Since when did the theatre become a proper place for a clinic of horrors and the vivisection of moral ailments?" (Williams 3)

But, World War I presented horrors that could no longer be kept out of *any* arena, and social criticism of poverty, war, racism, and the denial of individual value in pursuit of profits became subjects that the theatre could not deny.

THEATRE BETWEEN THE WARS

New theatres that developed before and during the war, when touring had become less profitable, provided opportunities and audiences for new plays and playwrights. Theatres like the Goodman in Chicago (1911), the Provincetown

Players (1915), and the Washington Square Players (1915; reorganized as the Theatre Guild in 1918), as well as a growing number of community and Little Theatres provided access to the theatre for people across the country. The professional theatres were organized in a more open and receptive manner than their commercial Broadway counterparts. Although they retained a traditional theatre structure, there was not as much concentration of power at the top of the hierarchy. Many of the theatres characterized themselves as "collective" in terms of a supportive atmosphere, a personal investment by each member of the permanent company, a commitment to collaboration, and a sharing of limited income. It is interesting to note that even in these early stages of collectivization there were debates over the place of democracy in the arts, even among those devoted to socially conscious drama, and over the ability of a group with an equal division of power to run a theatre that had been controlled for so long by a dictatorial director.

The Theatre Guild discovered a compromise solution—one in which the director and actors kept their traditional provinces while a board of directors directly supervised their work. This remains somewhat unusual even by today's standards, but the structure was radical seventy years ago.

> It is a commentary on the times that when Walter Pritchard Eaton wrote the official history of the Theatre Guild, in 1929, he felt impelled to refer to the Board of Directors as "soviets." This did not mean that they had fallen into the clutches of Moscow. But many new and stimulating ideas were coming out of Russia, and among them one which captured the interest of artists was that of group, or collective, creativity....It included the establishment of a permanent company, a program of training, a directorial board with a common point of view, and if possible a permanent house. A sense of purpose, too, helped unify these companies, whether it was simply to do good plays or to experiment with form or to bring on the revolution.[4]

What did come out of Europe and Russia in those years was particularly exciting. Expressionism was seen as an escape from stifling commercialism and a perfect vehicle for social criticism, while the performances in 1922 and 1923 of Konstantin Stanislavski's Moscow Art Theatre in New York were to revolutionize American acting techniques.

During and after the Depression, when capitalism seemed to have failed, and communal living became a necessity for many, the new theatre structures that had been introduced in the 1920s grew rapidly, especially among ethnic, foreign language companies and the vibrant workers' theatre movement. Foreign language companies, such as the Yiddish-speaking Artef (Arbeiter Teater Verband) and the Erwin Piscator-influenced, German-speaking Prolet-Bühne, were promoting cultural democracy and leftist politics in plays of high quality. Each remained closely attached to its community, yet provided a broader social perspective for its immigrant audience. The Prolet-Bühne was more openly

Marxist than almost any theatre producing in the United States today.

The most vibrant theatres in the thirties were part of the workers' theatre movement, of which Hallie Flanagan wrote in 1931: "The power of these theatres...lies in the fact that they know what they want. Their purpose is clear...to make a new social order" (Williams 43). The most influential of these was the Worker's Laboratory Theatre (WLT). Originally formed to do skits to help the Worker's International Relief obtain funds for unemployed workers, the WLT became a driving force not only in the labor movement, but toward a new vision of theatre as socially motivated, collectively organized, and community anchored.

The WLT's plays were mostly agitprop, simple and direct explanations of events and calls for action, performed where unions were involved in confrontations rather than in theatres, but their method remains strikingly modern. Believing that theatre makers are workers and theatre making a trade, they developed a collective process that allowed anyone in the company to participate and develop in any area of production. "They formed committees, one to study acting, another to oversee directing, a third to produce plays. Anyone could belong to the playwriting committees, which found basic subjects in news items or current events and then chose certain phases of a subject by vote for inclusion in a sketch. The actual writing of dialogue was assigned to one person. The finished script was submitted back to the committee and finally to the membership" (Williams 42).

The group was unlike commercial theatres in another important way: It contributed to its audience's life through political action other than just play production. WLT members were involved in organizing, in bringing theatres together in national festivals of cultural workers for the exchange of ideas, techniques, and scripts, and in publishing a magazine, *Workers Theatre*, that grew to have a circulation rivaling theatre journals today. As did the Prolet-Bühne, it encouraged the formation of new groups and fostered debate about how the workers' theatre should operate.[5]

For WLT members there was no separation of art and politics, and the theatre remained at the center of political and aesthetic controversies of the time: debates between those who believed that form should be more or less complicated, who believed that bourgeois theatre techniques should be used more or less frequently, and who believed that acting style should be more or less impersonal (role- as opposed to character-oriented). Ultimately, the motive of both sides on any issue was a desire to create theatre that was accessible while maintaining its aesthetic integrity, and this agreement about purpose led to a peculiarly American style of political theatre—epic and individual at the same time.

There was much discussion as well about the proper organization of theatre companies. John E. Bonn wrote in *Workers Theatre* in 1932 that theatre makers must have the "spirit of action" within themselves if they wished to inspire others, and that this spirit comes from political training "of each member and political orientation of our entire work....Keep a strict Proletarian Discipline. A group member who is convinced of the political necessity of our work cannot act undisciplined and irresponsible. *Collective Method* based on political education and on voluntary discipline generates the best results" (Taylor 40). While a number of workers' theatres did organize as collectives, few defined their methods carefully enough to achieve such discipline in spite of good intentions. The Theatre Union, a most influential workers' theatre, was never a collective, and even the WLT reorganized to increase discipline. The Theatre Collective, an offshoot of the WLT devoted to productions of more elaborate leftist plays, did maintain a collective structure, but was not a successful producing group. It was, however, very influential as a training center for cultural workers.

As the debates continued, individual theatres began to achieve more sophisticated results with their own methods. The Group Theatre, which was organized in 1931 to produce socially relevant plays using Stanislavski's Method as an acting approach, was beginning to get a great deal of critical attention because of the high quality of its writing and acting. Political concerns invaded Broadway in *Of Thee I Sing*, the 1931 hit musical, and in 1933 the Theatre Union generated great excitement with its prolabor, antiracist play *Stevedore*.

This play, which had a racially mixed cast, dealt with the exploitation of black workers and called for black and white union solidarity. It was created using a collaborative method that relied on the traditional playwright and director, but allowed for a great deal of input from the actors and the community at large. In fact, dock workers were asked to read and comment on parts of this play before it was put into rehearsal. The audience was large, diversified, and multiracial, and it behaved in an unexpected manner: "Some of the actors noted that the very speeches they had called 'soap-box' were most loudly cheered—and it was to be the pattern for most of the Theatre Union's productions" (Williams 116).

Nevertheless, socially concerned theatre makers were dissatisfied. In 1933, an article appeared in *New Theatre* magazine, the voice of the League of Workers Theatres, which stated "that the members of the League had all been much too narrow in their plays, and repeated what had been said in the past; ...that they were going to have to break down the cliche of form in which, as one of them had put it, 'In the first act we suffer, in the second we pass out leaflets, and in the third we go on strike'" (Williams 123–24). Yet it was a play that made the most of a similar pattern that would rock both workers' and commercial theatre in 1935: *Waiting for Lefty* by young Clifford Odets.

Only two years later, though, the Group Theatre that had supported Odets was essentially dead, destroyed by its inability to resolve power struggles and by financial stress. The Theatre Union had folded, and the WLT after an unsuccessful attempt at a full length play finally burned out. Will Lee, a member of WLT's core company, the Shock Troupe, noted reasons for its demise that were strikingly similar to those mentioned today by some disbanding collectives: "We seemed to have all grown to a certain height together, creatively, and now we all leveled out. We all knew we needed stronger creative leadership and it wasn't around. During the five years or so we lived together we never had any rest, or any time off, and we only slept for a few hours a night for months. We were broke, hungry, and exhausted. We started to run out of steam" (Williams 170).

What had taken the place of these groups was the huge, nationally organized Federal Theatre Project under the direction of Hallie Flanagan who, although in academic theatre at the time, had been associated with the workers' theatre movement from its inception. The Federal Theatre Project was the first American national theatre and was popular in every sense of the word, playing in its heyday to over 400,000 people each week for an average admission price of fifteen cents. (It is worth noting that ticket prices were higher, but 87 percent of the admissions to Federal Theatre productions around the country were free.)[6]

The pressure to produce for so many performances forced the Federal Theatre to create a new form, the "Living Newspaper," in which current events, actual speeches, and created scenes were combined to relate and explain the news of the day. The creation of these plays was collective. Although Arthur Arent did a majority of the actual scripting, "without the living newspaper staff this form so suited to his writing talents would never have been devised" (Taylor 147). Unfortunately, but not surprisingly, the Project had to battle censorship attempts from the beginning. Its rocky history and battles with red-baiting conservatives have been amply documented, but its great influence on theatre since that time deserves acknowledgment. The Federal Theatre Project and the workers' theatre movement between the wars left a legacy that many now take for granted.

> Today, the fabric of the theatre, the films, and the ubiquitous television is so shot through with the threads of the socially-conscious theatre and the forms it established over twenty-five years that no one any longer sees the connection. Yet it exists. The experimentation of the expressionists, the insistence that theatre should have a meaning, the realism of the Group's acting, the irreverence of the workers' theatres, the acceptance of social and political comment, the breaking down of the proscenium, all worked to change the atmosphere and even the structure of the theatre (Williams 255–56).

New forms, new spaces, and new connections with the nontraditional audience and the working people of this country, as well as nonexploitative, collective, collaborative methods of play creation and production continue to be the legacy of the theatre of the twenties and thirties, and continued to find currency in the hands of people's theatres into the 1990s.

THE FIFTIES AND SIXTIES

The radical spirit that motivated socially conscious cultural workers between the wars was defused as the national energies began to focus on the turmoil that was to become World War II. After the war, anti-Soviet phobia and the activities of Senator Joseph McCarthy and the House Un-American Activities Committee helped to crush what was left of the political opposition in this country. There seemed to be a deliberate desire to "decreate the experience of the Thirties and by doing so help establish the social paralysis necessary for the carrying out of cold war policies" (Taylor 191).

There remained, however, the belief that social issues were the legitimate province of drama, and there continued to be a political consciousness (if not conscience) in the theatre. Arthur Miller's *The Crucible* was commercial theatre's rebuttal to McCarthyism, and plays and pageants such as Ben Hecht's massive Holocaust production in Madison Square Garden, *We Will Never Die*, presented anti-Nazi and antiracist themes.[7] The theatre retained some public dimension, but for the most part was neither activist nor openly class conscious.

The fifties was, after all, a period of pressure for conformity: repression replaced depression, cars replaced culture, and Elvis Presley's hip gyrations replaced Woody Guthrie's lyrics as the musical call for freedom. Yet the seeds of the political theatre that was to blossom in the sixties were being planted, and the issues that were to galvanize the left again—civil rights, women's rights, unionization, and antiwar sentiments—were becoming more and more pressing.

Much of the theatre of the fifties was a continuation of the work begun by the Group in the exploration of character and acting technique. Realistic plays plotted in the tradition of Denis Diderot's domestic tragedy, but concentrating on the psychology of the protagonist became the norm. The Greek notion of fate had been replaced by Freudian unconscious forces or genetic structure. In the thirties and forties, in spite of the social consciousness, much concentration was on the fate of the individual character as determined by social and economic forces. (This was particularly true outside the workers' theatre movement, but even the work of Odets became character centered after *Lefty*.) The fifties presented audiences with idealized goodness (William Saroyan and Thornton Wilder) or self-destructive brooding (Tennessee Williams), and even the social problem plays of Miller and the tragic masterpieces of O'Neill concentrated on individual morality or emotional angst. The breaks with this world of realistic, if somewhat extended, character and its concomitant Method acting, were soundly rejected by audiences and critics alike. One need only examine the reactions to Samuel Beckett's *Waiting for Godot* to get a typical example of the response any experimentation was likely to receive. In spite of that, the work of the absurdists and those aligned with them, like Jean Genet, has had enormous influence on both alternative and establishment theatre in the sixties and beyond.

In the early sixties, though, political and artistic undercurrents reached the surface, and the increased activism of society as a whole was reflected in the theatre. Political theatre boomed; experiments in form occupied many of the most creative theatre makers, while others revitalized the dormant street theatre and agitprop forms as political weapons, and collective creation became the method of choice for many socially concerned cultural workers.

Once again, much of the earliest impetus toward change came from Europe. The theories of Antonin Artaud were accepted by many experimental theatre makers as the road to escape from the ordinariness of the plays and situations of the fifties, to the collective unconsciousness of the audience, and to the magic of ritual and spectacle. Others were influenced by Brecht's apparent rejection of the traditional relationship of actor to character and by his call for a politically responsible epic form.

The writings of Mao Tse-tung, Herbert Marcuse, Antonio Gramsci, and Karl Marx were examined with an eye to understanding a new aesthetic based on a materialist analysis of capitalist repression. Later in the sixties the work of Jerzy Grotowski influenced a number of collectives by providing a radically new way of training, concentrating on the actor as he or she manifests him- or herself in the performance, rather than exclusively on the character being performed. Grotowski's work also supported the movement toward freedom of expression and physicality that had already begun in the United States. Productions directed by Peter Brook, particularly his *Marat/Sade*, revealed the strength of ensemble work and hinted at the extent to which Artaud's ideas could be used to structure audience and performance relationships. Finally, the Living Theatre returned to America with four productions it had developed in Europe, and introduced new ways of integrating content, collectivization, and form with radical politics.[8]

The thrust of what came to be called *alternative theatre* in the sixties was antiestablishment, both in terms of politics and of the theatre itself. One wing of the movement concentrated on moving out to the people. These "guerrilla" theatres were often aligned with a particular interest group or oriented towards a particular issue—primarily concerning the war in Vietnam. Often their members came from outside the theatre, and their political goals were considered to be of primary importance.

Guerrilla theatre was responsible for revitalizing agitprop and for reaching new audiences. These groups would play at political rallies, demonstrations, and even in laundromats, imitating the hit-and-run tactics of guerrilla warfare. Their desire was to galvanize action against the war and its corporate supporters or, for some, in support of civil rights or some other movement. Most, unfortunately, were short-lived. They either disbanded when the war ended or lost their members to other forms of political work. Their legacy is in an expanded audience, in freedom from traditional and inaccessible performance spaces, and as training grounds for many who were later to see how a concern for aesthetics and activism could combine to produce the people's theatre of today.

Some groups that began this way have, however, continued to produce. In 1959 Ron Davis founded what has become the San Francisco Mime Troupe in order to use his performance training outside of the stifling commercial venue. During the early sixties the company attracted a great number of nontheatre people as performers and moved into San Francisco's parks, where it performed commedia dell'arte-style left-wing propaganda plays for free. The company tried a number of approaches to production styles and organization, including collectivism, as it matured. The Mime Troupe is still a leading force in the political theatre movement, now as a multiracial, multiethnic theatre presenting relatively didactic, vaudeville- and melodrama-influenced plays-with-music about working-class issues and seeking working-class and university audiences. Although most of the scripting is done by Joan Holden, the essential nature of the company has remained collaborative and democratic.[9]

In 1965, while the Mime Troupe was still attempting to define a structure that would enable it to "teach, direct toward change and be an example of change" (Davis), Luis Valdez left the company to assist the United Farm Workers (UFW) in its efforts to organize farm laborers. He formed El Teatro Campesino as a propaganda weapon for the union, and traveled from field to field, performing *actos*, didactic political skits characterized by stereotypical and exaggerated characters wearing signs to identify themselves to their audiences, on the back of a flatbed truck. These collectively produced plays focused on the situation of the audiences, presenting political and economic analyses of their situation, and calling for collective action through the union as a means of change. Not only did the workers respond (the UFW grew in size and power as a direct result of Valdez and Campesino's work), but the performers decided to follow Valdez's lead into more complex and sophisticated drama. While El Teatro Campesino is no longer in the forefront of the Chicano or political theatre movement, the theatre has continued to thrive. It now has a large, modern facility of its own, and has achieved commercial success with Broadway and film productions of its musical, *Zoot Suit*, and Valdez's examination of the Chicano working-class in *La Bamba*, the film biography of rock star Ritchie Valens.[10]

There were a great number of other theatres in operation at this time that were performing for large audiences in the streets. The Berkeley Radical Arts Troupe in California, the Burning City Street Theatre in New York, Bodacious Buggerrilla, City Street Theatre, and numerous others were working as collectives to create performance pieces that had a striking political punch. In New Orleans, the long-lived Free Southern Theatre was forming as part of the civil rights movement through the collaborative efforts of several northern theatre innovators and John O'Neal, who still performs plays that are celebrations of the hardships and the positive values of African-American culture.

In spite of all this activity, which was as vibrant in many ways as the workers' theatre of the thirties that it resembled, we tend to think only of the other wing of the alternative theatre movement: to think of the theatre of the sixties as a time of radical experimentation with form, with acting approach, and with mode of creation. In many ways, it is to this experimental theatre of the sixties and early seventies that current people's theatres, and particularly collectives, trace their roots. However, the alternative theatre of that time differed greatly from the political theatre before or after it. For one thing, the connection between theatre makers and the broader society was tenuous at best. One must remember that the workers and intellectuals were frequently on opposite sides of debates about the war and many other issues in the sixties: often not because of substantive differences, but because of the hazy definition of patriotism that remained as the legacy of World War II and the cold war mentality, and also because of differences in life-style. While "Peoples' Theatre groups in the 1930s publicly endorsed Communist ideology while members continued to live as practicing capitalists in private[, in] the 1960s and 1970s groups conversely tended to softpedal "leftist" polemic while practicing marginal lifestyles and employing collective techniques in creating their art (Jenkins 315–16). Theatre makers were not seen, either by themselves or their audiences (or hoped-for audiences), as workers.

Second, the theatre revolt in the sixties was more self-reflexive and more concerned with theatre makers and their art than their politics, with their relationship to themselves rather than their audiences. "What else could be expected of genuinely dissatisfied but self-involved workers who were the product of an increasingly self-involved profession that served an intensely self-involved, elite, isolated audience" (Paterson, "Working Paper" 14). It is not surprising, therefore, that experimental theatres chose forms that were even less accessible, based on an aesthetic that concentrated on the creators and shocked or alienated the audience. Ironically, this made the theatre even more elitist and limited further, but did not change the composition of, the audience. Undoubtedly, some of the impetus for this kind of attitude came from the atmosphere of confrontation in the streets while some was motivated by a genuine concern for social change, but the real thrust of experimentation in the sixties was toward freeing the artist *from* his or her audience and the demands of its expectations to allow great latitude in exploring the development of the actor and the forms in which he or she could perform on stage.

This concern of artists for their art was not necessarily politically regressive; it was a healthy and necessary step in the evolution of American alternative theatre, and still provides a route for development in all theatre venues. Guerrilla theatre was producing excitement, but very little lasting work. There was commitment, but no innovation and little growth. In addition, life itself was becoming more theatrical, especially in the political arena. Frequently, events with a purely political thrust were more theatrical than the theatre performances in the street, and the distinction between the work of making theatre and anything else was disappearing. Yet to many people the theatre was worth protecting as a separate and identifiable product that celebrated culture in its broadest sense.

This is not to say these artists and critics did not see themselves as antiestablishment. Many felt that the dominant forms of creation and presentation were repressive regardless of content. Unfortunately, this often led theatre makers to a glorification of form that was even more mystifying, more thoroughly concerned with theatre as performance and exhibition than as interaction, than before. One need only read Marcuse's rather romantic justification of art as being necessarily oppositional if it is original and nonconformist to see how far even the most intellectually demanding leftist theorists would go to try to make sense of sixties experimentation.[11] While it may be argued that this critical bent is an extension of the Marxist aesthetic defining art as "creative intervention" rather than reflection (Georg Lukacs), or of Pierre Macherey's persuasive argument about art deforming reality so as to parody and thereby reveal its truth, it at times came rather close to defending art for art's sake.

Perhaps it was the pervasive activism of the period, the frequently heard call for unity, or the more general breakdown of social convention that prevented such a defense. For whatever reason, there remained even among experimental theatre workers a desire to form connections, to create positive tension between the performers and the audience that would break down the accepted rigidity of theatre behavior. For many this meant audience participation: from the Living Theatre's attempt to dissolve entirely the difference between performer and audience, on one extreme, to the OM theatre's gentle hand-holding with audiences in church pews and The Performance Group's radical change in the physical relationship between audience and stage.

The Performance Group (TPG), founded by Richard Schechner, developed the concept of *environmental theatre*, in which the entire space inside the theatre is part of the ambiance, if not the actual performance area. The audience was fragmented, with different groups sitting in a variety of areas and having a variety of perspectives on the action. Sometimes audience members were invited to move between areas during the action to change that perspective or to become part of the play itself. TPG was also devoted to new methods of actor training and new performance styles, many of which have had an impact on all forms of contemporary theatre. Its updating of Greek tragedy in *Dionysus in 69*, and its drawing of parallels in *Commune* between the Sharon Tate murder by the Manson Family and the massacre of Vietnamese civilians at My Lai, generated a great deal of excitement and influenced a number of experimental and more overtly didactic theatres.[12]

Although The Performance Group had a definite sociopolitical context for its work, its goal was not to reach people in the same manner, or to reach the same specific ends, as the more politically oriented street theatres. The concern of TPG was the process of creation and how it could be sustained as part of the performance event. In its search for a means to bring the audience into the creative act by exhibiting the performer as artist rather than hiding her or him as character, TPG made use of the methods of Grotowski, of shamans in primitive cultures, and of any ritual that seemed to contribute to the movement of the group.

The reliance on ritual as a guide was typical of many theatres of the sixties, because ritual was seen as a way to reconnect each actor with his or her own inner drives, with the collective unconsciousness, and with the roots of the theatre itself. The level of participation—of almost total involvement in the creative act—during a ritual freed the actor from the strictures of craft without removing the tools of performance. As with collective organization, ritual was seen as a means of reintegration into the process of creation that had been taken from theatre makers by money-makers who controlled established venues in America.

However, because the work of theatre making is so unusual to the audience, adding an additional layer of rituals foreign to audience members did not lead to a return of any primeval relationship, but only to greater distance between performers and theatregoers. Theatres began to exhibit the process of theatre making instead of the product, thereby taking away one more indication that those in the theatre are cultural workers who produce something that is an integral part of society's activity. In addition, the reliance on the type of transformation necessary to participate in a ritual drove wedges between performers whose politics demanded careful analysis and those who felt that some sort of spiritual revitalization was the way to discover progressive truths, and it helps account for the dissolution of several collective theatres.

Nevertheless, performers did need to search for new means of presenting social and human problems on stage. The theatre of the establishment, of heroes discovering ways to salvage the status quo or remove those considered unfit to remain in society (even if that meant their own deaths), was failing to satisfy its practitioners or to represent a progressive political and economic perspective. "The theatre of character, of problems and resolutions, the theatre of beings uttering intelligently formed, balanced sentences, the theatre of significant scenes, of fortuitous events, was no longer working for many of us" (Sainer 15). It became necessary to develop new performance theories to promote the creation of theatre that would inspire audiences to respect themselves and their own ability to create a society that is supportive of their needs and cultural prerogatives. (This can be seen as the political core of much sixties experimentation.) First, however, it became necessary to create a working ambiance that would support such development, and for many groups, that meant collective structure.

However, the sixties was a period of crises, and the pull of particular events and issues that demanded immediate attention was not always conducive to the sustained development needed by collectives. The Pageant Players, the Company, and other groups were torn apart by political debates. The group that left the Company formed the Provisional Theatre in 1972, a collective devoted to political theatre, that disbanded in 1984. The Pageant did not survive, and the Living Theatre lost its following. The work of Richard Schechner continues into the 1990s, but in a direction that is less influential on the new political theatre movement.

A most influential theatre of the period was the Open Theatre, which was under the direction, although in a collaborative sense, of Joseph Chaikin, a veteran of early Living Theatre productions. The Open Theatre developed a highly physical acting style through actor input and disciplined training, but discovered that its work could not move to the stage without the assistance of playwrights. Claude von Italie, Susan Yankowitz, and others worked with the group and created scripts that could be performed by other companies. This allowed the Open to spread its work in much the same way that the workers' theatres shared their scripts. Yet it is for its highly individualistic creations, such as *Terminal*, that the Open is remembered, and also for its carefully documented actor training approach. Nevertheless, the Open Theatre can be seen as a transitional group, becoming decreasingly self-indulgent and increasingly representative of and concerned with its audience.

The proliferation of the ensemble—of groups and not individual artists— in the sixties was perhaps the most significant development in recent theatre history. The number of theatres with a political or people's orientation was staggering, and although many were short-lived, most contributed to audience expansion. The number of experimental groups was large as well, and each of them functioned both to train artists and to push theatre beyond the limits of form and content established by the commercial power structure. Collectives fostered a new sense of freedom and support and, by removing their members from repressive hierarchies, promoted serious social criticism and sustained growth. Although few survived the end of the war in Vietnam and the dissolution of radical student groups that had provided focus and support, their members have become leaders in the development of a new people's theatre as it has moved towards grassroots connections, working-class audiences, and the support of cultural democracy.

THE SEVENTIES AND EARLY EIGHTIES

The people's theatre of the past fifteen years or so has been a logical continuation of the work begun by both guerrilla and experimental theatre makers in the political turmoil of the sixties. As would be expected, when the sense of crisis and confrontation of the sixties passed, there began to be a realization that problems and solutions were more complex than had been perceived before. Jerry Rubin perhaps best summarized the dichotomies of the sixties and early seventies by saying "You're either part of the solution or part of the problem." However, contemporary political theatre makers have begun to realize that there are more levels to consider and more people to reach.

Throughout the seventies, collectives with progressive political goals quietly proliferated. Feminist theatres such as Alive and Trucking and At the Foot of the Mountain, both in Minneapolis, Lilith in San Francisco, and Spiderwoman in New York, created moving analyses of the plight of women and discovered images that were very much outside the pall of Western machismo. The Boston Theatre Group began to explore ways in which classical texts could generate images of contemporary struggle. In San Francisco, the Plutonium Players were formed to produce antinuclear street theatre, and later created the nationally known Ladies Against Women; while in Seattle, the Theatre Picaro was working for families to reinforce the value of self-trust and impulsive action. The Street Theatre in Ossining, New York, began to produce plays that helped prison inmates see themselves in new ways, while the Roadside Theatre in Whitesburg, Kentucky, brought traditional Appalachian stories to the stage in an effort at cultural ecology and the Dakota Theatre Caravan brought theatre to rural South Dakota. At the same time, David Olson brought what he had learned in Colombia to St. Peter, Minnesota, and founded the Cherry Creek Theatre which integrated its work into small-town life to such an extent that when it sponsored a Gathering of people's theatre makers and artists from around the country, almost the entire town participated in the event.[13] The United Mime Workers finished their stint as students and began their sophisticated explorations of economics and theatrical form, while Chicano students in Santa Barbara, California, were forming El Teatro de la Esperanza to reach beyond the bounds of the university.

Meanwhile, groups like the Provisional; the New York Street Theatre Caravan; the People's Theatre of Cambridge, Massachusetts; Theatre X of Milwaukee; and the San Francisco Mime Troupe continued the efforts they had begun in the sixties. And they continued to grow, as did their audiences. New alliances began to be formed, particularly with working class audiences and organizations, and new theatres began to build on them.

In 1976 the Iron Clad Agreement was founded in Pittsburgh, and only four years later it was able to mount a season of seven new plays, created specifically for working class audiences and staged 180 times for about 30,000 people.[14] Although not fully collectivized, the Iron Clad is much more democratically structured than most traditional theatres. The Modern Times Theatre, founded in New York in 1977, is a collective that since 1983 has supported a company of six year-round.

Near the end of the decade, Word of Mouth Productions (WOMP), a collective of working women creating productions for other working-class women, was formed in Boston, and Split Britches began to collectively create pieces in the East Village in New York City that would challenge the heterosexual male's dominance of theatre and would soon play to audiences all across the United States and Europe.

For these theatres and others like them, the impetus was mostly sociopolitical, but their expanding diversity (what some call a response to our postmodern sensibility),[15] increasing sophistication as artists, and developing relationships with their audiences allowed for a resurgence of the challenge begun in the sixties to the organizational and presentational strictures of mainstream theatre.[16]

The debt to experimental theatre is most easily seen in the continuation of the exploration of form. Theatres such as Otrabanda in New York and the United Mime Workers continued to experiment with radically new ways to communicate, while groups like the Play Group and the Dakota Theatre Caravan searched for means of making relatively direct contact through easily recognizable manifestations of their audiences' lives. A group such as Theatre X, although it is not often as closely associated with people's as with "alternative" theatres (a term that has come to mean apolitical), has continued to work as a collective, to explore questions of actor vulnerability and responsibility, and to create pieces that challenge audiences both in the United States and abroad. For them, social responsibility begins with individual responsibility, and their plays tend to focus on the consequences of individual action. They are empowering without seeming to be at all didactic, and yet they are striking in their variety of style and innovation of structure.

In this way, Theatre X and groups that are more openly didactic, like The Talking Band (made up mostly of members of the Open Theatre), or more devotedly ethnic or issue-oriented, have sustained the belief of the sixties (and the thirties) that the theatre must be an educational tool. However, this understanding is far more mature than it was only a decade ago.

The work of A Traveling Jewish Theatre (A TJT) of San Francisco, a small collective, provides a typical example. A TJT performs original creations about the Jewish experience specifically, but really about issues that dominate much of the contemporary people's theatre movement: "cultural diversity, celebration of life and language, victory over despair, the power of the theatre to revive the souls of the oppressed" (Weinberg 6). More important, it is clear from the work of A TJT that oppression is not a necessity and that the power to change society lies in the hands of the audience. The group begins, as did ethnic theatres in the thirties, with a particular audience or theme and use it to communicate to a mass audience. The same could be said of any of a number of feminist theatre companies, companies that explore racial issues, and theatres whose major focus is on discrimination due to sexual preference. It is in the historic and situational specificity of these works that their breadth of appeal lies—not in what the mainstream bourgeois theatre defines as "universality."

The difficulty, of course, is that theatre that seeks change must reach an audience that is bombarded by the rhetoric of bourgeois hegemony through the mass media and has been educated to be without historical sense or revolutionary commitment. It is for this reason that people's theatres have sought to make connections with the communities from which they draw their audiences and whose interests they represent.

The need for complexity and connectedness helps account, as well, for the resurgence of collective companies. It has been necessary since the sixties for theatre companies that wish to have any real impact to analyze conditions in a rather complex manner and yet to produce accessible and entertaining works that present that analysis clearly. This is a particularly difficult task when the position taken is outside the dominant ideology. In a collective, the model for the desired social structure can be used as a context for these arduous explorations;

moreover, the temptation to allow easy clarity to replace intellectual and artistic integrity is much harder to succumb to when the scrutiny of the collective center can serve as a balance to the quick fix of an individual moment.

In addition, the process of the struggle of collective members is very much like the struggle of the working class, from whom people's theatre audiences are often drawn. The community of and around the collective provides a place for reenfranchising the cultural worker and reconnecting the theatre maker to his or her audience. The collective member's revitalized sense of community helps him or her discover images that will appeal to and yet disturb whatever audience the theatre initially attracts: images that will "remain vivid in the mind of the spectator, and serve to displace traditional concepts which are the products of ideological repression within a system" (Moreno 38). Change only comes from dissatisfaction with the world as it is and a belief that it can and should be different.

Finally, there is room in a collective for a full exploration of the emotional responses of a variety of people to each situation. Audiences respond to emotion on stage, and can be led to disempowering conclusions by careful manipulation of those emotions. The collective structure mitigates against this by filtering personal response through the center of the collective process. In addition, the variety of responses of individuals in collective rehearsals brings, even to an agreed-upon political philosophy, a human and exciting diversity. When playwright Sidney Howard was asked in the late 1930s which political outlook he felt gave the greatest "creative stimulation," he responded: "Any consistently conscientious outlook on life may be guaranteed to make a bore of any man....Revolutionaries and fascists are permitted to be bores, but not dramatists" (Williams 127). Collective diversity and growth are constantly stimulating.

In the United States the number of collectives is growing but is still relatively small, and collective work is still developing as part of the artist's continued dissatisfaction with traditional theatre and her or his need to return to the fulfilling sense of belonging to a community. As late as 1977, Mark Amitin, who had long been involved in political theatre, stated that people with education in theatre at the college level "have to understand that they can never make truly people's theatre because they are intellectuals, and they probably come from the bourgeois class" (Jenkins 370). This elitist concept, that training and intelligence separate an artist from the people and that there is no way to join a community if an artist's background is bourgeois, is part of what prevented the theatre from being as powerful a political tool as it might have been in the late sixties and early seventies. Such attitudes isolate artists from the people by the very fact that artists know how to do what they are doing. In the collective, however, the isolation of expertise and of background is decreased, allowing each member to feel more involved in her or his own work and in the surrounding community.

FOUR REPRESENTATIVE THEATRES

The chapters that follow present the histories, trace the methods, and evaluate the productions of four collectives that have succeeded in creating theatre for particular communities and diverse audiences.

El Teatro de la Esperanza is a highly structured and rather large group whose central concern is exploring the problems of the large Chicano minority in the United States. The Dakota Theatre Caravan was a smaller group, also highly structured, that had as its major focus the lives and problems of rural peoples. The United Mime Workers had a much more flexible structure than the other two groups, and yet produced the most formally complex compositions of almost any people's theatre. Their target audience was rather generalized, but their scripts often dealt with the world of the workplace. Split Britches is a feminist collective with a distinct working method that is known particularly for their challenge to the traditional theatre's heterosexual imperative. Although their original East Village community was mostly lesbian, they play to and challenge a wide variety of audiences on both sides of the Atlantic. All four groups were or are thoroughly collectivized.

Each chapter is organized chronologically, and descriptions and critical evaluations of particular plays are interpolated where appropriate. The chapters also contain detailed sections describing the method that each collective uses to create its productions. I have tried, whenever possible, to give a sense of what it is like to watch or participate in the creative process employed by each group. Although a careful description of technique can reveal a great deal, it is the special sense of the center that is the province of collectives, and the personnel of each group determine the texture of that center.

NOTES

1. Split Britches, while it has not changed members permanently, has had temporary changes of performers, several managers and designers, and often modifies the group members' working relationships.

2. For a fuller study of the European backgrounds in the nineteenth and twentieth centuries, see Eugene Van Erven, *Radical People's Theatre*.

3. See the transcripts of the debate in Darko Suvin, "Organizational Mediation: The Paris Commune Theatre Law."

4. Williams 51. As history repeats itself, the Actors' Guild of Lexington, Inc., in Kentucky has made the radical (in some circles) decision to organize its permanent staff of eleven members, including the artistic manager, producing manager, and all business and technical coordinators, collectively. Each one has "an equal vote in all artistic, administrative, and management matters of the company" (bylaws). The theatre, however, uses many volunteers and hires directors who work in a hierarchical manner with casts chosen for individual productions of challenging texts that are written in a traditional manner by a variety of established playwrights. It is a successful compromise between democratic decision making and hierarchical production practices, with a broad audience and strong production record, but it resembles commercial theatre far more than people's theatre.

5. For a full account of WLT's history, see Douglas McDermott, "The Workers' Laboratory Theatre: Archetype and Example."

6. For a more detailed study of the Federal Theatre Project and other theatres of the period, see Morgan Himelstein, *Drama Was a Weapon: The Left-Wing Theatre in New York, 1929-1941*; Dwight Steward, *Stage Left*; Karen Malpede Taylor, *People's Theatre in Amerika*; and Jay Williams, *Stage Left.*

7. See Robert Skloot, "*We Will Never Die*: The Success and Failure of a Holocaust Pageant" for a more complete study of this production.

8. It is worth noting that in the Living Theatre's inaccessible political analysis, and in its desire to obliterate the distinction between performer and audience, were contained self-contradictions that were really the seeds of its own failure. Ultimately, the Living Theatre seems to have been on the furthest fringe: influential in exploring limits, in training performers who later worked in other theatres, and in shocking audiences, but providing little lasting contribution to politics or performance in the way it intended.

9. The early years of the Mime Troupe's history are documented in R.G. Davis, *The San Francisco Mime Troupe: The First 10 Years*. See also Joan Holden, "Collective Playmaking: the Why and the How," "The Melodrama is the Message," and Daniel Friedman, "Contemporary Theatre for Working-Class Audiences in the United States."

10. The early years of ETC's history are documented in Betty Diamond, "'Brown-Eyed Children of the Sun': The Cultural Politics of El Teatro Campesino."

11. Herbert Marcuse, "Art in the One-Dimensional Society."

12. See Richard Schechner's *Environmental Theatre* for a more complete history of TPG and a full articulation of the theory.

13. The Gathering brought together people's theatres and artists from around the country for nearly a week of performances, criticism, and collective development of ideas suggested by talks on topics of concern to people's artists in the summer of 1981. The atmosphere was supportive, respectful, and joyous. Each person (and the community he or she represented) was given due respect, and nothing that happened was deemed unimportant.

This is unlike many of the competitive or elitist conventions held by other groups. Compare, for example, my description of the Gathering, "Unity in Diversity," and accounts by Arlene Goldbard and Don Adams, "Vital Signs: The Gathering and Alternate Roots," and John Rezmerski, "Small Town Stereotypes Come Tumbling Down in St. Peter," with Michael Kirby's "Editorial: The Third-World Theatre Festival in Seoul," in which he wrote: "Related to this was a pervasive sense of inferiority. The implication seemed to be that the Third World was not as "good" as the first two worlds (whatever they were). The main topic of the symposia was the influence of the East upon the West, as if Eastern theatre could only be validated and authenticated if it had influenced the West....The value system by which Third World theatre was deprecated seemed to be primarily financial." (130)

14. See Daniel Friedman, "Contemporary Theatre for Working-Class Audiences in the United States" for information on many of the theatres mentioned above.

15. See Philip Auslander, "Toward a Concept of the Political in Postmodern Theatre," and letters in response to this article in later issues of *The Drama Review* by Richard Schechner (31,no.3), Philip Auslander, Johannes Birringer, John Bell, and Richard Schechner (32,no.2) and Philip Auslander ((33,no.2).

16. For an examination of the way in which audiences and theatre makers participate in a "theatrical formation" that allows for the creation of responsive audiences and response-generating genres, see Bruce McConachie, "Reading Context into Performance: Theatrical Formations and Social History."

3

El Teatro de la Esperanza

When an artist creates because of an external need, in conformity with principles, norms, or rules imposed from above, what had been a movement, a vital force, a conscious and sincere reverence for certain creative principles, becomes a formal, external, and therefore false, loyalty. What was alive becomes congealed, inert.

Sanchez Vazquez

The Chicano is a victim
of a subtle and complex
Form of Oppression
Which because of particular racial
and historical factors
Differs from traditional forms
Yet results in the same end
The exploitation of one group
For the benefit of another.

Prologue to *La Victima*

El Teatro de la Esperanza has one of the most thoroughly codified and most complex organizational structures of any collective theatre in the country. Not only does Esperanza have a specific (although evolving) methodology for conducting the collective creation of a play, but it also has a completely structured administrative and interpersonal committee system. It has managed, with varying degrees of success over the years, to balance the often conflicting needs of individuals, families, collective decision making, and organizational necessity without ever interrupting its real function—that of making politically relevant theatre.

Esperanza was not always a collective, however. It started in 1969 as Teatro Mecha, one of the many student groups that began to perform Chicano theatre after its revitalization in the late sixties by Luis Valdez's El Teatro Campesino. Although it was not until this period that Anglo culture became aware of the existence of this movement, Chicano theatre traces its roots directly to the Christian missionary drama of the sixteenth-century Spanish conquerors of Mexico and through them to the pre-Columbian ritual dramas of the Aztec and Mayan civilizations.

The theatre has always been an integral part of the lives of Central Americans, not only as religious ritual, but also as a means of entertainment and secular education as well. Pre-Columbian traveling troupes called *tlaquetzque* (those who make things stand out) toured widely before the conquest. Jesuit missionaries, in a pattern often repeated in other areas, adapted this and other existing forms to Christian theology, eventually leading the Indians away from their traditional religion and culture and their indigenous "pagan" theatre. According to Jorge Huerta, director of Esperanza during its earliest years, this "progression from native ritual to Christian drama demonstrates the vital role played by theatrical presentations in the colonization and subjugation of the indigenous peoples of Mexico and the South West. The didactic theatre of [the teatros] is directly related to the Spanish religious dramas that were imposed upon a thriving culture of rituals, dances, songs, and myths" (Huerta, *Chicano* 187). Ironically, that same missionary tradition now motivates a Chicano theatre that is attempting to *undo* the cultural imperialism of the past.

It is important to realize that the Anglo conception of Chicanos as merely an unassimilated minority composed of Mexican-American (or, even further from the truth, Spanish-American) immigrants is false and has been a factor in the ongoing struggle of Chicanos against racial oppression. A far more accurate view would be to see Chicanos as "a militarily conquered people [who] became victims of racism, and of political and economic oppression....[Seeing the Chicanos] as an internal colony of the United States makes clearer the way in which cultural oppression and political/economic oppression function as one" (Diamond 25). After all, it is in the interest of the conquerors to devalue precolonial history and to foster the belief that Chicanos should be happy as Frito Banditos, working for the culture that purportedly rescued them from Indian "barbarism."

There had been some resistance to forced hegemony since the mid-nineteenth century. Latino theatres toured the United States even before the great influx of refugees into the Southwest during the 1910 Mexican Revolution, helping to maintain Mexican and Puerto Rican identities and community solidarity, but they had little impact. During the twenties and early thirties Hispanic theatre had some commercial success in the Los Angeles area, but it was not until "the '60s, in the wake of the tremendous impulse toward re-evaluation of basic beliefs forced upon us all as a result of the civil rights movement and the

Viet Nam war, [that] there came a cause which generated sufficient fervency among Chicanos to precipitate a national movement, '*La Causa,*' the cause of Cesar Chavez and the United Farm Workers Union."[1]

The modern Chicano theatre movement began when, late in 1965, Luis Valdez left the San Francisco Mime Troupe to form El Teatro Campesino (Farmworkers' Theatre) as an organizing tool for the UFW. Campesino's rise was meteoric, and the form it created for reaching its nontheatregoing audience, the *acto*, became the mainstay of most of the dozens of Chicano theatres that followed it. The *acto* is a highly stylized, short, didactic, comic piece that demonstrates a practical solution to a specific problem, in a style that Valdez called a cross between "Brecht and Cantinflas." Performances were characterized by actors wearing signs naming their roles, exaggerated gestures, stereotypical characters, and collectively created skeletal scripts. According to Valdez, the *acto* had to "Inspire the audience to social action. Illuminate specific points about social problems. Satirize the opposition. Show or hint at a solution. Express what people are feeling" (Valdez 196). They always emphasized a social vision of a social reality.

Most Chicano groups that followed Valdez were formed by students, for students, and performed *actos* about student issues. Like Campesino, these groups were by and in a community: people's theatres in the fullest sense. But, the "people" of the student community are very transient, and although many of these companies were part of organizations of Chicano student civil rights activists, most dissolved when the members of the groups graduated college. The major exception is El Teatro de la Esperanza.

THE STUDENT YEARS—1970–1974

In April 1969, Chicano students from all over California met in Santa Barbara to plan for the improvement of educational standards and opportunities for Chicanos. The group created *El Plan de Santa Barbara: A Chicano Plan for Higher Education.* In it they expressed a determination to improve the lot of Chicanos with a fervor and optimism that can still be heard, although tempered by experience, more than twenty years later in the voices of the members of Esperanza:

> For the Chicano the present is a time of renaissance, of renacimiento. Our people and our community, el barrio and la colonia, are expressing a new consciousness and a new resolve. Recognizing the historical tasks confronting our people and fully aware of the cost of human progress, we pledge our will to move...against those forces which have denied us freedom of expression and human dignity. Throughout history the quest for cultural expression and freedom has taken the form of struggle (Huerta Evolution 196).

The students organized for battle. They formed MECHA, the *Movimiento Estudiantil Chicano de Aztlan* (Chicano Student Movement of Aztlan, the mythical home of the Aztecs, the "land to the north") which, because of nearly one hundred Chicano students with scholarships through the Educational Opportunity Program, had a very strong chapter at the University of California at Santa Barbara (UCSB).

Later that year, Juan Arroyo and Mike Cordero, two student members of a Mexican dance group who had been inspired by seeing performances of Campesino, created *actos* and performed them for incoming students to help with orientation. The response was so positive that there shortly arose Teatro Mecha, a group of fifteen Chicano students who, with help from an Anglo graduate student in theatre, dedicated themselves to "the education and politicization of *La Raza*....As a committee of MECHA, the teatro found that it had a real responsibility to the organization to perform and function as a didactic arm of the student movement," and the pressure for quick and appropriate productions was great.[2]

The University and MECHA were very supportive, and in July 1970, Jorge Huerta, who was soon to become the first Chicano with a Ph.D. in theatre, came to UCSB to work with the young *teatro*. During that summer, Title I provided funding for Huerta and seven students to do a ten week project that included three days of rehearsal and two days of community classes each week. This close attachment to the community was to serve the *teatro* well, possibly keeping it alive while most student groups failed, but would lead within a year to an acrimonious split from MECHA.

During the next school year Huerta taught a workshop course in which he screened and trained members for the *teatro*. That spring also saw the formation of TENAZ (*El Teatro Nacional de Aztlan*), a national coalition of Chicano *teatros* created to coordinate the political, cultural, and social aims of the rapidly growing *teatro* movement, as well as to provide a forum for the exchange of ideas and skills. At first, Campesino was the only nonstudent company and Valdez was the undisputed leader of the movement, which had swelled to nearly one hundred theatres by the mid-seventies. Their manifesto, written in 1973, is indicative of the political concerns that have always been part of Esperanza's creed, and of an attitude and ideal to which Esperanza is struggling in the nineties to cling. It is reprinted here as a statement not only of the principles of Chicano theatre, but of people's theatre in general.

Manifesto del Teatro Nacional de Aztlan

> Teatro Chicano was born of the social struggle of *la Raza*; given birth by workers, who remain workers. It is a renaissance: from the old comes the new. Theatre is the mirror of the spirit of the Movement. It is a mirror of Tezcatlipoca which reveals the evil we are

> surrounded by; it is the Spirit of Quetzalcoatl in which we find the goodness and the Hope of *la Raza.* Teatro is the voice of the *barrios* [Chicano areas or ghettos in North American cities], of the community, of those at the bottom, of the humble, of the *rasquachis* [the down-and-out, a term frequently used to refer to poor but flamboyant Chicano youth].
>
> The Workers of the National Theatre of Aztlan are committed to a way of Life/Struggle helping the people to understand the why of their individual and social problems and to search for solutions. Let our theatre be the human rainbow: let it create theatre for all of the people—for children, young people, old people, women, students, workers, farm workers and even for the sellouts. It should be nurtured in the cultural roots of our past in order to plant seeds of liberation in the present and to reap the victory of our people in the future.
>
> The organization of TENAZ, which will work with all oppressed peoples, must develop a humane revolutionary alternative to commercial theatre and mass media. It is also necessary that we work and unite with all theatres struggling for liberation wherever, particularly in Latin America. It should serve as a tool in the Life/Struggle of la Raza by developing theatres as community organizations.
>
> The theatre should go to the people and not the people to the theatre.

The thrust of the manifesto—the connectedness of *teatro* to the struggles of the people—was part of the basic belief of several of the members of Teatro Mecha in 1971. MECHA's goals were also the betterment of *la Raza*, but the general attitude of its leadership was that by virtue of their education and training, students should be a guiding force for the community, advising and directing, but with limited participation. The *teatro* members, on the other hand, were far more interested in active involvement, such as helping to convert an abandoned warehouse into La Casa de la Raza, a Chicano community center in Santa Barbara. In June, the leadership of MECHA demanded that one of the actresses in the *teatro* be removed because her political attachments were not to their liking. Estella Campus, Joey Garcia, Salvador Ortiz, Emiliano Peña, Diane Rodriguez, Jose Saucedo, and their director, Jorge Huerta, renounced their ties with MECHA and in July chose the name El Teatro de la Esperanza (The Theatre of Hope).

The new company began work on several projects immediately, the most important of which was the building of a theatre in La Casa. Santa Barbara was to have its yearly "*Spanish* Days" festival, at which businesses and the town council completely denied their *Mexican* heritage in order to lure in tourist money. In response, the Chicano community organized a Fiesta du la Communidad and, on August 10, 1971, presented the first performance of Teatro de la

Esperanza as part of the festivities. Seven hundred people were in the junior high school auditorium to watch an evening of Campesino written *actos*, music, and "Juan's Epitaph," a "performed poem" by Joey Garcia. Two days later, the same show was presented in "el Nido" (the Nest), the theatre Esperanza had constructed in La Casa from old pallets during the previous month.[3] They followed this with a tour of surrounding communities for free—they felt they had to earn the right to charge, but became so popular so quickly that self-respect and admission fees both came soon.

From the beginning, Esperanza evidenced the concerns that have characterized their work ever since: clarity, currency, and a devotion to a broad community of Chicanos, and further, to the working class of which they are a part. Consistent with the demands for political involvement in support of the community and artistic freedom that had precipitated their split with MECHA, the young teatro was not afraid to make changes in Valdez's *actos. Los Pelados* (The Underdogs or Nobodies) was about the exploitation of illegal aliens and American employer duplicity. Esperanza changed the dialogue to reflect Cesar Chavez's reversal of his support for the controversial Dixon-Arnett Law and the Rodino Bill, both of which would have penalized employers for hiring undocumented workers. One of Campesino's most popular actos, *Los Vendidos* (The Sellouts), in which Miss JIM-enez [sic], a secretary from Governor Ronald Reagan's office, is tricked out of the $15,000 she brought to Honest Sancho's Used Mexican Lot to buy a "Mexican type for the administration," ends when the victors head out for a party. Esperanza rewrote Valdez's ending, changing it to a decision by the Mexicanos to use the money to build a community center. Company members further involved themselves in the Santa Barbara Chicano culture by getting advice from a local *vato* (flamboyant street tough) on refining the physical style of the character Johnny Pachuco.

During the next school year, Huerta's class in practical Chicano theatre techniques and the Teatro were nearly identical. The first two quarters of the school year were used to prepare original material for a performance on May 4, 1972, at the *Cinco de Mayo* festival, a celebration of Mexican liberation. Hoping to establish its own image independent of Campesino, while still keeping its political concerns intact, El Teatro de la Esperanza presented a bill of one-acts written by members of the class.

The first, *La Trampa sin Salida* (The Trap without Exit) by Jaime Verdugo, was an *acto* based on reports in a Chicano underground newspaper "that Los Angeles County Sheriff's officers were killing *pachucos* (swaggering street "toughs") in their jail cells and reporting the murders as suicides" (Huerta, "Evolution" 302). In typical *acto* style, *La Trampa* uses masks, exaggerated villains, a "one-way" sign to direct all blocking, and a call to join "*El Movimiento*" at the end. Nevertheless, this play was in many ways more sophisticated than other *actos* in its richness, variety of incident—including job hunting, an argument at home, a fight, a murder, and a very funny scene in which a sociologist pays Johnny Ray for each "correct" answer in a study to prove that Chicanos are mentally inferior—and breadth of thematic concerns. Although the play stresses a chance for salvation in solidarity, the movement is not seen as the universal panacea. The main character, Johnny Ray, looks and moves like all other *pachucos* (identical masks and costumes ensure this and make a class comment on identity and affectation) and is harassed at every turn; yet it is not he but his friend Jesse who is murdered, a direct comment about the capriciousness of both the authorities and death itself. Moreover, Johnny is certainly not a pure hero: he is constantly in conflict with someone, even his own friends and brothers, and directly with the audience, forcing it to question its own responses to Chicano stereotypes.

The second play on the bill was *Panfila la Curandera* (Panfila the Curing Woman), a six-minute farcical *acto* about the positive aspects of barrio folk medicine, as seen in conflict with Mr. and Mrs. Fatkat and their high-priced doctors. Its importance at the time seemed to lie in its positive approach. In his introduction to the play in its published edition, Jorge Huerta stated that "this should be the beginning of many more *positive* statements about our people; statements that can help renew and uplift our indigenous pride, without having to cut anybody else down in the process" (*Anthology* 30). In retrospect, the fact that it was created improvisationally but based on the script of Antonio Lopez, a member of the group, was more significant in that it foreshadowed the collective work to come.

Brujerias

The final play, *Brujerias*, was to establish Esperanza as the second leading *teatro* in the Chicano movement and its author, Rodrigo Duarte-Clark, as a leading Chicano playwright. It was performed in October at El Primer Festival Internacional de Teatro Latino-America in San Francisco, to which Esperanza and Campesino had been invited as the representatives of Chicano theatre. The following year it was made into the first film of an original Chicano drama: written, directed, filmed, and acted by Chicanos speaking "Spanglish," a mixture of English and Spanish unique to the bilingual Chicano community.

Brujerias is a light comedy poking fun at the superstition of two old Mexicanos. Its sharpest barbs are saved for the church, whose greed and dogma serve only to foster their foolishness. The plot is simple: Dona Petra, who covets Old Juana's house, calls the Immigration and Naturalization Service (INS) to report Dona Juana as an illegal alien. Don Rafael, her husband, believes that Dona Juana is a witch and, overreacting to simple natural events because of her own guilt, Petra comes to believe it as well. Together they go to wise old Tia Olga for guidance, and she tells them to bribe a priest to get holy water to sprinkle in their house to protect them from witches at night. Petra and Rafael follow her instructions, but drop the holy water vial accidentally. When they return to Tia Olga's to tell her about Juana they find that the old woman was neither a witch nor an illegal alien, and that she has moved anyway.

Thematically, it is not only Petra's greed that perverts her belief, but also her attempted collusion with *la migra* (the immigration officer). The history of acceptance and then deportation of undocumented Mexican workers in the United States and the use of the INS to implement this cruel exploitation had made the mere mention of *la migra* anathema to a Chicano audience. That Petra uses the INS to further her own greedy ends is almost unthinkable. Nevertheless, both main characters are basically good people, and since no actual immigration officer or priest appears on stage, there is no evil symbol.

This was not the only departure by Duarte-Clark from the conventions of the *acto*. Clearly, the play at least mildly chastised Latinos: an attitude almost unheard of in earlier Chicano theatre. In fact, this play was attacked by the "politicos" for reinforcing racial stereotypes (at the same time as these identical political complainants approved of the portrait of the *pachuco* in *La Trampa*). The theatre was upset by this but, convinced that *Brujerias* was a strong play and a vehicle for social comment, they decided to revise it to clarify its political content. This established a pattern that is still occurring in Esperanza: that of modifying works with the goal of political clarity, based on the criticism of aware and concerned audiences.

> [Actually] Rodrigo said he had not written this play to make any kind of socio-political comment, but we saw a good opportunity to satirize our superstitious compadres y comadres [compatriots] with his comedy. Yet, when we first produced it, most people did not catch any of the comments we were trying to point out. Taking our cue from the Greeks, we decided to add a chorus in the form of El Espiritu [de la Supersticion] . . . to comment upon what the characters do and say in an effort to point out the social and political motivations for their actions. (Huerta, *Anthology* 40)

Unfortunately the Spirit, who appears on stage to do an opening song, deliver explanatory narration, and make on-stage sound effects, was only mildly interesting theatrically and merely redundant verbally. The speeches, like many of those attempted for political clarity in other Esperanza plays, were never integrated into the flow of the events, and the character was dropped for the film (in which naturalistic causes of the sounds were shown, and a scene with the priest was added) and for later performances.

The interruptions by El Espiritu were purposefully designed to alienate audiences from the flow of the plot and, like Brecht's titles, to clarify. This early experimentation was not, however, based on a feeling that a Latino audience was unable to understand and interpret the messages of Esperanza's plays. Rather, it was a conscious attempt to implement what the group saw as the basic tenets of Brechtian theory: that the audience should be forced to think by performers who were "demonstrators" more than actors. Never did Esperanza deny the value of emotional attachment to characters by their audiences. In fact, some of the finest moments in the company's plays are points of emotional wrenching that verge precariously on the edge of melodramatic posturing. This balancing act is the result of conscious technique modified by a clear understanding of the needs of Esperanza's nontraditional audiences, and it is one of the greatest strengths of their performances.

The *teatro* has always been concerned with a system of checks and balances that would prevent its plays from wallowing in emotion at the expense of progressive ideology. Members often speak of their plays in terms of thesis and proof, and discussions of purpose relate to political as often as to dramatic necessity. Esperanza seeks to clarify causes in their plays and to present a picture of people fulfilling, often unwittingly, roles that have been forced on them by the circumstances of American capitalistic society, and not merely of idiosyncratic (although psychologically full) characters. In response to a question about the tension between the emotional and political purposes of Esperanza's plays, Rodrigo Duarte-Clark replied:

> I'm concerned with the *kind* of thinking. A lot of people are moved and forced to think, forced to question some things about their own existence. But...the kind of teachers that we are...makes people think and question, but the questions have not been developed enough. So when I say thinking, I mean a specific kind of critical thinking.
>
> I think the problem in the U.S. is that people don't know how to question. They might be able to rebel...but they don't know how to ideologically attribute something. It's not just the issue, but how to think about the issue. (interview)

Esperanza continued performing during the summer of 1972, and by August of that year had built El Auditorio, a 140-seat theatre in La Casa that became a multiuse auditorium for the community and Esperanza's rehearsal hall. Several members of the company also worked with the Trust Company, a community group developing creative outlets for juvenile delinquents. The students returned to the university with high hopes, but scholastic demands prevented them from creating any major work other than the film of *Brujerias*.

The *teatro* did open another trilogy of originals for the Cinco de Mayo festival of 1973, but none of the plays showed a great deal of growth from the previous year. *Los Pelados* was an imitative *acto* that dealt with immigration laws, "actually an urban version of *La Quinta Temporada* (The Fifth Season)" (Huerta, "Evolution" 366-67), one of Campesino's most popular *actos*. Racism was the subject of *La Cucaracha* (The Cockroach), and the rise of the Chicano movement was chronicled in Jorge Huerta's *Renaciamiento de Huitzilopochtli* (The Renaissance of Huitzilopochtli). The most important development that year was a growing sense of self-confidence and a desire to find a working method that was reflective of the political concerns of the group.

During the Summer of 1973, *El Teatro de la Esperanza: An*

Anthology of Chicano Drama (a volume edited by Huerta and containing the six *actos* previously mentioned, with introductions, production notes, and photos) was published. Esperanza was a great success at the TENAZ sponsored Fourth Annual Festival de los Teatros Chicanos in San Jose, California, and began to assume leadership of the movement in which they became the only extant, full-time touring *teatro*.

By this time, the Chicano theatre had developed several fairly distinct forms in addition to the *acto*.[4] The insistence of Valdez on the importance of the *mito*, a religious form, led to an unpleasant split between Campesino and TENAZ (and the entire rest of the Chicano theatre movement) not too long after. Esperanza, on the other hand, was aligned with forces that would keep it writing in forms that are far more responsive to the immediacy of events in Chicano life.

For one thing, Esperanza had been very successful both in maintaining its student group atmosphere and in finding from that perspective issues that touched a broader community. Very early in their work the members began to see positive and immediate effects. For example:

> an acto recreating a high school counselor who tells the Chicano student he cannot go to college because "your people work better with your hands," aroused the audience's indignation as well as recognition that many of them had also suffered this form of discrimination in the schools. When high school students witnessed this acto they began to question the validity of the counseling services available to them, if any, and would approach the platform after the presentation and ask how they could get more information about colleges and universities. (Huerta, "Keeping in Touch" 38)

At the same time, the flush of pride in just being a Chicano performing on stage for other Chicanos was becoming less important as the group became more experienced, and there arose a real desire to be something more. Jose Saucedo, the last member of the original company to leave the group, remembered making his own decision to push the group toward fuller participation in the community. He had seen Teatro Experimental de Cali (TEC) from Colombia the year before. "I said to the group that, 'I want to do this.' And one day we can become what they are for their country. What they are for the Columbian people, we can be for the Chicano people. We can take theatre and reflect our communities' problems, entertain, and at the same time educate" (interview).

In 1973, the group incorporated as a non-profit organization, severed ties with La Raza Libre (a rather radical student group that had given them support and funding after the split from MECHA), and began to work with the support of their own NEA grant. "For many of the actors, Teatro had been their source of self-education and change from identity as Mexican-Americans to Chicanos. Emelio Peña put it this way: 'I didn't even like to hear the word Chicano. I thought it was something vulgar, lower class. When I became involved in the Chicano movement in Teatro, I began to appreciate what I had—my culture, my heritage, the language'" (Cless 12). They began to search for an appropriate subject for a full-length play, not a very difficult task considering the widespread oppression of Chicanos then and now.

Guadalupe

The immediate inspiration for the group's next play, *Guadalupe*, came from a 1973 report by the California State Advisory Committee to the United States Commission on Civil Rights entitled *The Schools of Guadalupe... A Legacy of Educational Oppression.*[5] Guadalupe provided the perfect subject for a docudrama, the form on which the company had decided. It was a typical barrio: 80 percent of the population was Spanish-surnamed, a small group of wealthy landowners controlled the poverty-ridden population, and teacher brutality and insensitivity had already been documented by the government itself. In addition, it was close enough for firsthand research and had already been rocked by battles between a group of parents and individuals who sought to maintain the feudal economy under which many Chicanos suffered.

Research on *Guadalupe* began in January 1974 with the report and was followed by the reading of local newspapers and court transcripts, interviews with the residents who were involved in the struggle, and attendance at local events. Information was then shared in the group, and improvisations were begun to flesh out actual incidents and delineate the motivations of composite characters. The piece was collectively written, directed by Jorge Huerta, and premiered in Santa Barbara on Cinco de Mayo, 1974.

The play, consisting of thirteen scenes and an epilogue connected by narration sung to the music of well known *corridos* (popular ballads)

> was based on the concept that the problems with the local elementary school in Guadalupe, California began with the wealthy agriculturalists and filtered down through the police, the local judge (who was the husband of the school principal), the school principal, the teachers, the John Birch Society, and the local priest. "Those of you who follow Cesar Chavez or join his union will go directly to hell!" This massive opposition to educational and social equality was most visibly an issue of unionization. The hypothesis was that the educational system was operating to keep Chicanos down on the farm and was geared to "de-Chicanoize" the Chicano population of Guadalupe. (Jenkins 53)

The goal of Esperanza was to effect change in this repressive conspiracy, and it succeeded.

The scenario is based on the actual efforts of a parent group to improve classroom situations for their children, who had been forbidden to speak Spanish, beaten, and placed in classes for the retarded because they could not speak English. To end the protest, the controlling powers of Guadalupe orchestrated a "community confrontation" by inviting a John Birch representative to a parent-teacher meeting in order to incite the parents. Three weeks after the meeting, which ended in the expected shouting match, nine parents were notified of their arrests by mail, found guilty of disturbing a public meeting, and sentenced to jail or probation. The harassment so frightened the town that all protest was silenced.

Guadalupe begins as if this meeting were in progress. Marcos Cortez, the speaker, calls to the guards to take their places and begins haranguing the audience for being ungrateful to school administrators, for allowing their children to "run wild like animals," and for being led astray by MECHA, the Brown Berets (militant Chicano activists), and the UFW. The cast shouts back from their places in the audience, until Cortez, "ashamed to call myself Spanish," unfurls Nazi, Communist, and UFW flags claiming that Chavez should be compared to Hitler. The cast begins chanting "Que viva Cesar Chavez," trying to get the entire audience to join in. Suddenly there is a drum beat and everyone freezes. The actor playing Cortez announces: "This parent-teacher meeting took place on March 16, 1972 in Guadalupe, California. The following events led up to this meeting," while a "demonstrator/actress" from the audience makes the same announcement in Spanish. This is the first of many sociopolitical statements with factual support that serve as transitions in the play.

At this point the cast gathers on stage to sing a song admonishing the audience to take action based on what they are to hear. The final line, "*E-scuchen este hecho y pongan atencion* (Listen to the truth, and pay attention)," is both driving and demanding. The next scene is also a song in which each verse or group of verses introduces a problem which is then demonstrated in dialogue while the music continues. The actors pantomime being *campesinos* (farmworkers) at work while singing and break out of their activity to demonstrate an inclusive list of problems, all of which exist but many of which comprise only the distant background of this play, unfortunately dissipating the strong opening focus.

The play proper concerns four separate elements in two plots. In the central action, the parents/workers decide, partly in response to a student walkout, that in spite of the risk to their jobs (and the wrath of *la migra*) they will organize as workers and as concerned parents. Eventually, two of the parents are sent as representatives of the committee to the school superintendent, who blames the children for lying and being stupid, and says that he is doing just what they asked him to do the last time there was a problem. For example, he is preserving Chicano culture by not allowing Chicano students to use silverware, "and letting them eat with their hands as they are accustomed to at home." The final time we see the parents is in a scene that is played simultaneously with a secret meeting of the school board at which both groups plan strategy.

The second element in this plot is the children. In the two strongest scenes in the play, the audience sees students being abused and humiliated in school. In the first, a student is mistreated by a teacher who lectures the class on the need for subservience, while on the opposite side of the stage a priest is exhorting kneeling parishioners to be faithful and obedient. The scene begins with the simultaneous recital of the Pledge of Allegiance and the Lord's Prayer and ends, in a moment of extremely effective staging, as the kneeling parishioners become *campesinos* and sing a song titled "A Life of Slow Death," drawing an analogy between spiritual, political, and material enslavement. In the other school scene, a student who was named Guadalupe after the Virgin of Guadalupe is not allowed to give a report on her name because it is not about the town and because she wants to use Spanish. It is significant that the only person in the classroom who cannot speak Spanish is the teacher.

The final element in this plot concerns the two town gossips. They always enter to a light theme song and provide comic relief as well as political comment on the action. They support the forces of personal safety and inertia, showing interest only in gossip that will damage others.

The subplot, while not really tied to the main plot except by the intimation that dropping out of school is the root of social evils, concerns a drug addict, Jesse, who sells his wife's favors for a fix. Jesse is the brother of one of the students involved in the walkout and the son of one of the strike leaders, Virgie.

The penultimate scene is an extended repetition of the opening scene. The scene is not identical, however, as it uses freezes and drum rolls between selected indicative lines to control the pacing and build tension. The final scene includes a policeman reading a report to the court, an impassioned speech by Virgie, as if she was at a demonstration protesting the arrests and sentencing, and a final song calling for united action.

Guadalupe was extremely effective in all ways. Most important to the members of Esperanza at the time was the fact that it caused several changes in actual social circumstances. In the town of Guadalupe, the parents' committee renewed its struggle. Shortly after, a cast member was hired as a bilingual/cross-cultural specialist, and six other positions in that category were added to the school system. Several other audiences reacted with calls to their own school boards for bilingual programs, and in East Los Angeles a parent group organized to investigate complaints in their area and to demand educational reform. In a jungle village in Veracruz, Mexico, hundreds of *campesinos* joined a local farmworkers' organization immediately after seeing a performance. Audiences everywhere expressed a new understanding of systemic exploitation and thanked Esperanza for making them feel less isolated. Mexican viewers were so impressed that they persuaded Esperanza to do a videotaped adaptation which received national airing in Mexico, and an interesting documentary about the documentary was aired on West Coast public television stations.

Guadalupe was successful on stage as well, even though the dialogue is frequently overly economic, consisting of skeletal conversations and lacking color and texture. It is a compendium of Brechtian devices, each used in a naive but straightforward manner. Suspense plays no part at all in this drama—the play begins with the climactic meeting—yet the extensive use of narration over music serves to focus audience attention on the evolving story. The highly episodic structure, with interruptions for political statements, is used to provide a cumulative sense of oppression. In addition, the use of expository scenes that are not necessarily dictated by the story (e.g., an argument between the gossips over involvement and a fight in a bar between Mexican and Chicano workers) further emphasizes the sense of universal systemic abuse requiring a remedy that includes the entire population.

The staging techniques also serve to remind the audience that it is in a theatre where analysis is more important than empathy. Tableaux and simultaneous staging, pantomime, and symbolic settings make theatrically exciting visual comments on the dialogue and action. The constant presence of the actors, changing costumes and roles in front of the audience and reacting naturally from the sides to the actions on stage, reinforces the sense of actors as workers creating a useful product.

The performance contains a variety of acting styles, a device still used by Esperanza as part of a form that they hope will more easily reach an audience than straight psychological realism and will more clearly draw the political roles in character relationships. In *Guadalupe,* the antagonists are portrayed naturalistically, patterned on assumptions made about actual townspeople that were gleaned from interviews. The gossips are more caricatured and stereotyped, but still portrayed in a relatively realistic mode. The villains, however, use highly stylized movement and all wear clear plastic masks that give them personal anonymity, thereby focusing instead on their positions in society. The result is that the system itself, and not the individuals within it, becomes the real villain and the economic motivation for systemic repression became eminently clear. This was further emphasized by the casting of the same actors in the roles of different characters, thus implying that they represent analogous evils, such as teacher and drug pusher, grower and priest.

The stylistic variety and the complexity of the issues (coupled with the fact that there is no easily chanted solution proposed at the end to replace critical reaction with revolutionary fervor) made great demands on the young performers. Chicano critics at the time frequently praised the actors for their "energy" and "commitment," euphemisms for a lack of skill, of which direct mention would be inappropriate in a political review full of well-deserved praise for the play. The videotape reveals young, rather inexperienced actors who are so clearly moved by their desire to communicate the seriousness of their message that questions of acting technique become secondary. The standard of effectiveness was at that time more applicable than that of aesthetics.

And yet the staging is innovative, and structurally the play is quite clever and effective. Its appeal was so broad that it simultaneously received praise for dispensing with Brechtian objectivity to achieve an emotional appeal that would attract a Chicano audience already alienated by the very unfamiliarity of the theatre, as well as for the fullness of its Brechtian approach, replacing empathy with "conscious questioning" in an "artistic expression for [the Chicano movement's] political and cultural ideologies."[6]

However, the group did not bathe in the glory of *Guadalupe* for long. Most of the members graduated college that year and were looking toward the future. They had gone to their audiences, asking for criticism at the end of each performance and had collectively developed a second version of the play for 1975. The group had become a more cohesive and a more overtly political unit during the creation of *Guadalupe*. Both Jose Saucedo and Rodrigo Duarte-Clark talk about the educational aspect of the research process, creating a clearer understanding of the reality of the nonstudent Chicano population in terms of politics, social issues, and aesthetics.

> In *Guadalupe* there was a great deal of research that went into the play that helped us to develop the thesis, but also helped us to actually encounter characters, encounter theatre stuff. Esperanza always had the reputation of not being one of the most political groups in TENAZ [since *Brujerias*]. And in the case of *Guadalupe*, when we were doing research, it was research that was new to us. We were actually finding out things. We had not come up with an ideological answer and then we were going to fit the information into that form. (Duarte-Clark, interview)

Consequently, the conclusions were genuine and the company wanted to do more.

Perhaps most significant was the development of a collective process and the resultant departure of Jorge Huerta. Saucedo, in a typically self-deprecating fashion, described the decision to become a collective in terms of an equality of ignorance among group members as well as a collective feeling fostered by the type of training and group decision making under Huerta's directorship. According to Huerta, the fact that four of the eight *teatro* members had completed their degrees in theatre and the other members had been with them at least two years or more gave the group the expertise to make artistic decisions collectively. In any case, collective organization became a political necessity in response to a desire for a more equitable and egalitarian system in which workers of both sexes shared power, rewards, and responsibility. The process of collective creation developed by Esperanza is a direct reflection of its political and organizational philosophy.

THE METHOD

In workshops on collective playwriting, Esperanza divides its own technique into thirteen parts, although several occur simultaneously. Moreover, at different points during the creation or rewriting of a piece, there may be a good deal of modification in methodology. As with any viable group process, regardless of how tightly organized this one may seem in the explanation, there is great flexibility and room for change depending on changes in personnel, specific abilities and interests, and the goal of a particular production.

In addition (and it seemed during observation and interviews that the members of the company were not aware of this themselves), Esperanza has developed cooperative modes of behavior in group interaction that facilitate progressive discussion from the center. For each discussion the group sits in a tight circle, or a semicircle with a separate facilitator if the topic is a particular person's presentation. Those wishing to speak raise their hands, but usually do not speak until recognized by someone else. In this way the function of facilitator floats around the circle, with each person concerned not only with evaluation of an idea, but also with making certain each other person who needs to can speak. The focus remains on the idea, not the presenter, so there is little defensive behavior. Digressions are frequently prevented by such comments as "What's really important is..." or other such direct calls back to the central topic. The atmosphere, while gentle, is intensely critical.

Unfortunately, this process is affected by time, by the need to meet ever-tighter deadlines because of financial pressures and the group's struggle to keep the sense of movement alive in Latino theatre in the United States and Latin America. During the ten days I was in Santa Barbara, deadlines were approaching and the group became progressively more tense: "push" replaced "drive," there was less idle talk during breaks, and less socializing. Nonetheless, the process continued.

The process begins with what might be called the selection of germinal ideas. Each member of the group presents what he or she feels are two of the most pressing community concerns, and each is then assigned to do preliminary research on someone else's ideas. From its very inception, then, the process depends on assumptions about the importance of objectivity and the ability of shared or group investigation to achieve it.

The second step is the actual research, consisting of reading, interviews, and whatever other methods of information gathering are applicable. This step culminates in presentations of the findings to the entire group and the selection of what seem to be the most significant areas for further research.

Step three is more detailed research into these areas and a second presentation to the group, this time with a conscious attempt to give an objective summary of gathered information. At the end of this phase the final topic, which is frequently a combination of related concerns, is selected, and other important topics may be placed into subgroups for possible inclusion. Research is then completed as the fourth step. Everyone in the company studies the same topic from all sides, aware that disputation will enable the creation of functional characters as both protagonists and antagonists. Even this early in the process, the group is aware of its audience, and considers that audience's awareness of oppression and knowledge of the "villains" as well as its need for an introduction to new patterns of thought.

Of all the groups I examined, step five is unique to Esperanza. It consists of the creation of a written statement of a political thesis: a paragraph-long explanation of why the play is being written and what it will say. It is this step that necessitates Esperanza's artistic organization and contributes to the texture of its plays. The thesis, however, is both an asset and a liability. When used as a guide for excluding, for making certain that only scenes that keep the story inside a certain political framework are included, it can help create a strength of clarity without damaging either the continuity of the story or the richness of the characters. It is this combination of political clarity and human complexity that ensured the success of *La Victima* (The Victim), the first play written after the process had been fully articulated.

However, when the political statement is used to determine inclusiveness without an adequate consideration of theatrical viability, or when it does not account for the community's sense of political reality, it can lead to difficulties. The sterile, propagandistic bar scene in *Guadalupe* makes an important and provocative thematic statement, but it is clearly not cast in the same mode as the remainder of the play and should have had its content more delicately integrated into the fabric of the story, even at the expense of a degree of clarity. This problem arises again in *Hijos* (Children), a far more mature work.

What follows is the selection of a coordinating committee of three whose task it is to oversee the actual creation of the performance. The artistic coordinator's functions include serving as the outside directing eye, and scheduling and organizing improvisation work and rehearsals. The playwriting coordinator's task is to regularize the text, removing any evidence of stylistic differences between the various writers and translating the dialogue into the unique bilingual language of Esperanza: a language that attempts to make the complete text understandable to monolingual as well as bilingual audiences by putting indicative phrases in each language without the repetition that direct translation would necessitate. This person also oversees the entire writing process to make certain that each scene fulfills its function in the movement of the story line and is frequently called on to write transitions between scenes.

The final position is that of political coordinator, who ensures that each scene fulfills its function in the proof of the thesis statement. He or she keeps attempts to keep the character and situational conflicts in each scene in accordance with the political orientation of the play as a whole. As one can imagine, the major debates in the process are between the last two coordinators. Differences that they cannot reconcile are brought before the group for debate and decision. The difficulty is that much of the disagreement is interpretative and, even though both the playwright and political coordinator have previously agreed in principle to the statement they want the play to make, the desired audience reaction, and even the appropriate style, there are disagreements over many specifics about direction and degree.

For several years, the same three people assumed these functions. Jose

Saucedo coordinated the direction, Rodrigo Duarte-Clark did the playwriting, and Jose Luis Valenzuela provided the political thesis. There was, it seemed to me, a fundamental difference between the ways in which Duarte-Clark and Valenzuela approached the creation of a piece. This caused tension that was at times quite creative, but at times led to impasses that account for some of the weaknesses even in Esperanza's strongest plays. Duarte-Clark's focus was on dramatic viability, and he turned to on-stage improvisation as the appropriate way of testing choices.

Valenzuela sought a somewhat different type of on-stage excitement. He frequently talked about the concept of images as defined by Enrico Buenaventura, director and playwright of Teatro Experimental de Cali, to whom the theatre is a tool for revolutionary change that must mirror (read, "clarify") reality by an "analysis of reality and its stylistic representation, [not] the accurate reproduction of the content of reality....We think that concrete reality approaches its own transformation when, through us (actors, playwrights, directors), it generates out of itself contradictory images, which, by recreating it, by depriving it of its 'ordinariness,' by laying its mechanism bare, begin to transform it" (Espener 45). Buenaventura is as well interested in clarity, but the symbolic, transformational action of images—action that is expansive, that objectifies unspoken subjective reality and its causes or perceived causes—almost necessitates a degree of ambiguity.

However, Valenzuela perceived his function to be the removal of ambiguity. He evidenced a desire, therefore, to tell an audience *why* things were being done, a more comprehensive and rather different species of explanation than the telling of a revealing story. During discussions Duarte-Clark frequently posed questions or looked for ways to ask them while Valenzuela posed answers or looked for ways to tell them. It was revealing to watch this dynamic at work during the development of new version of *Hijos* in the context of the collective. Eventually, though, the debates disrupted the social order of the group by challenging the assumed basic values, and Valenzuela had to disassociate himself from the company.

After the coordinating committee is chosen, it meets to perform step seven, the writing of the basic scenario. This scenario consists of a broad description of the story line in dramatic terms. Each proposed scene is listed with an indication of its dramatic and political structure. This is then brought to the group for its acceptance and for the eighth step, the choice of a style. Traditional theatre forms are examined for appropriate presentational devices while improvisations on the scenario begin to flesh out scenes and suggest necessary or supporting characters. This method is an attempt to develop sophisticated yet popular forms that are "built to communicate with the majority of people" through images, language, and structures "that emerge or surge from the particular cultural context" (Duarte-Clark in Guerra 116), without dissipating the ideational clarity. When the attempt succeeds, Esperanza's plays exhibit a conscious control over form without oversimplification.[7]

The next step consists of refining the scenario, defining the characters to a point from which they are easily identifiable, and finalizing the political structure. Step ten is casting. There are normally no auditions. Instead, the group considers each actor's abilities in an attempt to showcase strengths, use experienced actors where they can support newer performers, and make everyone look good. Although acting abilities differ in the cast, Esperanza's conscious attempt to avoid creating its own star has served the company well. In political terms, plays are structured to contradict the hero theory and to focus on a class analysis of history. In addition, their political position has led the company to seek balanced characters, giving women a number of good roles which is very unusual in Chicano—or any other—theatre, allowing for complexity in relationships and causality, and presenting a high degree of ensemble work during performance: in essence, expanding the center into the performance itself.[8]

The development of characters and dialogue through improvisation follows. Each scene is assigned to a director and a writer, who are both chosen because they express an interest in a particular scene, and sufficient actors to play the required characters. The director sets up the improvisation, defining the situation and ensuring that the improvisational scenes fulfill the necessary functions. He or she may attempt to lead the actors toward a specific concept, but tries, regardless of personal approach, to remain as objective as possible vis-à-vis the purpose of the scene, and invites input from others who are working on the scene in order to foster clarity. The writer records the improvisations in preparation for the next step.

It is the job of the actors at this point to maintain a critical perspective. Frequently they will be asked to improvise characters that they will not play in performance, in which they are aided by earlier group discussions about the final scenario. In order to help the actors find the key elements of the roles and conflicts, the director will frequently suggest a situation or location that is analogous to the scene specified in the scenario. This frees the actor from the demands of a specific character and allows for a fuller exploration of possible relationships and reactions. The group has no qualms about modifying the scenario to incorporate discoveries made in this way, as long as new elements do not compromise the political thesis.

During the next step, each writer takes his or her records of the improvisations and scripts the assigned scene. The script is studied by the actors who will play the characters in the final staging and then read by them to the entire collective. The actors are free to make modifications to specific lines to conform to their understanding of the characters, but they basically keep the scene intact. After the reading, the scene is criticized in great detail by the group and sent back to the writer for revisions. The reading and critiquing process is then repeated, and the writer creates a third draft if necessary. This draft is then read for the entire company and either accepted or assigned to another writer who begins scripting again.

This is the most emotionally draining part of the process. It is the writer's obligation to consider the wishes and artistic decisions of the collective as binding. For this reason, she or he is not allowed to defend the script. Just as will occur in front of an audience, the work is forced to stand on its own from the beginning. This is not to say that explanations for decisions are not given while seeking ways to improve the dialogue. What it does mean, however, is that a writer's intentions are removed from consideration until the scene is criticized in terms of what it actually communicates (applying Friedrich Engel's "principle of contradiction" to the process itself), the needs of the scenario, and the expectations of the entire collective. Although this can easily bruise a writer's ego, it is also a fine training method and has led to the discovery of writing ability in several of the company members. It provides, as well, an arena in which a central concept in Esperanza's definition of collective action can be tested and revitalized in terms of a relatively concrete product: "Give when it's your turn to give; accept when it's your turn to accept."

When all scenes have been accepted, they are given to the playwriting coordinator for a final revision. Up to this point, each writer has been writing in the language that is most comfortable for him or her. The writing coordinator recasts the dialogue in an effort to make the play comprehensible to monolingual audience members. He or she is also responsible for stylistic consistency as well as for finding an indicative idiom for each character's speech. In view of this process, it is frankly amazing to find that Esperanza's plays show a degree of stylistic consistency that is often missing in the work of groups that rely exclusively on individual playwrights. This is a testament to the clarity of intent shared by the group throughout the writing process as well as to the skill of Duarte-Clark in reflecting the wishes of the group, usually without pandering dramatic necessity to political pamphleteering.

The final step in mounting the production is the staging. Each director stages his or her own scene, and again it is the coordinator's job to smooth over stylistic differences. One must remember that each member of the collective has had input into almost every section of the work, and that the concept (at least in terms of style and topical focus) was a group decision. Therefore, no one at this juncture is likely to have maintained an attitude that is really out of line with the consensus view, and the scenes are presented in very much the same style from the beginning. Also, various actors have improvised these scenes, so many people have rather clear perceptions of what needs to happen on stage from both an acting and a dramaturgical standpoint. The tremendous amount of input, rather than dissipating focus as it might for a more hierarchically dependent group, provides for a relatively rapid progress.

It is at this point as well that the group works on creating the transitions between scenes. These are more than mere segues for Esperanza. Because its audiences are frequently very unfamiliar with even the convention of the intermission, Esperanza creates transitions that keep the action moving, even if they necessitate the creation of an additional story or, more frequently, a framework justifying the telling of the central story. In one way this is an extension of the distancing techniques used in *Guadalupe*: what were just factual statements in that play had become fuller commentary and expository songs in *La Victima*, an entire cantina in *Hijos* in which an important debate necessitates the play, and a cabaret in *El Pulpo* (The Octopus) that provides an atmosphere of unreality in which the allegory of the core play becomes an acceptable form. In *Loteria* (Lotto) traditional figures from the popular Mexican picture-bingo game provide coherence and accessibility. In addition to providing such a framework, these transitional acts allow the performers to create an intermediary persona who then becomes the actor/demonstrator, in the Brechtian sense, of the story.

There is actually another step in Esperanza's process; one that many people's theatres use: the act of going to the people in the audience after each performance, gathering reactions and criticism, and rewriting with an eye toward clarifying the play's message first, and making it more easily accessible second. It is extremely difficult to respond to audience demands and yet challenge their political and aesthetic preconceptions. This has been a concern of Esperanza since they added the Spirit of Superstition to *Brujerias*, making the message too clear. "Now," said Ruperto Reyes, "we give the audience what they give us. And as much as they ask of us, we ask of them" ("Workshop").

THE COMMUNITY BASED COLLECTIVE—1974–1978

The period from 1974 until 1976 was a time of relative stability for Esperanza. During the eighteen month run and tour of *Guadalupe*, the group formed a highly cohesive unit experimenting with communal living, and systematizing their collective methodology. By this time almost all members of the company had completed their education and several were involved as teachers in Santa Barbara and surrounding communities. All had either been born in Mexico or were the children of recent immigrants. Most importantly, every member shared a political commitment to the betterment of the Chicanos' lot through theatre.

The group decided to continue the method of collective creation developed during the writing of *Guadalupe*, but to move to a broader perspective than that allowed by the documentary and *acto* forms with their relatively one-dimensional characters. "We were trying to get away from the notion that human beings are good or bad. They respond to conditions, and they live in a context. [*La Victima*, their next play] wasn't a documentary. It was a kind of historical analysis—presented in the form of an opinion" (Duarte-Clark, interview).

The company had begun to explore a more clearly defined Marxist analysis of history and was developing a class consciousness that, while recognizing the uniqueness of Chicano culture, was also cognizant of the exemplary nature of the Chicano working experience. "We're trying to show the Chicanos and Mexicans in this country that they are scapegoats for capitalism," explained Jose Saucedo in 1976 (Huerta, "Keeping in Touch" 44).

La Victima

The specific impetus for choosing the theme of *La Victima* was the "illegal alien" scare early in 1976, the bicentennial year. "We felt the irony of that celebration of independence in a country where many people live without independence, particularly economic independence. [Undocumented workers] live in terror, waiting to be picked up and deported, and their only crime is not wanting to be poor" (Petrinka). The mothers of three of the company members had been deported in the past and the issue was therefore one of personal as well as political concern.

In January 1976, Esperanza began intensive research about colonialism worldwide and its relation to race and the class struggle.[9] The company then formed study groups, assigning a different historical period to each, and discovered in this way a pattern of mass repatriations coinciding with economic recessions since the 1920s (a pattern so clearly repeated under the Reagan presidential administration in early 1982 that the group remounted *La Victima* for an international tour of Latin America, Cuba, and the United States). A decision was made by the collective to trace three generations of a single family, scripting of scenes was assigned as in *Guadalupe*, and three and a half weeks later, on May 5, 1976, *La Victima* premiered at the University of California at San Diego as a work in progress. As expected, several scenes were rewritten for purposes of clarity, but the play has remained intact and relevant to the present.

La Victima opens with the prologue quoted at the beginning of this chapter, followed by an expository song with plot-line lyrics sung to the tune of a popular *corrido*.[10] At the end of the song, a quotation is recited in Spanish and English to provide historical context and motivation for the first scene, and a title is placed in an easel stage right. This introductory method is repeated for nearly every scene. No attempt is made to integrate the songs or quotations into the action of the play: they are *about* what the audience is seeing, not *of* it. This simple Brechtian method, used, as it was in *Guadalupe*, to focus the audience's attention on the story and its import, rather than on the characters, is especially important in *La Victima* since the scenes are played naturalistically and are highly emotional.

The first scene takes place in 1913 as a family is waiting by the train tracks to flee to the United States from the ravages of the Mexican Revolution. The second scene, entitled "The First Deportations," takes place eight years later at a dance at which Amparo, who was only a child in scene one, meets Julian to whom she is later married (between scenes). The scene is essentially a comic interlude, making fun of Amparo's attempts to talk to a boy away from her Papa, and including bits of pidgin English to indicate the rising degree of assimilation. Papa's warm old country concern for Amparo is gently chided, but it remains humane and touching. His attitude is ironically juxtaposed with his grandson's very American and inhumane treatment of her at the end of the play. Scene two ends with the harassment of Chicanos and Mexicanos at the dance by local police performing as an INS raiding team. Amparo we learn, escapes, stays in the United States and happily raises a family.

The next group of scenes focus on Sammy, Amparo's son and the victim of the title, covering the time from the Depression through the end of the Korean War. In scene three Amparo sings Sammy a song about how her love will always be with him to comfort his loneliness, just before Julian enters to announce that he, like the fathers of Sammy's friends, has been laid off and will have to return to Mexico. Sammy is separated from Amparo in the confusion of boarding the train and is left in the United States. The intensely emotional "Repatriation" scene is very short and physical, using slow motion and stop action to create tableaux and break the rhythm of the previous, dialogue-dependent scenes. Until this moment the pacing has been steady, reflecting the slow but sweeping tides of events and the waves of people who are washed back and forth across the border. The wrenching change of style in this scene marks a shift to the new rhythm of the military industrial drive of life in the United States, a sense reinforced by the fact that the next scene, titled "The First Mexican-Americans," is almost completely in English.[11]

Sammy, who has been adopted by the Mendoza family, is Americanized in the next two scenes as he proposes to girlfriend Clara on the night before he leaves for Korea, and is indoctrinated in the army. Sammy seems to have been pushed into his future, creating a crisis of self-identity, a theme often dealt with in Chicano drama. He is forced to deny his *Chicanismo* (Chicano identity) in the army and finally to assert his love of country by screaming, "Kill the Communists!" as he shoots fleeing civilians.

The next group of scenes returns to Sammy's real family. Antonia and Meno, Sammy's sister and brother, return to the United States, where they banter about a dance and Meno complains about his job: a parallel to the second scene, implying that even if superficial circumstances have changed, things in the sixties are the same for Chicanos in the United States as they have always been. Antonia is fighting for change by organizing workers, but Meno will have no part of it because of their need for money and his fear of *la migra*. As in other places in the play, there is a long comic interlude followed by a sudden emotional shock. In this case the humor is provided by Meno's attempt to avoid the pushy Rosita, and the shock is a telegram announcing Julian's death and Amparo's need to return to the United States

The following section of the play is the most didactic and, unfortunately, the weakest, containing much political, expository, and even emotional dialogue that is sparse and statement-oriented. A scene in which Amparo is smuggled over the border ends with Antonia livid over abuse from a border crossing guard, who actually asked only routine questions. She has an attitude that is easily understood, but is not justified by the circumstances in the play. This is followed by a debate over the necessity for a strike that degenerates into name-calling between Meno and Antonia. Amparo stops the argument by explaining that disunity among the poor is the reason for the problem. There is no doubt that in the political terms of the play, she is correct, but the validity of her having such an insight, which she later denies by trying to keep Antonia from going to the picket lines, is questionable. The difficulty is that Esperanza has not found a way to integrate a portion of their historical analysis which instead is introduced in an inconsistent manner. It is hard to account for such an awkward decision when one considers that the same information could have been given through a song or informational quotation. It is especially disturbing here since the congruence of plot, politics, and character in the remainder of the play is one of its great strengths.

As soon as the focus returns to Sammy, there is a qualitative improvement in the dialogue and a corresponding clarity of theme that was not apparent in the more didactic sections of the play. In scene eleven, Sammy is promoted from his position as Immigration and Naturalization Service interrogator to a leader of raids. The exposition is so well integrated in this section that we learn how his twenty years of service, his daughter in college, and the INS claim that aliens are taking away jobs from American workers make the pressure to take the position clear and insidious.

At home Sammy is not sure about the job, but his wife Clara pressures him about the salary and the weight of all the accoutrements of his American dream. Clara also expresses concern over their daughter Janie's "weird classes about Mexican American history" and the "Chicano Power" bumper sticker on her car. When Janie enters, Sammy is reluctant to tell her about the promotion, and when Clara does, he and Janie begin to argue. Janie says she doesn't like Sammy's job and Sammy responds by listing all the material benefits she has gotten from it.

JANIE: Dad, you're deporting Mexicans.
SAMMY: I deport illegal aliens. I don't care if they're Colombians or Mexicans.
JANIE: We're Mexican!
SAMMY: We're American citizens and don't you forget that!
JANIE: Why do you deport them?
SAMMY: Because it's my job, that's what they pay me for.
JANIE: How can you deport your own people, father?
SAMMY: I do it so we can eat, so we can live.
JANIE: You father...
SAMMY: So you can live...

JANIE: You of all people...
SAMMY: So you can eat...
JANIE: You should hate what you do.
SAMMY: I'm proud of my job!
JANIE: Who separated you from your mother?
SAMMY: Shut-up! (*SAMMY slaps JANIE*). (356)

It is a powerful scene, recalling for many audience members arguments with their own parents or children in which the value of their actions and dreams were challenged by the other generation.

The scene switches to the now-violent picket line. Amparo, fearful for her children, goes to join them, and is taken by the INS during a raid led by Sammy. He has the feeling she is familiar and so decides to conduct her interrogation himself. The scene is titled "The Rejection."

The interrogation completes all the cycles at which the play had hinted. During the questioning Amparo, recognizes Sammy and recounts the circumstances of their separation without directly saying that Sammy is her son; Sammy, however, refuses to acknowledge her, rejecting all that she has come to stand for in the play and in his own mind. The scene, like the first, is entirely in Spanish, recalling the flight from all that is Mexican that began the cycle in the first place. Sammy is again pitted against a woman of another generation, who echoes the same challenges as his daughter.

AMPARO: You [the INS] have compassion for no one.
SAMMY: It's my work, Madame. It's my work.
AMPARO: It's your work to separate families?
SAMMY: No!
AMPARO: How would you like to be separated from your mother?
SAMMY: Get out! Take her out of here! Take her out of here! (362)

The interrogation is also the completion of the process that was begun in the sixth scene, "The Indoctrination," except that now the women and children are not distant "commies" but Sammy's own family. Finally, it is the absolute acceptance of the system—Sammy will not say that Amparo's emigration was wrong, only illegal—and of the role in it that Sammy will play.

"The individual who chooses to take part in the process of dehumanizing others, inevitably begins the process of his own dehumanization" (363). With that statement begins the final scene, titled "The Victim." Sammy wakes up screaming, reliving in a nightmare the separation from Amparo, but Clara convinces him to regard Amparo's deportation as another routine case. Sam begins repeating, "She's not my mother," in an effort to convince himself, but he fails as a vision of Amparo begins to sing as she did when young Sammy was afraid. He collapses, recreating exactly the physical scene of the separation, except that instead of crying for his Mama, he is crying, "I hate you!" In the work's final moments, Clara comes to Sammy. She has by now, however, come to represent the materialistic American dream rather clearly, and her attempt to comfort Sammy provides a rather ironic intrusion. The play ends with the entire cast on stage singing a song that calls for unity as the only road to change.

La Victima is a moving and challenging play for non-Latino audiences as well as for Chicanos and Mexicanos. It is an effective demonstration of its historical statement—that deportations accompany recessions—but more important, it raises many questions about personal definition, self-identity, and the corrupting influence of the capitalist system. By presenting a main character who is both villain and victim, and whose personal and circumstantial motivations are clearly drawn, Esperanza challenges audience preconceptions about individuals as good and evil.

One must remember that in the *acto*, *la migra* was practically the devil incarnate, and in *Brujerias* even contact with the INS by phone was enough to make one believe in all kinds of evil forces in the world. In *La Victima*, however, we are forced to see an INS agent as a human being. No one can forgive Sammy for killing civilians in Korea or for deporting his own mother, yet one cannot help but sympathize with his dilemma. In this way, the play places the blame on the system, thus finding a way to make the experience of the Mexican immigrant in the United States, and especially the experience of this individual, representative of wider systemic oppression.

In some ways, Sammy is admirable: He is dedicated to fulfilling the implied promise to his work, acts honestly according to the dictates of a now accepted indoctrination, and sincerely believes that what he is doing is right. However, these very qualities lead him to suffer great personal loss, feel guilt and confusion, and find it increasingly difficult to maintain a sense of his own identity—problems more universal than deportation. According to Duarte-Clark:

> "Plays like this have always existed in the theatre. Immediately *Antigone* comes to mind—when you have to choose between things that are equally important or emotionally valuable. In the case of Sammy in *La Victima*, he has to choose between what has been taught to him—his duty to his country—and deporting his own mother, his own flesh and blood. And the two things pull on him with quite a bit of strength and I think people can understand that about human beings—the emotion and the pain" (interview).

The reflection of the Greek tragic tradition is consistent with other elements of *La Victima*, including a certain sense of inevitability; however, for Esperanza it is history driven by economics that replaces fate as the determining factor. This analysis is clarified by the inclusion of the introductory quotations to each scene. These have the oracular effect of saying "Since such-and-such is true, how could anything else happen?" It is further emphasized by the long narrative songs which tend to point the rush of time and the need to focus on the circumstances when we are given the opportunity to study specific moments.

La Victima continues to show the influence of a certain concept of Brechtian theory. As in *Guadalupe*, each actor plays more than one role and changes costume and character in plain view of the audience. The intrusion of statements, title cards, and songs into action that is performed on a set of platforms and boxes are all calculated to remind the audience of the analytical nature of the script. Yet *La Victima* is not as dependent on the idea of actor as demonstrator as was the company's earlier work, and it makes use of other theories and traditions as well, an indication of the success of the group's study of history and theatre, as well as its collective confidence.

The most obvious shift from its earlier work is the company's use of a realistic acting style, reflecting both audience desire and Esperanza's concern for a more complex analysis of the person in society. In addition, there is a conscious use of the elements of melodrama, especially coincidence and heroic calls to duty. The tradition of the reunion of abandoned child and parent is savagely twisted, however, leaving the poor widow out in the cold. The play, then, sets up all the conditions for a heroic act and joyous conclusion, but does not become entrapped. Finally, the play uses a motif that is not closely associated with the Chicano experience to develop an image of hope and disappointment: the image of the train. In the first scene the train is a means of escape, hope, arrival at a new level of experience. The railroad provides employment for Chicanos later in the play, representing the positive drive of industrialization. However, it is the same train—the same system—that separates Sammy and Amparo, and cuts Sammy off from any possibility for connectedness.

La Victima was, and still is, phenomenally successful. It fulfills in a very real way the goals of political theatre: It uses a sense of historical background to clarify socioeconomic situations and to fight cultural colonialism; and it is both popular and progressive, or, in Buenaventura's terms, it uses "popular themes as a means of communication to structure real experience in such a way as to reach the audience directly" (Espener 46). That is, it is accessible without being nostalgic or folkloric and without slavish adherence to the conventions of commercially accepted and recognized forms.

THE TRANSITION TO FULL TIME—1978–1979

Ironically, the success of *La Victima* was the catalyst for the dissolution of the collective that created it. Many requests for performances were fulfilled, but when the company decided to accept an invitation by the International Federation of Independent Theatres to perform *La Victima* as the U.S. representative to the Festival of Theatre and Open Art in Poland in September 1978, a decision that necessitated performances in New York on the way and a tour of Yugoslavia and Sweden while in Europe, some of the company members had to risk or give up other jobs. When the group returned in November it was decided that a full-time commitment was essential for the survival and growth of the company. This resulted in the loss of several members and created a need to rebuild a committed collective that took several years to meet.

At the same time, pressure began to mount from other sources. The company had obligated itself to open a new play in March 1979. In January of that year the group received funding for several positions under the Comprehensive Employment and Training Act (CETA), enabling it to hire actors for the next play, but requiring the company to present one or more children's theatre pieces, a music show, a full-length major work, and a series of one-acts over the next year. In addition, the first national tour was scheduled for the spring and the company was sponsoring the Tenth Annual Chicano Theatre Festival, to be held in Santa Barbara in June.

For three months the company was composed of just men who worked on creating roles for men and women in *Hijos: Once a Family* (Children: Once a Family), Esperanza's next major collective creation. When the CETA money became available, the company was expanded to thirteen and split into the children's tour and the *Hijos* company.

The children's plays were very well received and, although they deliver clear messages about social organization and personal worth, they are also quite entertaining. The first, *Working Together*, is about the value of collective work. "Long ago," the narrator tells the audience, "there lived four musicians who together played the prettiest music ever heard in Melodyland.... And the people of Melodyland lived with this beautiful music in harmony" (np). Each musician, however, decides that she or he can make it on their own. Not only does each fail, but the town itself begins to experience great strife. Realizing the error of their ways, the drummer tricks the other musicians into playing together at a masquerade party. As soon as they cooperate, all the townspeople stop fighting and live happily ever after. The play uses many pratfalls and a great deal of music in a clear and well integrated piece.

The second play, *We All Have a Talent*, provides a balance for the first by stressing individual value and respect for one's own abilities. In this play, a jealous witch casts a spell over the town singer, preventing him from making his beautiful sounds. Doctors, who charge a great deal of money, fail to revive his voice, and only a *curandera* (woman folk medicine healer) realizes that they need other help. She sends the man's son to a wise man who tells him that the only way the spell can be broken is to show the witch that she has some ability of her own and should not be jealous. The son helps the witch discover her ability to dance, she breaks the spell, and they all live happily ever after.

The music show, as well, is quite good. From its beginnings in 1979 to *La Muerta Viene Contado* eleven years later, it has developed into a major part of Esperanza's touring repertoire. The songs, which are mostly in Spanish and political in nature, are gathered from various parts of Aztlan. They are extremely well performed, often in complex harmony, to the accompaniment of guitars and congas. Many of the numbers are introduced with political statements, and several are illustrated with pantomime performances or, more recently, unified with complex "images" à la TEC.

The failure in this tremendous creative push was *Hijos*. An attempt was made to stay with the same collective creation process, but it became extremely difficult to teach it to the cast and have it in use at the same time. In addition, the speed with which the play had to be created severely limited the time that could be spent on research to develop a thesis and plot that were based on community input and contact. Moreover, the older members of the company seemed to feel that the documentary form was no longer aesthetically viable. Finally, because there was little experience in terms of knowledge of other company members, the writers did not know what characters could be included in the script.

To complicate matters, the narrower participation of cast and community was linked to a more intimate subject matter than in any of the previous works: the family. In general, the topic became the destruction of the family and the thesis was that the cause of that destruction was "this capitalist society." Questions were never answered about intent—Was this a purpose of capitalism or merely a by-product?—or about motive—Was this done to maximize exploitation of the individual, or was it merely accidental? "The vagueness of the material led to a vagueness in the plot." Instead of presenting the "proof" of a discovered hypothesis or raising questions about people in a historical context, the first version of *Hijos* was "just a story—dealing with an issue through a story" (Duarte-Clark, interview).

Hijos: Once a Family

Called "the first Chicano soap opera" by a friend of one of the company members, *Hijos* was a highly melodramatic account of a family's disintegration presented in a realistic acting style. The mother blamed the failure of the family on the father, who in turn blamed it on the pressures of "the system" and his children who, he claimed, drove him into alcoholism. The mother died in the middle of the second act, but it was not until the third act that the son realized the error of his ways and rescued the father from the degradation of a nursing home in a "heart-rending" climax. Audiences accepted it, but the politics were unclear and it seemed as if the children were at fault for not maintaining the family tradition.

The second version of *Hijos* was written in the six weeks following the original production. It was restructured as a play within a play, with the external story creating a pretext for telling the tale of the family, thus enabling the company to concentrate on the political message rather than just wallowing in emotion. In addition, the form was for them a new extension of their investigation of Brechtian performance: now it was the character from the external story who was the "demonstrator," but this time a demonstrator with a clearly documented point of view.

The external story takes place in Art's Bar where workers from an electronics factory are arguing about that night's strike vote. Manuel, a strike leader, has just died. Enrique, a new worker, is afraid to strike because he needs every penny he can get to support his family. To assuage their doubts, the patrons of the bar decide to reenact Manuel's life, taking various roles, each portraying, when possible, the character with whose sympathies they are most closely allied.

As with the earlier plays, *Hijos* is episodic; it is divided into twelve scenes with a return to the cantina for commentary at each break. The early scenes effectively use freezes and montage to introduce Manuel, bring him from Texas to Los Angeles with his family, and present their economic troubles. Much of the remainder of the play traces the disintegration of Manuel's life. He is refused a raise because he has been branded a troublemaker for asking questions; his working son leaves home while his daughter is demanding college tuition. His youngest son, Bobby, is dating the evil boss's daughter. He says that the family embarrasses him and moves out.

In the factory, workers are getting sick and leaving work, thereby losing their pensions, because of poor working conditions. Manuel, who is nearly crushed by family and financial pressures and by the growing realization that working in the factory will never provide a way out of poverty, demands a public airing of the issues, and becomes a leader of the workers. Unfortunately, he lacks the support of his family because they each have financial and personal concerns. Bobby even comes back to support his future father-in-law and argue against the strike.

Finally, himself ill, Manuel appears to be a broken man, still willing to strike for his dreams, but seemingly aware that his family's situation is hopeless. In the final scene of his story, he comes home drunk and, though barely able to walk, performs a *danse macabre* with his wife, dying in her arms.

Nevertheless, the reenactment convinces Enrique of the rightness of the strike. Even before the final scene he delivers an impassioned speech about the need for united families as a means of defense. The message is clear, but the conclusion is not necessitated by the action. This is the major problem with the play: There is not a sufficiently clear delineation of the external forces that drive the children and are, therefore, responsible for Manuel's downfall. As a result, there is no real motivation for any growth of awareness by the cipher-like characters in the cantina, whose scenes are mostly of the "let's see what happens next" variety, and rarely provide a real framework for the analysis of Manuel's tale.

The play suffers as well from a certain set of assumptions that are not really supported in the body of the story. Almost everyone can see the family as a support structure, but it is not universally accepted that the departure from the family to gain wealth, power, or status is necessarily tragic. The denial of one's own heritage and culture is shown as despicable, but the necessity of that denial in order to gain other goals is not blamed clearly enough on the political and economic system.

Actually, the entire structure of the play seems somewhat contradictory. The characters in Art's Bar should be realistic; they face an immediate dilemma and have a clear purpose. However, they are given no biography and often deliver such predictable statements that they seem like attitudes rather than people. On the other hand, the Manuel story is supposedly acted out by bar patrons who would be likely to overact and rely on histrionics in their portrayals, thereby creating caricatures in the internal play, but their acting is restrained.

One might debate, as well, the play's uncritical and politically questionable support of Manuel's ideals. His dreams are illusions: The family is not a refuge from a socio-economic denial of the worth of the individual; the family is not an "isolatable entity" that can be removed from class struggle; and the family cannot be taken to a safe place, because there is none. Besides, the capitalist ideal—the belief that honest labor can provide the financial means for a way out and that Manual could work his way free of circumstance—is known by Chicanos to be a lie.[12]

Company members are well aware of the problems of *Hijos* (they are as vehemently self-critical as any group I have ever witnessed) and although they began a major revision for their 1983 spring tour, they dropped *Hijos* from their repertory when time did not allow for a full rewrite. The group blames much of the difficulty with the play on its departure from the methods used to create the first two plays, especially the lack of time for thesis-oriented research and for discovery in the writing process. The first version of *Hijos* was the product of expediency and necessity, and the second of a search for political clarity.

REDEFINITION—1979–1981

Determined not to commit the same mistakes again, Esperanza began, late in 1979, an attempt to redefine a clearer and more inclusive method. The collective was beginning to seem a bit more stable, its financial support had increased, and it had defined a workable touring and administrative structure. At the same time there was a feeling that the company had lost contact with its community, was performing for too narrow an audience, and needed to experiment with ways of improving itself aesthetically. To these ends, the group began several projects that were unique in their history, yet representative of the risks that Esperanza has always been willing to take. Project one was a summer repertory in Santa Barbara, during which company members worked with community actors on *Brujerias* and *Commadre*, both by Rodrigo Duarte-Clark, and the members of Esperanza performed *La Orgia* (The Orgy) by Enrique

Buenaventura under the direction of Ecuadorian mime Jose Vaccas. Vaccas was also to train the company in corporeal movement and character analysis.

Although one company member calls the result "the summer wreck, not rep" (Olivara) because the time for leisurely training evaporated with the necessity of mounting all the plays practically without outside assistance, everyone speaks lovingly of their work with Vaccas and of the progress they made in physicalizing characters in their next play. He introduced to them as well a sense of historical perspective concerning character and not just situation, teaching them a charting method for discovering relationships to economic situations, other characters, and period while simultaneously considering age, activity and other motivational forces.

The second project was the restaging of *La Victima* for a national tour. Because the script was already firm, the group felt comfortable with a cast that had not participated in the collective creation, including a contract actor hired to play the lead, and with a director who was a relatively new member of the group. Although the production was very successful, it created two crises that tested the mettle of individual devotion to the collective ideal. In the first instance, the cast found it difficult to work within the limits of the director's concept and political understanding. The director was removed (actually demoted to technical coordinator). Duarte-Clark returned to the artistic component from his work on administration and writing a new play, and with Saucedo and Valenzuela, he formed an artistic committee to direct.

The second crisis had far more catastrophic dimensions. In the middle of the tour, relations with the actor playing Sammy deteriorated. His work was quite good on stage, but he had a different view of responsibility and refused to become part of the collective touring procedure. On the first day of a week-long vacation in New York, the company fired him, and the musician quit. Duarte-Clark, who was managing the office in Santa Barbara, flew to New York to assume the role of Sammy—only his second role as an actor. Saucedo returned to the office, and Valenzuela, who was in the cast as singer, learned the guitar music and stepped on stage to take over all of Saucedo's roles. The consensus is that the performances improved from that time on and the reception in New York supports that contention.

El Pulpo

The third project was *El Pulpo* (The Octopus), which was to be written exclusively by Duarte-Clark after definition of the thesis by the collective, directed by Jorge Huerta, and designed by John Seffick of the Provisional Theatre in Los Angeles. The play opened in November 1980, but was poorly received in spite of the fact that its theme had a broad appeal. The play was restructured and rewritten with more collective input and a new director was chosen from inside the company for the Spring 1981 tour, but the company still was not satisfied. The third version, which opened in August of the same year, was the first to receive popular acceptance, yet it was performed only three times and laid to rest with such finality that no one in the company is able to find a script.

El Pulpo is an allegory exploring the connections between exploitation in the Third World and the American working-class Chicano experience, described by Esperanza in the 1981 tour brochure in this way: "The age-old conflict of underdog and top-dog unravels itself, as an expose of contemporary events help a type of Chicano everyman realize his condition and how world politics affect his daily life....Although the specifics of the play are directly linked to the Chicano people, the universality of the production makes this an important piece for everyone."

The plot is clear, simple, and linear as opposed to the multi-leveled, episodic structure of previous stories. The Octopus (representing American corporations) owns a restaurant that has as its sole function catering to her insatiable appetite. The waiters and cooks (American labor) are barely fed, yet they prepare and serve a great deal of food appropriated from the "Village" (developing Latin American nations). When the villagers revolt, waiter Johnny Henry is sent to the village to straighten things out. While there he is made aware of the way in which the Octopus has exploited not only the villagers, but the American workers as well. Horrified at the way the Village is being run and the revolution has been crushed, he returns to the Restaurant and defies the Octopus. She sets up court and, by playing on their fears and racism, convinces the other employees to condemn Johnny Henry to death.

The play is performed without an intermission, but is divided into acts by scenes in a Cabaret that provide the framework for the allegorical play--within-a-play. In the first version, the transitional scenes were of robots who moved to "this stupid little music [and read] this poetry that was supposed to explain the action that was about to happen, but it was so abstract that a lot of the actors didn't know what it meant" (R. Reyes, interview). The second version used the cabaret with the intention of creating a justification for the internal play like *Hijos*, but the connection between the cabaret acts and the octopus was still nebulous: the acts were too abstract and, according to one member, "awful."

The company found itself in an awkward position. On the one hand, the group felt the need to experiment, to find a form that would appeal to the entire working class. In addition, the theme was meant to be universal and required research that was not community oriented, which led to overintellectualization and the loss of the emotional "catch" that had made Esperanza's plays so attractive before.

On the other hand, the company feared alienating their usual audiences which did not support experimentation or internationalization and requested more plays like *La Victima*. The politics of the play were clear, but audiences seemingly could not accept the form—a reversal of previous problems. According to Jose-Luis Valenzuela, the solution came from relinquishing control: "So the third version we say [forget] it, this show doesn't have a solution.' So the best we can do is make it as fun as we can for the audience. The politics are there—we were not worried about the politics for this show....So everyone went out and wrote again. It was a very rich experience for the group—it was very motivating" (interview).

The result was well received both critically and otherwise. The usual standing ovations returned, but the company had so soured on the show that they dropped it from the repertoire anyway. The final version, which I saw at the Gathering, was lively and polished, and though the cabaret had little to do with Johnny Henry's story, each play was given its due. The circus atmosphere made it easier to accept the blatant politicizing of the allegory and reinforced the sense of demonstration, strengthening the symbolic import of the clever theatrics of the play proper.

The production's reliance on pyrotechnics and visual razzmatazz was quite exciting. The cabaret performers clambered about on a large platform which later became the Octopus's throne, various scenes in the village, and finally a tank that actually rolled across stage as it crushed the revolution. Almost every review mentions the image of an apparently endless stream of scarves passing in front of the Octopus's face as a representation of her consumption, and the very funny illustration of business control of the government, in which the mayor is a ventriloquist's dummy.

The performance was also the culmination of the technique of rapid character transformations that had been begun in *Guadalupe* and *La Victima*, was used to great advantage in *Hijos* (during which the actors would revert with ease to their cantina personas even in the midst of an emotional moment), and was made an integral part of the production in *El Pulpo*. The degree of change is enhanced by the fact that some of the changes are of sex as well as character type. Power and knowledge are not given a gender in the play: the Octopus (who is played by a woman) is androgynous and the most aware leader of the revolt is female. But narrow-mindedness is given a gender: the male villagers reject an old revolutionary's good advice simply because she is a woman.

Equally important as the play itself to a complete study of Teatro de la Esperanza are the reasons why, in spite of great expectations and the return of Jorge Huerta, the process of creating the first *Pulpo* failed. The project was designed to modify the collective process to allow individuals to focus on specific areas in which they wanted to grow. Duarte-Clark wanted the mandate to write, to "improvise at the typewriter" on a theme researched and defined by the group, but there was no time for preliminary work. "So the writer, me, went into the process without it....We were creating a vehicle without necessarily knowing what the vehicle was supposed to carry. Although we all had notions of what it was supposed to be, there wasn't that basic unity that was very necessary to create the criteria by which to evaluate. So it was very frustrating for everybody" (interview). The lack of an idea from the center slowed the writing and dissipated the focus. As a result, director Huerta arrived before the script was completed, and became part of the critiquing and developing group. The company had hoped to avoid this; it had hoped to create a script without outside interference and without their normal concerns for staging and writing simultaneously.

In addition, when company members were not placed in their usual roles in the process, they became uncomfortable. "We—we meaning some of the people that have also writing skills—felt frustrated in not also writing....We all step in each other's areas because we're used to that" (Olivara). "In this case I was not on the [directorial] committee, but I guess I was trying to do the same thing—trying to have political clarity. And it frustrated Roddy probably a lot—I feel like I'm confessing myself—and frustrated me and frustrated the director" (Valenzuela).

Directing became a particularly sore area. Esperanza's method of long discussion, unselfish improvisation, and frequent reworking after group critiques creates a degree of responsibility for creative participation and interaction that is very rare in traditional director-actor relationships. It allows as well for a certain freedom which seems to be kept in check by a shared understanding of method, attitude, and focus, but not by regulations or rehearsal structure. The entire process retains the sense of togetherness and purpose that is a source of strength for the company (and is readily discernible by even a casual visitor), yet allows for open suggestions, even of acting specifics by fellow actors, while the director is shaping the scene. It is, though, very exclusive as it functions. While Esperanza is the most successful collective at incorporating new members, it was almost certain to fail at bringing in a director whose expectations were not consistent with Esperanza's standard creative process—or to work with a company whose process is much different than theirs, as they tried to do for their next play.

Additionally, an outside director has only one task with the company and cannot share the needs of the collective members to perform a several functions simultaneously. Because of Esperanza's various commitments, the company members faced the recurring problem of diversified focus during the period that required concentration on the play at hand: a reason for difficulties in both creative and interpersonal relationships. It is hard to imagine a director who has been brought in to concentrate on the staging of a particular script being able to tolerate this kind of multifocused company effort.

NEW CORE, NEW QUESTIONS—1981–1986

By the time *El Pulpo* closed, the company had begun more projects, but this time with a renewed feeling of permanence and a sense of broader political function. In August 1981 the group performed at The Gathering, and for some this was their first real introduction to Anglo and black people's theatre on a broad scale. Over the years the company had developed a Marxist perspective and an ever-growing class consciousness, and their rediscovery of their connectedness to the working class in general (several members mentioned being in tears during a performance of *If I Live to See Next Fall* by The Play Group from Tennessee, a play about race, worker exploitation and unionization in the South) was inspiring.

Esperanza had also by this time taken over the political leadership of the Chicano theatre movement in general. After *El Pulpo*, Duarte-Clark went to Minneapolis to help form Teatro Latino. Several members of Esperanza went to Cuba with a "Cultural Brigade" that they had cosponsored with Teatro Cuatro, a Puerto Rican theatre company in New York. The group's international work, and its place as liaison with the fine political theatres of Latin America, gained in importance. In 1982 alone Esperanza sponsored the first United States tour of Cuba's Teatro Escambray, sent a representative to a conference of Latinos in the arts and humanities from all of Aztlan and Latin America, hosted the TENAZ seminario, at which Chicano positions on national and international issues were discussed, represented Chicano theatre at the Third Festival of Latin American Popular Theatre in New York, and toured Mexico and Cuba performing *La Victima*.

During the same year, Esperanza hosted a mini-festival of new Chicano companies with the goal of critiquing and improving the quality of Chicano *teatro* on the West Coast. The company was not satisfied with its own development, though, and attempted to define a more mature collective creation method. To this end, Jose Saucedo spent almost a year with Teatro Experimental de Cali, and with a collective company in Venezuela, and Jose Luis Valenzuela began a study of, and presentations to the company about, collective creation. While in Cuba, Valenzuela participated in an international director's workshop and used the knowledge he gained there to restructure the music show.

Tecolote Visions

The year 1982 began with the production of *Tecolote Visions*, which was created and performed in collaboration with the Provisional Theatre of Los Angeles. Once again, in an attempt to broaden their sphere, and in spite of awareness of the group's idiosyncratic working method (which had grown as a result of their experience with *El Pulpo*), the company attempted to share in a creative venture with other theatre makers. To complicate matters, the Provisional was also a collective and had developed its own methods over thirteen very successful years as a leader of the political theatre movement in the United States. Neither the process nor the product were very successful.

The difficulties with the process seemed to stem from two areas. The first was a repetition of a difficulty with *The Octopus*: the Provisional was prepared to devote themselves full time to the project, but Esperanza had several other obligations. Therefore, the Provisional spent more time in early preparation and had a more fully developed script idea when the collaborative work began. (There was a play-writing committee to do the scripting.) As a result, much of the preliminary script came from the Provisional without the kind of political input that members of Esperanza were used to having.

Secondly, there is a very different ambiance in the working styles of the companies, as well as rather incompatible modes of exploration. The importance of group clarity before improvisation is central to Esperanza's work, and during staging the group demands that the actor communicate the company perception with an equal degree of clarity. For the Provisional, the theme was more a matter of discovery growing out of the text, and the actors were given a great deal of latitude to explore the text during rehearsal. In fact, the Provisional relied on individual discovery to a far greater degree in all areas than Esperanza. It is not hard to imagine the difficulty created when the main characters, one played by a member of each company, were on stage, as one was urged to expand while the other was attempting to respond at the same time he was being held in check.[13]

The reliance on individual work also necessitated a degree of discipline that the Provisional had fine tuned into a rigorous and concentrated warm-up and preparation period before rehearsals. Esperanza, on the other hand, "glides" into rehearsals, using music during warm-ups and taking time to establish that day's rapport so that a group attitude unique to that moment precedes the work. These differences created tensions with which, due to deadline restrictions created by financial necessity, the collaborative group was never able to deal. The resulting script has been described by one reviewer as a "picaresque fairy tale, using American Indian decor. An old man and his twin [children] are put through the trials of Job by evil contemporary society and they act out their story with the assistance of four desert animals—a coyote, a mountain lion, a skunk, and an owl (or tecolote)....It's a blend of 'Pinocchio' and the sanitized Indian tales so dear to Boy Scout camps" (Jones).

In spite of the relative failure of their last two plays, Esperanza continued to develop. In the spring of 1983 the company toured *Hijos*, *La Victima* (a particularly relevant play under the Reagan administration) and the music show, which had grown into a major production relying on "images" and physicalization to music.

In 1985 the company again collaborated with another theatre group. This time their joint work with the Ensemble Theatre Project, a production of Esperanza's adaptation of Dario Fo's political farce, *No Se Paga! No Se Paga!* (*We Won't Pay, We Won't Pay!*), generated much excitement among audiences and critics alike. The play, about two couples who resemble the "Honeymooners" of sitcom fame, a supermarket riot, and unionism, "travels easily from its original working-class district of Milan to East Los Angeles, from Italian to Spanish-laced English, and from what the playwright has called 'the dramatic problem of eating' in Italy's inflation-unemployment crisis of the mid-70s to the homegrown stomach problems of rollercoaster Reaganomics" (Marx, "Review").

Esperanza's production, which I saw during the company's 1986 Midwest tour, was quite exciting. The translation is crisp and very funny, the acting was much improved on all technical levels, and the politics were clear to multiracial, working-class audiences.

Discussions with company members about the redefinition of the collective process indicated great hope, and the adaptation seemed to be a sign of a solid, reconstituted collective. Jose Luis Valenzuela and some others left the company, recognizing that the differences in approach were irreconcilable, and the troupe moved to San Francisco, a city in which they felt they could establish a more solid base, building on a larger and more supportive working-class community.

The move was part of an attempt to solve several major problems. As with almost all theatre companies, Esperanza faced grave financial difficulties. For years, the company projected an operating budget as part of planning and granting requests, but then curtailed activity instead of borrowing or attempting further fund-raising if grants did not materialize. This kept it relatively sound, but prevented any long-range planning. California Arts Council (CAC) and NEA grants continued, but Esperanza was not able to raise its earned income to over 35 percent of its expenses during most of the eighties.

In 1983, though, a restructuring of the granting process by the CAC became as important as the amounts being given. In previous years the CAC gave Esperanza a specified amount of money to underwrite half the fees for a performance. The grant was given in a lump sum in advance under the proviso that a certain number of performances in specified geographical areas be given. This enabled the company to contact sponsors who needed to put only a relatively small amount of money up front. The new CAC system required that the sponsor pay the entire fee in advance and then apply to the CAC for reimbursement. This decreased the number of sponsors, effectively decreasing the CAC touring grant. During the *Tecolote* tour, for example, the companies were only able to collect $20,000 of a $37,000 grant because of a lack sponsoring groups with sufficient funds. By the time of the 1986 tour, fees had risen significantly. According to tour coordinator JoAnne Reyes, "People who have money don't want us; people who want us don't have the money" (interview).

This statement reflects a problem of image as well as finance. Political theatre is generally seen by those in the arts orthodoxy as boring, didactic, agitprop—something for which one does not want to pay. Political activists frequently see theatre as either frivolous or as a support arm for a largely volunteer movement—something that should be *freely* given. Anglos see Chicano theatre as separatist, with a very limited audience. Many Chicanos and Anglos think all Chicano theatre must look like sixties Campesino performances.

For these reasons, when Esperanza contacts organizations for support, they receive criticism from all sides. It is still very difficult for people in the leftist community to see that theatre makers are workers for change, too, and need to make a living from their work. The company has been charged with being too expensive, with not having a clear enough political statement, and even with being elitist because it holds auditions. Professional standards are seen by the Chicano community as selling out and polish and efficiency as co-opting: there were complaints after the 1979 TENAZ festival in Santa Barbara that the facilities were "too good," even though Esperanza had gotten them free of charge.

The result has been that most of the bookings the company receives are from Chicano organizations with university support. In order to resolve the dilemma of playing to an already aware, student audience, Esperanza instituted the policy of "community performances." For each performance that pays full fees in an area, the company actively searches for two smaller and poorer organizations for whom they will perform for a fee of $100 if they can be guaranteed an audience of fifty.

The desire to reach a broader audience, manifesting itself in the added work of performing essentially free of charge, raised several questions about political purpose, aesthetic form, and even location. An attempt was made to create a shared understanding of Marxist ideology in the company through workshops with the goal of developing a mode of dialectical analysis that would eliminate the necessity for so much political debate in the creation of a work. In addition, workshops studying form and structure were created to familiarize the entire company with the range of possibilities for modes of dramatization. The pressure of work cut these short, but the attempt to seek new people's forms that can communicate relevant information entertainingly is still an essential part of the company's planning.

That "relevant information" is, to Esperanza, the fact that many problems in the Chicano community are the result of broad based economic exploitation, which will continue until all exploited people/workers are willing to support each other's right to say "No." The difficulty, however, lies in the need to imply the audience's complicity in its own exploitation--a hard pill for struggling Chicano workers to swallow. In addition, Esperanza had moved away from its community in many ways. Local performances were very rare, local audiences were small, and activity with local groups was extremely limited by schedule demands and the need to spend so much time touring to earn funds.

As a result, the *teatro* had become less successful at talking to its core audience. Moreover, because it operated under conditions that further isolated it from the immediacies of community life, the company was less able to grasp immediate community concerns and use them as the basis of its work, as it had did so successfully in their its three plays. According to Rupert Reyes: "Our plays are missing the target. They're not missing the target, they're just—We haven't been community people in a long time. Most of us are from the university [or out of the area. We have certain ideas, but] the community we serve is still strongly, devoutly religious. They're still pro-capitalist. They're still sexist. They're still boss-worker oriented" (interview).

The solutions proposed for this problem fell into two basic categories. The first was "artistic" and included a more open relationship with the audience. Valenzuela's desire to lead Chicanos to a brighter future was seen as incompatible with the company's more general concern for participatory "consciousness raising."

> What does that mean? Do we hand them [the audience] a gift of knowledge—here's from us to you? [Is] that an elitist concept? Is it not our function to enter into a conversation, a dialogue with the audience? Is it not more our function to ask questions that we think are relevant and to see if they think they are relevant? In a sense to bring the participation of the audience in a more sophisticated wa...If you really do enter into a dialogue with the audience you find out that they don't agree with you in a lot of things, and many times for a very good reason....
>
> The way we write plays—we create a thesis and we mount arguments toward that thesis and then we present it in the play. But it's packaged, it's closed—it isn't asking questions. If there's an argument in the play, it's a fixed fight....We have become narrow. That really bothers me. (Duarte-Clark, interview).

The split in the company was ironically a mirror image of the one that caused Esperanza to break away from Teatro MECHA.

The second area of solutions to the problems of community contact was in the "social" category. The decision to move the entire company to San Francisco, where there is a larger Chicano community and more political and artistic activity, was particularly difficult to make because children were involved in the relocation.

Difficulties are compounded for Esperanza by the additional demands of managing a socialist life-style in the midst of a capitalist society. There is a constant need to balance the personal needs of the individual with the production needs of the organization. Some of the members talk of the collective in familial terms, and the mutual respect, love, and support of that type of group is certainly there. But the collective is also very demanding and critical, making certain that its processes are not interrupted more than necessary, yet always concerned with the growth of its members as part of the creative unit. The driving force seems always to refer to political necessity. To one member, the principles of guerrilla warfare apply:

> You will always sacrifice the individual for the benefit of moving the organization forward to achieve its objectives. But in our case, if the individuals in our organization cannot produce—like if we're losing

> people because they can't support their families, because it's just too hard for people to survive in the group—then it becomes necessary for the organization to make their conditions livable so that they can produce. As cold as that sounds—I mean, I'm not against the family concept. We have to raise our children in that manner, but it's towards a political objective. We are not an end in ourselves; we are part of a struggle that has not been realized and will not be realized for some time. (Duarte-Clark, interview)

To this end, Esperanza has made some difficult choices. It is necessary to note that this company is one of the few theatres of its type that has members with young children. To free women for full participation(an effort to combat sexism) and to allow both married and single members to enjoy a degree of freedom—as well as to permit equal fulfillment of responsibilities—Esperanza has collectivized child care. The system is complex and comprehensive, including fifteen-minute shifts during company meetings and planning for care during each moment of touring. The company even schedules a very late lunch to accommodate day care schedules.

Salaries, too, reflect need. "Many of our costs are predetermined by equity waiver requirements, specifically salaries, fringe, travel, and per diems" (CAC Grant Application), but the actual salaries do not fulfill professional standards year-round. What it all amounts to are minimal per diems, free board and lodging whenever possible, and minimal take-home per month for each full time adult in the company. There is an additional allowance per month for each dependent, and child care necessitated by company work is also subsidized. Outside income from teaching or advertisement work is usually donated to the company.

Nevertheless, living on the road is difficult on the children and on couples, who are sometimes split for several months each year. As the company ages, it takes more time to recover from a road trip, and this decreases the time available for creating new works. San Francisco provides the opportunity to perform more often at home and to tour less.

SAN FRANCISCO—1987–PRESENT

Since the move, Esperanza has thrived, although there have been some drastic changes. In a little over two years, company personnel changed almost totally. By the end of 1989 only Duarte-Clark and Illizaliturri remained in the reformed collective. Even Jose Saucedo, who had continued to study with other companies (including Groupo Nixtayolero in Nicaragua) left the collective to teach.

The company has remained committed both to broad social concerns and to the creation of an equitable collective structure, but it has found its recent inspiration in its roots, in more traditional Chicano or Latino culture. *La Muerte*

Viene Contado, the music show which was created at about the time of the move, uses the *corridos* form, but does not celebrate tradition uncritically. "Esperanza selected a *corrido* that tells the story of a woman who shoots a captain who has raped her and killed her brother. Other sections celebrated the role of women in the Nicaraguan revolution and dramatized Domitila's famous speech to the Women's Conference in Mexico City" (Yarbro-Bejarano, "Chicanas' Experience" 57). The traditional Mexican game *loteria* provided the title and character types for their next play.

The company's most recent piece, *La Cantata de Santa Maria de Iquique* (subtitled "A Bilingual Dance and Theater Adaptation"), builds on Chilean composer Luis Advis's "The Siege of Santa Maria de Iquique—A People's Cantata." The play chronicles, in eight scenes, labor unrest in Chile in 1907 through dialogue, song, and dance (a logical extension of Esperanza's physical image creation). A prologue and epilogue set in a schoolyard in Iquique in 1973 (the year that labor supported Salvador Allende against Augusto Pinochet's military seizure of power) provide the frame for and occasion the telling of the central story—a pattern reminiscent of earlier works. While the subject matter is historical and Latin American-based, the play is directed at working-class audiences in general, and is designed "to illuminate the courage and determination of the miners of Iquique, to honor their vision of a society of self-determination, and to remind ourselves that so many people all over the world are demonstrating the same courage and determination in their own communities" (American Festival, "Program" 11).

In addition to creating new pieces, the company fulfills its responsibilities as the resident theatre of the Mission Cultural Center in San Francisco, has continued to tour nationally and in Latin America (including an appearance at the first annual theatre festival in Managua, Nicaragua), has begun a program to develop new Chicano playwrights, and remains a central force in TENAZ.

However, economic and temporal pressure has changed the working methodology of the group. In an informal interview with Ruben Castro Illizaliturri after a performance of *Real Women Have Curves* by Josefina Lopez in Whitewater, Wisconsin on April 13, 1992, I was told that the need to produce new plays more frequently than the collective process allows has become paramount, and that although the company develops scripts like *Real Women* through workshops and other more-or-less collaborative means, it no longer creates its works collectively.

ORGANIZATION

The variety of Esperanza's activities has necessitated a complex structure that is functionally oriented within the limitations imposed by collectivity. The goals of sharing work equally while making use of individual expertise and maintaining the ultimate decision making power of the collective as a whole have been rather well met.

The overall work of the company is divided into two "components": the artistic, which has been described above, and the administrative. The latter consists of two full-time office workers, a support structure, in which each company member has specific responsibilities, and a committee system to deal with various continuing group activities. In addition, there are very specific tasks that are assigned while on tour on a rotating basis.

The most sensitive office position is that of tour coordinator. It is her or his job to represent the group to funding sources and sponsors and to schedule the itinerary for the most important source of income and audience outreach. She or he also handles promotional materials, advance contracts, and all the other exigencies of booking. Due to the nature of the job and the necessity of frequent quick decisions to generate bookings, the tour coordinator works alone, trying whenever possible to get group approval on community performances, but usually only going to the group with controversial requests. Again it is the political concern that creates controversy. For example, after accepting a booking in Houston in 1980, the company discovered that the performance was being sponsored by the Exxon Corporation. Rather than cancel a contract and miss the chance of playing for an audience they would have liked to educate, the company did the performance but refused any money.

The other office chores are the responsibility of the fiscal manager. It is the job of this person to coordinate the filing of grants and all necessary governmental forms, to handle correspondence and telephones, to pay bills and salaries, to maintain the vans, and to ensure that the technical elements of each production are properly rented or constructed.

This position is one of implementation, however, and is not as isolated as the tour coordinator. For example, although the fiscal manager writes checks and makes wage reports, another member of the company does the bookkeeping and a third member does most of the fiscal analysis and budgeting. These three people form the Finance Committee and meet to make the actual financial decisions about planning, hiring, personal requests for special support beyond salary, funding for special events, and so forth. They report at weekly staff meetings where the entire company votes on their recommendations.

Other committees perform functions necessitated by the collective structure. The Life Style committee is responsible for areas in which individual and group needs require compromise. It has dealt with issues as broad as developing a mechanism for airing personal and interpersonal problems that might have divisive results and creating a code of ethics for behavior while on tour, to problems as specific as cigarette etiquette in the van. One meeting considered the problem of attitude toward married company members touring without their spouses by others on tour and the resulting inadvertent isolation of people who were already disturbed by separation.

The Child Care committee arranges for and schedules child care and is responsible for parenting education and consistency in areas such as bilingualism and discipline. The Programming Committee schedules and promotes special events or tours of other companies and allows for the participation of supporters not in the company who act as local contacts in several areas of the country. In addition, special committees are often created to coordinate events that are not performance oriented (e.g., the Cultural Brigade to Cuba, or a TENAZ Seminario) or to perform specific functions (e.g., creating a political study group). Before the move, the company created an oversight committee that was directly concerned with long-range planning.

Although every person is on at least two committees and is expected to take initiative in his or her area, there are different levels of company membership with progressively greater responsibility. All performers are brought in as contract actors for a specific tour or production. Their maximum tenure at this level is one year, during which time they participate in all decisions that will affect the company's work during their contract.

After six months the person can ask to be considered for Associate Member status. If accepted by all Base Members, the person begins a six-month probationary period, after which he or she either is accepted or leaves. Associates sit on the board and participate in all votes except those concerning membership. The assumption is that these members want to remain with the company permanently, though this level is also probationary. At the end of eighteen months, the person can become a Base Member and participate in all decision making. The expectation at this level is of a "life commitment." No one in Esperanza sees their work as a step on the road to Hollywood stardom, a charge that has often been leveled at Chicano theatre groups since El Teatro Campesino became more involved in commercial ventures.

Esperanza has been very successful at bringing in new members without discontinuity. This can be partly attributed to a constant but slow change of personnel which has prevented the company from developing a dependence on specific personalities. The eighteen month assimilation period also gives stability as does the lack of attractive possibilities with other Chicano companies.

Most important, however, is the company's method of selecting contract actors in the first place. The process begins with an audition during which the group assesses performance ability. The concern here is for potential more than current level: the company has a strong historical perspective and is always concerned with growth and change more than immediate success. An entire day of conversation and interviews follows. The auditioner is asked about life-style, personal commitment, ways of dealing with interpersonal relationships, child care philosophy, touring and time expectations, thoughts on collectivism, and political affiliation. The interview is given significantly more weight than the artistic audition.

This accounts, though, for one of the problems with which Teatro de la

Esperanza must deal if it is to continue to grow as a politically effective and theatrically viable force: that of training. The phrase "Bad art is bad politics" is often heard in company discussions, and bad art is also bad for income. The company will either have to devote more time and money to fund-raising or create such a fine reputation that more organizations with funds will recognize their name. The company has always relied on the latter option and it could be very inhibiting if a shift in focus became necessary.

This is especially true when one considers the recent return in the United States to attitudes and misconceptions that characterized the periods of open discrimination and exploitation of the past. The problems of Chicanos are the same as they were when Esperanza began. There is still student remedial placement due to language, and bilingual education is very much an issue. Economic exploitation, supported by INS harassment of undocumented workers, lack of support for the very high Chicano percentage of Vietnam veterans, repressive church doctrine, government scapegoating and redbaiting, still occur. The problems of infighting and drugs, unemployment, and the lack of support by those few who have "made it" financially are getting worse.[14] In addition, the Chicano theatre movement is faltering.

There are, however, positive pressures that will make Esperanza progressively more important, provided the group can concentrate on political and artistic endeavors. The people's theatre movement in the United States is receiving more attention, and Esperanza's role as the Chicano explicators in the movement is essential. The growing consideration for our intimate connection with Latin America and the fact that Esperanza is a bilingual liaison with those countries is of rising importance. Finally, there is still a need to confront the old problems and the new issues of sexism, homophobia, and the experience of the Chicano middle class.

Esperanza is still striving to fulfill what it sees as its function in "preparing for the change" (Saucedo). The company seems to subscribe to the theory of George Lukacs that theatre is the genre most naturally produced by social antagonisms—that it, like life itself, is a matter of the definition and resolution of conflict. *Teatro* is, therefore, not only a means of changing society, but a necessary part of life. As such, it is respected as life's work. In the words of Jose Saucedo, "I know I do theatre because I love theatre. And yet I know I do theatre because I love politics. And what I want the group to be is best in both" (interview).

NOTES

1. Diamond, 32. For a more comprehensive analysis of the roots and renaissance of Chicano Theatre, see this source, as well as Jorge Huerta, *Chicano Theater: Themes and Forms*; Jorge Huerta, "The Evolution of Chicano

Theater;" Nicholas Kanellos, "Two Centuries of Hispanic Theatre in the Southwest;" and Joanne Pottlitzer, *Hispanic Theater in the United States and Puerto Rico.*

2. Huerta, "Evolution" 202. *La Raza* literally means "the race," but it is more generally used to refer to Chicanos as distinct from other Hispanic groups.

3. Simultaneously, the group was doing scholarly community work, creating a bibliography' and conducting tutorials with La Raza Libre. Esperanza has continued to do community work beyond theatre ever since.

4. Other forms included: the *corrido*, which was like the *acto* in structure, but a longer and less concentrated form whose pieces were based on a particular song rather than a story; children's theatre, frequently performed by children; "nostalgia theatre-non-politicak," entertainments that were hotly debated because of their claim that merely representing Chicano past without presenting a political analysis is progressive enough to justify the presentations; and the *mito*, "the content of [which] is the Indio Vision of the Universe. And that vision is religious as well as political, cultural, social, personal, etc. It is total" (Luis Valdez quoted in Diamond).

5. *Guadalupe* is published in Jorge Huerta, ed., *Necessary Theatre: Six Plays About the Chicano Experience.*

6. The first comment was made by Novoa and Valentin, reviewers, and is quoted in Huerta, *Chicano Theater: Themes and Forms.* The second is from Ellen McCracken, "Review of *Guadalupe*," p.554.

7. Marxist critic Terry Eagleton, in *Marxism and Literary Criticism* noted that form is a "complex unity of at least three elements: it is partly shaped by a 'relatively autonomous' literary history of forms; it crystallizes out of certain dominant ideological structures...[and] it embodies a specific set of relations between author and audience." (26) Esperanza's creations are almost textbook examples, though their plays embody, in addition, the relationship of the artist to the process of creating the work: that is, they embody their own mode of production in their scheme of representation.

8. For more detailed analyses of women's role in Chicano theatre, see Yvonne Yarbro-Bejarano, "The Image of the Chicana in Teatro," "The Female Subject in Chicano Theatre: Sexuality, Race, and Class," and "Chicana's Experience in Collective Theatre: Ideology and Form." Also see Joanne Pottlitzer, *Hispanic Theater in the United States and Puerto Rico.*

9. Jose Saucedo, interview by author. Research for this project was particularly intensive. The influence of reading from works such as Franz Famon, *The Wretched of the Earth* and Albert Manni, *The Colonizer and the Colonized* is quite apparent.

10. *La Victima* is published in Jorge Huerta, *Necessary Theatre: Six Plays About the Chicano Experience.*

11. Unfortunately, the use of English or Spanish for verisimilitude causes some difficulties for monolingual audience members. In addition, much of the humor on which the coherence of these scenes depends is in Spanish.

12. See Yvonne Yarbro-Bejarano, "Teatro Esperanza: Hacia una teoria del teatro chicano," for an analysis of these and other thematic concerns of this work.

13. Matters were further complicated by the great difference between the leading actors. Candace McGlaughin was possibly the most talented actor in political theatre at the time. Her experience, stage sense, and range are quite impressive. On the other hand, Ruben Castro Illizaliturri was a relatively inexperienced performer who had been trained in mime in Mexico, but was unable to speak English with fluency. Illizaliturri has since received very good reviews for his work. See also Susanna Halpert, "The *Tecolote Visions*: The Dynamics of a Collaboration."

14. See Jorge Huerta, *Chicano Theatre: Themes and Forms*, for a more extensive discussion of this topic.

4

The Dakota Theatre Caravan

> For the great majority of working people, our art, besides being inaccessible on account of its costliness, is strange in its very nature, transmitting as it does the feelings of people far removed from those conditions of laborious life which are natural to the great body of humanity. That which is enjoyment to a person of the rich classes is incomprehensible as a pleasure to a working person, and evokes in him either no feelings at all or only a feeling contrary to that which it evokes in an idle and satiated person...But if art is an important matter, a spiritual blessing, essential for all people,...then it should be accessible to everyone. And if, as in our day, it is not accessible to all people, then one of two things: either art is not the vital matter it is represented to be or that art which we call art is not the real thing.
>
> Leo Tolstoy

> This is serious stuff, I know, and it scares me some to be right honest, but, dang, we gotta learn how these kinda things happen. I told you, you push us in the ground, we'll grow out here, right where they don't want us, like volunteer corn. Volunteer people, you might say.
>
> Rollie in *Dusting Off the Thirties*

In the mid-seventies, Doug Paterson, a professor of theatre at Willamette University in Salem, Oregon, realized that he had become disenfranchised from the people of his great Plains home and that much of the theatre he had been trained to teach and produce was *designed* to exclude from its audiences the 98 percent of the public who do not attend. Paterson was "angered by the endless mystification of Broadway which absorbs young artists and strangles most of them, depriving the home areas of their vitality [and] insulted by that unspoken and spoken elitism which says good theatre can't be made there or made in these little out-of-the-way theatre groups" (Paterson, "Theoretical Questions" 9). He resolved to return to South Dakota, his place of birth and his home for twenty-two years; to go to an area and a people who had no theatre, to discover what was important to them and why, and to create a theatre piece that would be a relevant, respectful, and vital expression of the culture of rural midwesterners. He hoped in this way to reach audiences who had been deprived of indigenous and meaningful theatre as part of the exploitation of their work and the denigration of their cultures by the eastern urban establishment.

The key to the creation of such a theatre piece was the formation of a cultural alliance with the audience, an identification with the people of the rural Midwest, and the establishment of a theatre group that was a working part of the community. However, it was not enough to merely respect and reaffirm the active culture of the people or simply mirror their history and attitudes. The assumption was made that these people were capable of being theatre audiences because they were capable of making rational and critical choices, capable of responding to challenges to their imaginations and views, and capable of being just what they were—real people rather than the cretins of the Hee-Haw and Petticoat Junction stereotypes promulgated by the established arts and media. It followed naturally that theatre for this audience would have to be noncon-frontational, but at the same time challenging, raising questions, for which the answers might suggest paths to progressive change in the lives and attitudes of audience members.

The decision was made, in other words, to form a South Dakota people's theatre. "To this extent, the [Dakota Theatre] Caravan was to become a very political theatre, but the politics of the company would be woven deeply into the plays and into professional practice. The most obvious political alignment of the company, however, was with the rural people themselves, for...what we reflected was the daily politics of rural America" (Paterson, " Theatre for a People" 10).

THE SUMMER COMPANY—1977–1978

In 1976 Paterson submitted a grant proposal to the South Dakota Arts Council and to the Alternate Futures project of Willamette University. The objective of the proposed project was to create a play based on the concerns of the people of rural South Dakota and to tour it to small towns throughout the state. The play was to be created after information gathering through research and interviews by a company of six, organized collectively. "The Caravan was not begun to be part of a movement or to compete with the cultural palaces. It was begun as an experiment, one which sought to make a theatre specifically for a people who had no indigenous theatre of their own, that respected them, their work, their lives" (Paterson, "Theoretical Questions" 5). Funding was granted to support an eight-week project in June and July of 1977.

On May 20, 1977, four men and two women met in a small room on the campus of Yankton College in Yankton, South Dakota, to form a company to create such a play. One of the people was a student at Yankton (Robyn Sue Schmidt, from Minnesota), another was a student at the University of South Dakota at Vermillion (Rob Christensen), and two were Willamette students (Mary Patton and musician Doug Daniels). The other two were teachers (Paterson, and D. Scott Glasser, an Equity-affiliated actor from New York teaching at Willamette, whom Paterson had met while completing his graduate work at Cornell). In spite of the relationships implied by the differences in position and training, "it was understood that everyone would have the right to voice their opinion on any aspect of work, that all money belonged to all of us and would be spent as we decided, and that it was important that we work toward power-sharing in all areas of work and that [no one] remain the leader" (Paterson, Theatre for a People" 4).

It was agreed on that the company's work would respect its audiences' beliefs, but would not "tail slavishly after oppressive points of view,...which must be confronted and opposed in our relationships with one another, in the works created, and in the relationships with the audience" (Paterson, " Theatre for a People" 4). The members of the company believed that new modes of organization were necessary in order to realize the capabilities of the group and its audience.

> We believe that it was a thorough-going conscious decision made by all of us to work collectively, and that in no way was it a fluke, an evolution, or a warm fuzzy feeling inside. Second, we believe that this approach to work, demanding as it is and difficult as it sometimes can be, enabled the Caravan to do what it has done; authoritative and hierarchical arrangements, we are convinced, would have cramped and perhaps even prevented us from doing much in very little time. (Dakota Theatre Caravan, "Dakota Theatre Caravan" 9)

Collectivism was an appropriate manifestation of its principles of nondivisive, responsible, and shared work. In this way, the Caravan, by a deliberate, revolutionary act, became an experiment in a social relationship of the kind that philosopher Herbert Marcuse insisted "could lead to self-determination at the very base of human existence, namely in the dimension of necessary labor." Certainly a social structure of this sort "would continue to depend on a division of labor which involves inequality of functions...necessitated by genuine social needs, technical requirements, and the physical and mental differences between individuals. However, the executive and supervisory functions would no longer carry the privilege of ruling the life of others in some particular interest" (*One-Dimensional Man* 44). They articulated nonsexist, nonracist, nonageist, and nonelitist principles in order to enunciate their freedom from, and negation of, what they felt were destructive attitudes that were operative in society in general and theatre in particular.

Combating elitism was of particular concern. It seems to be an accepted axiom that there is little work and less money for theatre makers because there is a very small audience for the theatre. As a result, the theatre seeks a wealthy, elite audience, resulting in its own lack of vitality, exclusiveness, irrelevance, and high level of unemployment. "It is a sacrifice for most theatre performers to practice the trade they love most, relying on that destructive cliche of the starving artist to validate an indefensible system" (Paterson, "Popular Theatre" 12). The Caravan hoped to find support among a ^population for whom the commercial theatre had no concern.

The collaboration was extraordinary, proving the value of the detailed theoretical analysis that predated its formation, and thirty-four days after its initial meeting, the "South Dakota Variety Theatre Caravan" opened *Dakota Roads: The Story of a Prairie Family* in Salem, South Dakota. The audience of eighty sat on the grass in the public park, unaware that thousands of people would be seeing this play over the next eight years, yet acutely conscious that something very clearly connected to their own lives was occurring on the stage.

That first summer, even the company was interested only in performing its play in as many towns as possible to return to the people of South Dakota the stories they had collected in the creation process (described later in the chapter). By writing letters to the mayors of small towns throughout the state (the average population was 2,500), the Caravan was able to arrange a four week whirlwind tour, performing the play twenty-two times in twenty towns in twenty-seven days. All performances were free, although "Associate Producer Harry the Hat" was left on stage after performances to help pay the company's meager expenses.

The Caravan's touring procedure was rather unusual, the result of their particular talents, the nature of the towns in which they performed, and the error of sending publicity packets third class, frequently causing materials to arrive in towns several days after the performances were over. To counter this, the company would arrive in a town as early in the morning as feasible. They would meet with the contact person and be introduced to their hosts: the people at whose homes the members of the Caravan would be housed. They would find out what preparations, if any, had been made, and begin to drum up an audience.

At noon, company members would gather on the town's central intersection and perform a half-hour music show, which was planned as an added attraction originally, but turned out to be essential for advertisement. All the Caravan members could sing, and their unusual combination of guitar, harmonica, and trombone provided them with the ability to draw some attention. During and after this show, they would announce that night's performance. What followed was "papering the town": distributing leaflets to as many businesses as possible and to anyone they passed on the street.

After setting up the performance space, which, for *Dakota Roads*, consisted of a twenty foot semi-circle defined by a yellow clothesline laid on the ground (most performances were given out of doors), the company tried to rest from 3 until 5 P.M. and eat from 5 to 6. As they had done in Yankton during the creation process, the company would sometimes sing for their supper--arrange to perform at a person's home or to swap stories after the show in exchange for dinner. This enabled the Caravan to make new contacts and to become a more integral part of the town, and these informal sessions provided much information that was to find its way into their plays. Besides, it cut down on expenses.

At 6:30 P.M. the company would begin warm-ups. The first year, techniques that had influenced Scott and Doug were used, including Robert Benedetti and Maxine Klein's approaches to developing the actor's ability to make on-stage transformations. The company's familiarity with these modified Stanislavskian techniques, the lack of time for additional training, and the technical poverty of their productions help account for the style of "theatrical realism" that remained the hallmark of DTC's performances.

After forty-five minutes, the cast members set up the neat piles of props and costumes they would use to define the sixty characters that they were to portray during the performance, and prepared to welcome the audience. The performance lasted from 7:30 until a little after 9:00 P.M. (without an intermission), after which the cast cleared the performance area, fulfilled any musical or other after-performance arrangements they had made, and tried to get enough rest to begin again the next day.

After eight weeks of work like this for $100 a week, the company decided to come together again for the summer of 1978. They hired a manager to handle scheduling and touring; replaced Daniels with Pat Erwert, another guitar player from Oregon; took two weeks to mount the show, and with the help of a South Dakota Arts Council (SDAC) grant that enabled them to pay themselves union-equivalent wages (this grant was renewed because of the great number of letters sent to the SDAC from around the state, toured to twenty-six towns (twenty-four of them new) performing *Dakota Roads* forty times in forty-four days. Although much better organized, the Caravan still performed music shows in the streets, papered towns, and sang for their suppers. By the end of July 1978, the Caravan had performed the play sixty-two times in forty-five towns to an audience of well over 9,000—without ever charging a cent.

Dakota Roads: The Story of a Prairie Family

Dakota Roads itself is epic in scope, tracing five generations of a German immigrant family from its arrival in the United States in 1856 to the return of the youngest family member in the 1970s to the quarter section of land that the family managed to save during the Depression. The topic was chosen to reflect the interest of the people of South Dakota, all of whom except for the Lakota Indians, are relatively recent arrivals.

Performances began with "May the Circle be Unbroken," the first of many songs that are integrated into the play, followed by an introduction delivered directly to the audience by one of the cast members. The speech includes a welcome to the audience, an indication of the goals of the Caravan's work, some exposition, and an explanation of the technique of casting one actor in several roles, all delivered in the idiom one might use over the back fence to a familiar neighbor. The device of direct, conversational address is used frequently in the play to indicate passages of time or introduce new characters.

The structure of the play is episodic, with each scene representing a significant event in the lives of the family members. Although it is the most musical, sentimental, and eclectic of the Caravan's plays, and although the company really tried to please a very broad-based audience, the events were not chosen merely because of their emotional or typical value. A materialist analysis of history in this play balances humor and pathos, and historic and human concerns, through the presentation of a highly individualized chronology created out of tales gathered from people in and around Yankton, South Dakota.

The tone is set in the first scene. The cast, rocking as if on a boat, listens to Otto and Gretchen Heidenreich, who are expecting their first child, discuss their fears. Another passenger sings a German song, reaffirming the need of these immigrants to somehow remain attached to their homeland's culture, and raising a lump in the throats of many audience members.

Suddenly Otto becomes agitated, as he sights land, and an actress in the pose of the Statue of Liberty moves slowly across stage, turning at the last moment to reveal a sign on her back reading, "Wall Drug 1409 miles." The laugh is short lived, however, as the new Americans are forced to change their names to Heiden because the immigration officer cannot pronounce their real names, and a passenger is sent back to Norway because, although he has family in America, he is eight dollars short of the required pocket money.

This rapid alternation of emotions characterizes all the plays of the Caravan, and was the group's conscious choice. Not only does the humor arise naturally from the stories of the people and from their need to maintain a positive attitude during hard times, but it also works to create a sense of perspective. The choice arises from the company's analysis of Brecht's opinion that sympathetic emotion, and not self-indulgent or politically obscuring pathos, arises from understanding. "You must know why you are asking the audience to cry at that moment or why you are asking them to laugh, and what it is you're asking them to do, and what they're crying and laughing about" (Glasser, interview). In other words, it is the responsibility of the artist not to destroy emotion, but rather to indicate its root causes at the same time that he or she allows it to work in the audience.

The next section of the play, as do all succeeding ones, begins with an expository direct address. This one, by Christine, the child born to the Heidens, traces the family's progress to Chicago. There she meets Eric Anderson and, after some banter about his accent, marries him. Influenced by railroad propaganda about the land of plenty, the Andersons move to South Dakota. On the train they learn of the hardships of homesteading. The scenes include a wedding procession, two short songs, and a great deal of information about the movement West. Despite this pastiche of incidents, there is a strong sense of continuity and specificity. The richness of detail gives a sense of a full and varied life, while the rhythmic structure of the dialogue and songs keeps the scenes coherent. The expository speeches are personal enough to develop characters and yet analytical or indicative enough to give the sense of the pressure of history and the westward expansion. There is a wave-like flow to the entire play that is only occasionally interrupted by contrivance in incident or dialogue.

The characters provide a central focus, not as movers and shakers, but rather as typical participants in the life of the times. There is no room for the hero theory of history in a class and economic analysis of events. This is reflected in the plays and even in role assignment: there is no star in the Caravan and rarely is there a "main character." This is a difficulty in any chronicle play, because there is a need to present both historical process and individuals with whom the audience can empathize in order to provide a "handle" for events. The play does not do this successfully during some sections—a problem corrected in a later version of the script.

The next segment's expository monologue, behind which the performers mime the action, gives the audience the history of "proving" a claim and of making primitive farms succeed without the assistance or planning of the Eastern powers that had pushed for the opening of new markets in the West. The succeeding scenes follow Christine and Eric into their "Little Old Sod Shanty" (a song that is used to provide plot and thematic continuity) and into the last quarter of the nineteenth century: through the "Children's Blizzard" and on to "the endless, treeless, colorless expanse of prairie, often unrelieved by even hills, [that] drove many to despair, and some to madness" (12).[1]

The next eight pages of Dakota Roads form a montage, a technique used by the Caravan in their plays to give a full sense of the history and life-style of a period, while making a relatively clear political and economic analysis of the events without long-winded explanations. These montages provide an excellent change of pace from the monologues by creating a different rhythm and, through that, a different relationship between the audience and script. There is a series of very short lines delivered by actors making almost instantaneous character changes, sometimes in short conversations and sometimes directly to the audience. At the same time, large amounts of history are condensed without being belabored. The Caravan is particularly adept at choosing specifics for these montages, which become, because of their juxtaposition with each other, symbols of an entire way of life.

This montage begins with the 1876 "Gold Rush" in the Black Hills, repeating the hyperbolic accounts of wealth that brought many settlers to South Dakota, but tempering their impact with factual anecdotes. The genocide of the Native American population is the next topic. The pace of this section replicates gunfire and war as the names of tribes, generals, and battles are recited from various areas of the stage, forcing the audience to rapidly shift focus as if it was being attacked. Periodically, the rhythm is broken to state a point of view or analyze the events, and these three- or four-line moments become extremely powerful. The montage continues through the policy of "manifest destiny," the floods and droughts of the 1880s, and onto statehood in 1889.

Although war is the topic of the next set of scenes, the play focuses on the family again in order to detail and analyze events. Christine's son Jonathan has joined "Grigsby's Cowboys" and later Roosevelt's "Rough Riders." During a scene about soldiers, we discover that Jonathan's wife and child died during a blizzard the winter before he signed up. "I took her outside, in the cold, and put her and the little one in the snow till the roads were open in the spring. Wasn't nuthin' else I could do" (18). In comic counterpoint, Christine convinces Eric to buy some items from the Sears catalogue, as the work again uses specific details of daily life to indicate major changes in society. This segment ends with Jonathan's return home and an expository speech in which Christine describes the prosperity attributed to the war while lamenting the effect events have had on her now cold and distant son. Jonathan is "different" now: [he said the] "poor Cubans were just a prize in a useless, bloody carnival. Those were his words. A useless, bloody carnival" (22).

The discussions of the place of war in the economy are particularly striking examples of the ways in which the Caravan has been able to "say things in a way that the people can hear them" (Nelson, interview). By carefully choosing details and allowing Christine and Jonathan to make statements that are revealing without being directly analytical, the play expresses the ironies of war and supports the thematic statement that eastern capitalists make their fortunes over the corpses of others--European immigrants, Native Americans, settlers, and now Cubans and young soldiers. The characters thereby retain credibility and are consistent in their degree of awareness; they are not suddenly made spokespersons for particular points of view.

The play moves rapidly through the next several scenes by interspersing short expository speeches with comic and active vignettes. Jonathan marries a "freethinking" woman named Rose, whom we first see singing a song about sexism and the poverty of a single woman ("The Wagoner's Lad," a particularly strong number that was written, as were all others in the play, during the late nineteenth century). Jonathan's nervousness before proposing echoes Eric's earlier accent problems, thereby creating a sense of human continuity despite changing times. A square dance follows, then a song about the lack of respect for farmers and their exploitation by middlemen which modulates the tone, and finally an exposition by Peter, Rose and Jonathan's son, which suddenly pulls the family out of the boom twenties into the Depression.

The Depression and Dust Bowl years are dramatized in another montage, this one using mostly stories and jokes gathered during interviews with people who had lived through the period. It includes tableaux, quick cuts, and factual statements and ends with a song about migrant workers. Eric's personal depression and death pave the way for the family's loss of much of its land. Jonathan and Rose move to the city. In a rather poignant scene, Christine decides to stay on the farm alone, certain that "The land will come back." This particular scene actually motivated one audience member to defy her family and remain on her land. She thanked the Caravan when she saw the troupe the next year for giving her the strength to stand on her own.

Very little attention is paid to the years from 1936 to 1968 in terms of analysis of events. What does occur, instead, is a sequence of expositions, radio entertainments (including "Who's on First"), and montages that end two generations later. The war is a short exposition during which we are told about Rose's son Peter. The fifties and sixties are treated via a montage that concludes with a monologue by Jonathan introducing Peter's daughter Christina. By the end of this speech Christina (the fifth generation) has become dissatisfied with life in Sioux Falls and wants to move back to the remains of the family farm, even though she, unlike the original homesteaders, has realistic information about the hardships involved. Unfortunately, in the rush to complete the generational cycle and sketch all the relevant history, much of the focus on the Heidenreich descendants and their place in the events is lost. Christina and Tom, the generation that will begin again, are not bound closely to the family and do not really represent the closing of the circle in spite of Christina's name.

The play ends with a scene in which young Christina opens a trunk full of mementos left by her great-grandmother Christine, after which the cast sings "May the Circle be Unbroken," inviting the audience to join in. Finally, a member of the cast delivers a thank you speech and removes the rope that defined the stage, thereby removing the barrier between actor and audience and inviting comment and conversation.

These last scenes are the weakest of any in the Caravan's plays. After such clear and specific analysis and action, Christine's motivation to move back to the farm is too nebulous, relying on sentimentalization and romanticization that had been so assiduously avoided before. Symptomatic of this lack of clarity is a section of particularly weak dialogue and a contrived ending in which all loose ends are tied up. However, historical chronicles are so often empty of any sense of human participation or of causal analysis in their recounting of events that the error of emotional overcompensation here seems a relatively minor flaw in an otherwise well-crafted, functional play.

Thematically, however, the play is consistently clear and well modulated. The most deliberate statement is the economic analysis of the history of the Great Plains: an indictment of the exploitation by capital of the Native Americans as well as the settlers. Tied to this economic cause is a view of war as imperialistic, of Native American genocide (and the related stealing of even the Heidenreichs' name) as profitable, and of sexism as part of the devaluation of labor that funneled money into the hands of the wealthy. Although relatively nondidactic in tone, the play does indicate the complicity, either through greed or lack of knowledge, of the settlers in their own exploitation. This is most clear in the song "The Farmer Is the One" (originally "The Farmer Is the Man," it was changed in recognition of the many women farmers) which ends by noting that farmers themselves forget their role in the structure of society and denigrate their own worth. One wonders, though, if the audience is led to notice that it, too, profits from militarism, or that despite a certain naivete, the Heidenreichs, too, profited from the system that supported westward expansion and Native American genocide.

Respect for the people who fought the moneyed interests and the natural elements to maintain a joyful life of hard work and family continuity in the Midwest is the most easily perceived theme, however. Life in South Dakota, the performance says, is as important as life anywhere, and deserves to be given its due. Home, rootedness, and the land are seen as valid reasons for staying—and yet, there is no indictment of those who need to move on. The play's passion, conflict, and questions without dogmatic answers are all designed to lead to a greater understanding of the people of South Dakota and their role in the economic system.

THE METHOD

Dakota Roads was not only a reflection of the concerns of the people of the Great Plains and the political beliefs of the Caravan members; it was also the direct result of a particular method of creation, necessitated by the part-year company organization.

> When the company gathers for the first day of a project, we have literally no idea what the play will be about....From this first meeting day until the opening performance takes between four and five weeks. We don't necessarily recommend this; it just happens to be the way we have found ourselves needing to work. The advantage of a very short invention and rehearsal time is that one can become very focussed, concentrated and productive as well as surprisingly creative. A further advantage is economic in nature: we can get the play made and in front of audiences quickly so that the audience and funding agencies don't have to support lengthy playmaking periods. (Paterson, "Playmaking" 16)

Another reason for the rapidity of its work is that the Caravan is a very product-oriented theatre. This is not to say that the method of creation is unimportant; collectivization asserts each person's power to modify the product, thereby demanding responsibility as a necessary part of all progressive endeavors. What it does mean is that to the Caravan, the creation and rehearsal process is only a step that must be completed prior to the performance of a finished script. Doug Paterson, in critiquing the theories of Richard Schechner, noted that "a progressive theatre requires the process-product dialectic in order for there to be a methodology of self-correcting criticism in theatre making. The theatrical work must stand on its own as a finished—though improvable—product" ("Progressive Critique" 16).

In conversation, almost every member of the company noted that "the play is the statement" and, though they make their working methods and politics clear to anyone who shows an interest, the perceivable point of view and analysis of society must come through the performance in order to have any impact. If the play is performed as part of the process of searching for a means to say what it is the company wants to say, then it is still an exploration and as such cannot be something for which the performers are held responsible. In addition, the audience is led to focus on the worker and his or her technique—on the activity of performing—rather than on the meaning and value of that which is produced, and this is necessarily elitist to the Caravan. (The United Mime Workers and Split Britches, as will be seen in Chapters 5 and 6, hold quite different views. In fact, the relatively traditional acting style and strategies of representation in the Caravan's work, except for the device of montage, which resembles the process of communication in the collective center, reveal less of the collective process than do the performance choices of any other collective I examined.)

Finally, the Caravan is committed to respecting the people's right to their own stories, to maintaining the vitality of their own histories. Yet it has chosen to take the risk of challenging these same people to see the mutability of society by clarifying the causes and asserting the historicity of the past. In the company's opinion, this can only be accomplished through the presentation on stage of a completed story with a beginning, a middle, and at least a possible end: a story that is the result of the process, and that would be obscured by watching the process itself. In other words, perhaps paradoxically, it is only the finished play that can reveal, to the Caravan's audiences, possibilities for change. "Recognition and relation to the past as present counteracts the functionalization of thought by and in the established reality. It militates against the closing of the universe of discourse and behavior; it renders possible the development of concepts which de-stabilize and transcend the closed universe by comprehending it as historical universe" (Marcuse, *One-Dimensional Man* 99).

The Caravan's process can be divided into eleven steps, each of which (with one exception) requires the participation of the entire company as a unit. Therefore, the process is sequential at the same time that it is organic and collectivized. The first step is the initial meeting, at which the topics of concern to the company, along with professional needs and personal preferences, are discussed. At this meeting questions to be asked of local residents during the first interview phase are determined. These include questions about basic factual information as well as queries about attitudes toward rural life and images of urban existence, descriptions of major local events or personalities, and community concerns.

The second step in the process is to conduct interviews of local people. It is the concern of the Caravan that these sessions not be seen as "cultural strip-mining," but rather as lively discussions motivated by sincere interest and a desire to promote a cultural alliance with these people. Some of the interviews are formal, arranged in advance with people whose names have either been provided by the contact person or suggested by previous interviewees. This can lead to a closed circle of acquaintances, so the Caravan members also do informal interviews, talking to everyone from the waitresses or waiters who serve them lunch to people they pass on the street and residents of homes for the elderly. Interviewees are told the reason for the interviews, assured that they will not appear as characters in the play and that nothing they say will be directly attributed to them, and asked some of the leading questions that were developed in the first meeting.

When the newly formed Caravan began its first interview set, one of the questions to which it received the most enthusiastic response was, "How did your family come here?" It seemed that people were intensely interested in their own and others' immigrant heritage, but really had no sense of what it was like for other families or what place their own family history played in the scheme of development of the country as a whole. This concern provided the focal point for *Dakota Roads*.

Step three in the process is a second meeting at which the members share what they have discovered during interviews. It is at this point that a pattern of concerns usually becomes apparent. At times, actual characters will have suggested themselves to members of the company, and these will be discussed as well as the group members' search for a list of topics on which they think they should focus.

The interaction during these sessions is concentrated and intense. As I watched the company use this technique during the development of a reader's theatre piece in Wall, South Dakota (to be discussed later), I was amazed by each member's ability to remember so much in such a short time, evidencing almost the ability to contain the center in each individual. The skills of listening and retaining have been finely honed in these people as an outgrowth of their respect for the stories they hear and for the tellers. (I was rather shocked to find this happen to me when, during my formal interview with Joe Nelson, he referred to specific statements I had made in an informal conversation with several people earlier in the week).

The fourth step in the process returns the cast to the streets to conduct a second set of interviews concentrating on the areas of interest defined in the previous meeting. Again the Caravan members attempt to keep the feeling of informal conversation in the interview, even though the direct questions are more specific. This is made possible because Caravan members feel that they do not have hypotheses to prove, but rather are trying to find out what is going on in the town. As Duarte-Clark noted about the work of Esperanza during the interview process used to research *Guadalupe*, it is truly exciting to really discover something. To do so, however, one must have the attitude that the source knows more than the researcher.

> It is our objective to create material which concretely reflects the lives of the people to whom we will be playing and whom we, more or less, claim to represent. Interviewing is a method whereby we can find not only facts about the area, but also different versions of these facts and, importantly, how people feel about these facts. It reveals contradictions, dreams, strong passions, assumptions, fears, and most importantly, revealing stories and life episodes. Our own assumption from the start was that it was in the life of the people that we would find the life of our theatre, and the interviewing process was one key to gaining access to this life. (Paterson, "Playmaking" 7)

This respect for and reliance on its sources remains apparent even during performance. As a reviewer noted in the *Los Angeles Times*, "The Dakota Theatre Caravan is a collective of six young people, and unlike the majority of such groups, they don't come at us as if they've invented, or just discovered for themselves, the history they're telling us about. The Caravan consists of fine actors who are sensitive to experience beyond their own—meaning, in this instance, older people, people who were there" (DTC press release).

At the end of these interviews, the Caravan has a great deal of information in notes (they do not record because the microphone is intimidating and because they do not have time to transcribe the tapes anyway), and a real sense of the core of attitudes and the rhythm of life in the town, and all this after only a few days. It is difficult to believe that so much can happen so quickly, but the members of the Caravan have succeeded in creating four plays in this manner, and all have been recognized by critics and audiences alike as accurate and high quality presentations. Not only is that the case, but in spite of changes in personnel, the method has continued to prove itself viable. In fact, Joe Nelson and Jeannie Zeck, who joined the company in 1981, continued to carry on the method as much as possible even after the founding members had left the Caravan.

I was fortunate to be able to participate in an abbreviated use of this technique to gather information for a staged oral history project in Wall, South Dakota. I watched an interview and then conducted one on my own, finding that the Caravan's procedure helps people open up in ways that are personal and revealing. I was frankly amazed to see that the townspeople were able to find ways to articulate their feelings in a specific and entertaining manner even after they had assured me that they had nothing to say and were really not very interesting, anyway. At a script development meeting, the Caravan members not only discovered the significance of individual stories, but also differences in attitudes and ways to use them to clarify the living history of Wall through variation and juxtaposition. When the performance was given, audience members were moved frequently not only to laugh and look knowingly at the person next to them, but also to nod their heads in both agreement and discovery.

The organizational meetings after the second interviews compose the "idea stage." During this step the Caravan searches for motifs, "our greatest source of a conceptual foundation for each play" (Paterson, "Playmaking" 8) and for a germinal idea that will form the core of the piece. It is the concern of the company at this stage that the play to be written remain the story of the people, even though the tales gathered will from this point on be modified and fictionalized. The group members are acutely aware that their knowledge is not absolute: that the stories are only shared and that the culture thus far revealed to them must not be appropriated exclusively for either their own use or the theatre's.

Perhaps because the research has dealt with individuals, the Caravan typically moves directly to a discussion of characters at this point. The main characters are individuated and made typical simultaneously. The Caravan avoids melodramatic stereotyping, but does try to make certain that each character is somehow a representative or an extension of an attitude, a people, or a profession. In this way, the company outlines individuated composites. These characters, because of what they would be doing and where they would be going, suggest certain incidents. Other events are chosen because they are indicative of the culture, history, or political realities of the period or place. Finally, situations are chosen to be consistent with certain themes and to elaborate on the core idea. These two steps, character choice and scenario building, take two or three days. The work is concentrated, the atmosphere open, and the people responsive, but the hours are long: by this point, sixteen hours a day for over a week.

The eighth step in the process is a detailed talk-through of the entire play over a period of several days. The scenario is expanded scene by scene, with discussions of exact incident, length and importance, focus and themes to be raised, characters and relationships (including the difficulties of casting each actor in several roles), setting, music or song, and even some specific lines or phrases. The characters are constructed through consideration of function, attitude, description, relationships, and speech (including rhythm, patterns, and key words or phrases). Everything is based on the input of every member of the company. The process of structuring the script is completely collectivized, and allows for the completion of the process later using the skills and talents of individuals to actualize the plans that were made by the group.

It is important to note that there is no active improvisation in the process and, as indicated by interviews with the company members, none is desired. One of the members even stated, "The getting up and moving with it is alien to us" (Zeck, interview). What is apparent from watching the company at work is that the discussions are "verbal improvisations," a thinking-through process performed with a group sensibility that is based on clarity of purpose, specificity of content, and absolute trust in every member of the company to contribute in a full and open way.

Each member of the Caravan is responsible for a particular task during stage nine of the creation process. During the last few years of the company, Glasser and Schmidt did the business work, Schmidt found the costumes, Nelson composed the music and lyrics, and Zeck and Paterson wrote the rough draft. Eventually, the script went to Paterson as "editor." "This focussing of all material into one hand at a certain point in the process has the advantage of giving an internal coherency and flow to the rough manuscript, some consistency of character and language, and formal cogency to the overall movement of the play, especially in regard to transitions" (Paterson, "Playmaking" 9).

There is a dialectic established between the company and the writers. Everything up to this point has been collectivized, but it is now the obligation of the writers to distill the work of the group into a readable and performable text. They must to move the process toward a specific product and allow the stimulation from the work done thus far to inspire their expansion of ideas into theatrical reality; in other words, they must realize the decisions of the center. This is a very different viewpoint than that of the experimental groups of the sixties whose collective work was the precursor of the kind of collectivized power sharing that the Caravan does. "The experimental theatre groups of the last two decades often proceeded without a prescriptive text as their generative source. The collective performances, based on rehearsal exercises, *group examinations of personal themes* [emphasis mine], and other innovative material, relied not on the structure of a play script, but rather on theatrical structures inherent in the groups' performance philosophies" (Tyler 12). The Caravan is also charting new theatrical territory for its audiences, but its main concern is the examination of social, economic, and historical themes, with the goal of understanding how these are tied to personal events and concerns.

DTC is also very concerned with high-quality writing, using language that is designed for the stage and that, simultaneously, provides an access route for the audience in a manner consistent with the European theatre tradition of a story well told—a tradition of which the group's work is a part.

This is not to say that performance philosophy does not play a role in determining the nature of collective performances. Because of the political nature of the Caravan's work, however, there is a concern for effectiveness, which the company believes cannot be achieved without an equal concern for quality and accessibility. In essence, the company accepts the traditional apparatuses of narrative development and character definition, directly asserting their political efficacity and implicitly denying that such representational strategies necessarily communicate an exploitative ideology. DTC has determined that the way it can most successfully reach its audience is through the style that Glasser call "theatrical realism" in a mode he described as "transformational" (interview). A number of influences have combined to create this unusual performance ambiance. Not only has there been a conscious attempt to use in the productions a particular analysis of Brecht, but also the non-theatrical analyses of relationships in the writings of Karl Marx and Mao Tse-tung (mostly through the work of Paterson). Interestingly, these combine with the grounding of the company members in various modifications of Stanislavskian training, thereby allowing for a highly individualized process for each actor yet resulting in a consistent and unified company style.

The style is based on a particular view of the acting company's relationship to the audience. The Caravan's performances are rather demanding, encouraging the audience to move away from its reliance on the media to show and tell everything, and instead "trusting [it] to be intelligent enough to imagine things in the play" (Glasser, interview). There is a resulting freedom from sets and props, from the type of consistency imposed by naturalism, and from the prohibition against a degree abstraction. Obviously, a style that allows for minimal sets, props, and costumes is appropriate for a touring company, particularly one that wants to pay a living wage, but the impetus for this style came from a desire to reach the audience, not just to make the process easier for the performers.

In fact, the transformational element is extremely demanding on the cast of each play, requiring actors to play several roles each and be able to return to a role after playing many others with enough consistency so that the audience is able to recognize immediately that this character appeared before. To permit this, the performers each wear a basic costume over which they put indicative pieces to create the look of a particular character. Frequently hats are a major element, although jackets, scarves, and props such as pipes or canes can also define roles. Many props are mimed, however, so the real work of creating a character must come from the actor. There is frequently no time to allow each persona to develop because some changes are made very quickly, perhaps with only one line during which the actor switches hats, and some characters have little more than a single speech.

Each actor, then, must develop a particular voice, stance, rhythm, gesture, attitude, and so forth for each character that he or she plays and must use these devices to create instantaneously "fairly real characters, even if they're extended a bit into comic characters" (Glasser, interview). The characters are defined functionally (and, as far as possible, emotionally and attitudinally) during the talk-through, but much development is left up to the individual actor. The collective process, though, enhances the reliability of each performer as an accurate interpreter of the collective will. The few times that one performer's private decisions seem out of synch with those of another, the actors try various modes of interaction, under the guiding hand of the person directing (Glasser and then Nelson), until they find one that works within the political and theatrical context of the scene.

While there has never been time to train the company as a whole to use particular methods of character creation, the performers have had a great deal of influence on each other and, since each has brought a particular type of experience to the Caravan, it is possible to see various theories of acting permeating the group's work. Most prominent to me were those that stress a sense of *form.* Since characters appear and disappear so rapidly in each play (there are over sixty in *Dakota Roads* and nearly fifty in *Welcome Home*), each one must be recognizable at first glance or from the first words, and yet have the potential to change, gain awareness, or make a decision.

The creation of a mutable form resembles what Michael Chekhov in *To the Actor* called the "psychological gesture," a reflection in a specific form of the "essence" of a character. For the Caravan members, however, this "essence" is not intuitively revealed as it was for Chekhov. Rather, it is a discoverable typicality that is determined to a great extent by the situational and political context in which the character has spent the majority of her or his life. Each character in a DTC play does retain the attributes of archetypicality, strength, and simplicity that Chekhov insisted are essential, but each remains both social and idiosyncratic.

Chekhov spoke as well of "transformation," although to him it was mostly a matter of finding the body that will trigger the psychology. The transformational approach of which the Caravan members spoke is more like that described by Robert Benedetti in his discussions of the relationship between acting and mask wearing.

> When the mask-wearer dons his mask, then he is literally *impersonating* in the root sense of the word: *im-persona*, going *into a new mask*. He is *trans-forming* himself, *going into a new mask form*, and we who watch project onto his new form a sense of new identity which, in fact, is a projection of *our own* consciousness into the new form suggested by his performance. It is our belief in the mask which permits it to seem truly alive or authentic; in this way the actor's transformation becomes the occasion for a "sympathetic" transformation by the spectator in his own terms [author's emphases].

In one way this is a statement of the relationship between the performers and the audience at a Caravan production, and it accounts for the fact that audience members frequently come up to performers after a play and tell them that they recognize particular residents of their town in some characters. Moreover, most transformations are made in full view of the audience in order to demystify the actor's craft and subtly reaffirm the company's assertion that reality can be changed by workers' conscious choices.

Finally, Maxine Klein's reformation of Stanislavski in terms of "intention," outwardly directed character action designed to generate reaction rather than play out emotion, influences the technique of Caravan members, and is revealed in their ability to enter the performance area in a specific and active manner.[2]

This is not to say that every performer has articulated these influences or has gotten them directly. Glasser and Paterson spoke of them specifically and use the language of these teachers in their acting and directing workshops, and in the descriptions of their own work. Zeck spoke of her Master of Fine Arts (MFA) training at the University of Minnesota where the writings of Chekhov are very influential. She also mentioned Uta Hagen as an influence and called Robert Cohen's *Acting Power* the book she "lives by" on stage (letter). Schmidt spoke of her own development as an actress in terms of particular challenges presented by her roles in Caravan plays and the influence of Caravan members. Most interesting in this discussion of influences was Joe Nelson's view. Nelson spoke of himself as an "instinctive" actor because he has had no formal theatre training, although he has performed since early childhood as a cowboy, a stunt man in films, and a musician and singer, yet his performance style, growing out of experiences in his native South Dakota, is very close to that of the other company members.

The writers, then, are aware of the stylistic possibilities of the performers and the necessities of touring as they write the play scene by scene. There is a great deal of concern for language that is clear without being overly obvious or contrived) and yet stageworthy. Paterson has a particular flair for incorporating the vernacular of the area and creating an individuated idiom for each character. As soon as a scene has been completed, it is read to the rest of the company for comment. Changes are made if necessary, most often because the actor who will play the character has some insights, and staging begins.

The writing and staging steps continue simultaneously until the entire play is completed. When he was in charge of directing the performances, Glasser did not see his function as traditional because of the amount of input that each member of the cast had, even during rehearsals. The director does, however, have full control over the stage picture, and the concept for blocking the entire play is usually his. The writers of the play try as far as possible not to be overly inhibited by staging or character contingencies. "We write the play and then find a way to do that theatrically" (Glasser, interview). The director takes the script as it is being written and, with a concern for the exigencies of staging and the need to define place and time without sets, blocks the play in varying degrees of detail on paper. Some scenes are given to the actors for development with just the direction to "play the scene down left," while other segments of the play, such as the montages, are very specifically preplanned to make certain that the staging reiterates the quick cutting freedom of film, and the style changes, time jumps, and mood shifts of these rapid-fire sequences.

The position actor/director is a particularly difficult one, although it is seen frequently in collective work because of the difficulty of giving control to an "outside" eye after the group creative work (as Esperanza's experience with *El Pulpo* proved). The Caravan relies on individuals to create their own characters, but does help with indications to each other of whether something "works." Ultimately, however (until he left the company), the directorial decisions were Glasser's, and this caused some tension in the work. Joe Nelson voiced his fears, at the same time that he expressed his commitment to collective work, that the quality of the work may suffer because there is sometimes no one to be a more-or-less objective guide. Glasser noted that he has been accused of "acting [i.e., performing] like a director," and that it is sometimes an effort for him not to slip out of character in a scene (interview).

What Glasser did to make the system work for him was to develop a very Brechtian dichotomy for his own acting work. In his directing workshop he responded to a question about emotion by saying, "I cry but not because I, as Oscar [a character in *Welcome Home*], am crying, but because Oscar moves me" (author's notes). During an interview he explained to me his concept of the actor's "running commentary" on his or her own work and the need to find tricks, "not tricks to do it for the audience, but tricks to get yourself into it." He was describing what seemed to me to be the ability of the company as a whole: to make things very "real" in terms of a focused and complete on-stage presence while at the same time being always an active audience for their own work.

This requires, however, that each company member also functions as critic for all work. In the early years this was formalized: after every performance the group members gave notes to each other commenting on the performance and suggesting changes (Bechtold 13). Now, however, there is an even greater reliance on each actor to find his or her own workable solutions to creative problems, although help is offered whenever it is requested.

It seems to me that the intense level of collaboration during the discussion stages almost requires that at some point control be returned to each individual in the company to use her or his training and personal discoveries in an idiosyncratic way. The degree of shared understanding, respect, and devotion to the task that is established during the other phases of script creation allow this individuation of creative roles to actually bolster the collective work, a phenomenon noted by members of Split Britches as well.

However, the Caravan's concern for high quality—clear, moving, and non-didactic—theatre demands that somehow the company find a way to constantly evaluate its work. The difficulty of finding a supportive critiquing method is encountered by most collectives and can be a source of some friction for even the most cohesive group. As Glasser described it, "not everyone can take criticism the same way. It takes us a whole season to get to understand each other's vulnerability. So sometimes we'll sort of walk on eggs in criticizing each other, 'til we get to know each other better and relax. And sometimes just that tension will cause tension, because people don't know quite how to read it" (interview).

Nevertheless, there is a positive attitude that every company member shares in her or his discussion of both process and product: arising, it seems to me, from the fact that the quality of the work and the respect for the individual's contribution are very high. According to Zeck, at the time the newest member of the collective, "I've never had an experience with a theatre company where

I was valued as much as a performer, as an individual, as a thinking person, and as a woman—and now it is difficult to go to another theatre company to do an audition and to be seen as another person at the cattle call" (interview).

The final step in the process is the return to the audience of the stories that it gave the Caravan in the first place. The stories have been fictionalized, the attitudes clarified, and the causes specified, but they remain those of the people of rural South Dakota. The company attempts not to distort by oversentimentalizing or romanticizing the picture of life in the Great Plains. To do so would be disrespectful and condescending and would require the company members to compromise their political beliefs, a thing they refuse to do. The characters in the plays have "foibles, follies, and difficulties," but at the same time they are, if not always admirable, at least respected. This allows the Caravan to voice political concerns to a very conservative, mostly white, rural audience ("Opposition in itself is unpatriotic around here" said Nelson); to present the real, not "official," history of their struggle; and to entertain and try to educate the very people that political theatres try to reach constantly—the people who do not necessarily agree with their political stance.

Following each performance, the Caravan invites comments from the audience. Sometimes particular criticisms are taken, new stories are inserted into the play, and greater understanding is gained on both sides. While it is hard to measure the impact of their work, the Caravan's plays do not call for specific action, sometimes individuals tell the Caravan about ways in which a DTC production actually changed their lives, or at least allowed them to discuss topics at home that were considered taboo before being raised on stage. Sometimes audience members reject the Caravan's message with the question, "What do you know, you don't live here." Always, however, the audience is entertained by high quality theatre, stimulated by the demystification of the actor's profession (the revelation that art makers are workers too, and not the owners of culture), and touched by the sight of their own lives on stage.

THE FULL-TIME EXPERIMENT—1979–1981

In mid-1979, the company, dissatisfied with summer-only work which prevented them from playing to farmers except during their busiest season and precluded more extensive touring, decided to become South Dakota's only full-time professional theatre. The company incorporated as the Dakota Theatre Caravan, a nonprofit, tax-exempt corporation, and arranged a Letter of Agreement contract with the Actor's Equity Association.[3] DTC received a $32,000 grant from the South Dakota Arts Council that provided them with salaries and benefits of only $142 a week (down considerably from the previous summer) for a six-month tour of a new play.

In September 1979, five performers (Robb Christensen was unable to make the full-time commitment and Dan Gilson became the musician) moved into a house in Sioux Falls to begin the process of creating the second Caravan play. They spent days researching and writing, and nights performing *Dakota Roads* for two weeks to raise some needed cash. A little over four weeks after their initial meeting, the company opened *Dusting Off the Thirties* in Watertown, South Dakota, on October 9. Three hundred people were in the audience that night for the premier of this play about the experiences of three working-class people during the Depression.

The company toured *Dusting* and *Roads* through the end of January 1980. During that time they did seventy performances in over fifty towns to a combined audience of more than 18,000 people. Although they had to change managers in December, the tour went smoothly, and it appeared as if the Caravan was going to be able to sustain itself full time.

In February 1980, the company was in residence in Milbank, South Dakota, working simultaneously in the schools and with the community at large. Each performing member of the company was charged with organizing a specific area of work: some taught with a theatre and literature focus in the schools, some conducted music education programs, and others helped the town develop and stage a centennial play using community performers.

The decision to participate in this sort of pageant creation was unique for the Caravan. There has been in the people's theatre movement a debate over whether companies should perform *with* or *for* the people with whom they align themselves. The question is a fundamental one, involving concerns over the relationship of a people to its culture and the appropriation of that culture by outsiders who distort and exploit it. Paterson expresses a belief in Augusto Boal's concept of theatre maker as *animateur*, leading people to make their own theatre, while other Caravan members, although recognizing the value and effectiveness of theatre with the community, believe that DTC can only fulfill its potential doing theatre *for* their audiences. "Some of that's selfish. Most of the people involved in the Caravan have been people who do theatre professionally, who do theatre full-time, and, I think, we all have a vision of what theatre can do, the magical feeling of theatre,...and it's hard to do that unless you have people who are trained, who have skills in that profession, to that degree...(Glasser, interview).

To Schmidt, however, the value of performing for the people lies in their relative passivity, allowing the Caravan to "prod them gently, and yet open their eyes a little bit[;]...to present them with questions that they may not have thought about in the way that we present it" (interview). The Caravan has satisfied its own obligation to the people by residencies during which members can become part of the town, discover the stories as sympathetic members of the community, and then return the stories to the people in a manner that moves them toward progressive change. And their plays do reach people: the Caravan developed *Welcome Home* during a five-week residency in summer 1981 in Miller, South

Dakota, a town of 1,800. They opened the tour with three performances there during which over 2,000 people attended.

In March and early April 1980, though, the Caravan went back on the road, but began having difficulty arranging performances outside of its home state. It was booked for four performances and eight workshops in Oregon, but then had to return home. In mid-April, the company began what was to be one of its biggest failures, its residency at the Little Wound School on the Lakota Indian Reservation in Kyle, South Dakota. The company attributes the fact that little was achieved to inadequate planning and lack of preparatory discussion before DTC's arrival. Not only were the students with whom they were to work ill-informed, but the Caravan had no idea as to how they could best contact this group. Although the workshops were structured to provide a progression over a twelve-day period, everything from attendance to cleaning the workshop space mitigated against success. The concern of the Caravan in its written report to the South Dakota Arts Council was not, however, to place blame or to vindicate their own work, but rather to note areas of difficulty because of their fear that other cultural or artistic groups visiting under the SDAC program would develop or confirm racist attitudes, blaming problems on students as Indians, rather than as participants in an inhospitable schedule.

In May 1980 the company again toured the West, performing to small audiences in Minneapolis and then, at the Provisional Theatre's space in Los Angeles, to audiences that increased in size every night and to an enthusiastic press. DTC participated in a Depression workshop in Bakersfield, California, later that month and finished the spring tour with performances at the People's Theatre Festival in San Francisco. Management difficulties were beginning to press on the company's spirits: planning problems had marred their out-of-state tours and the great amount of work had burned out several company members. On the night of their final performance, a thief broke into the company car and stole all the baggage. The Caravan took the summer off, Paterson returned to Milbank to help remount its centennial pageant, and it was understood that no obligations were to be made beyond the already scheduled fall tour.

In August, the company hired its fourth musician, Paul Harper, and toured *Dusting* and *Theatricks*, a one-hour variety piece composed of a montage of "bits" to illustrate to students the different elements that are involved in theatre. The reputation of the Caravan was growing in small towns across the Midwest and even in the circles of the arts orthodoxy which the company had not purposely sought to attract. The result of the latter was a prestigious grant for the Fall 1980 tour from the Affiliated State Arts Agencies of the Upper Midwest, which chose only five companies that year. By December, however, divisions had marred the company's cohesiveness, and by the end of 1980, there was no longer any full-time professional theatre in South Dakota. There was, however, the nucleus of Paterson, Scott, and Schmidt, who were determined to be at work again the next summer.

Dusting Off the Thirties

Although the 1979 company was not able to stay together, it did create a rather fine play in *Dusting Off the Thirties*. When the collective met for the first time that year, members only knew that they wanted to write a completely different type of play yet retain the same performance style. They also knew that the section of *Roads* that had generated the most positive audience feedback was the Depression montage. They attributed that to the fact that the montage had purposely "aimed for the gut" and was the most emotional, and therefore most easily accessible, section of the play; consequently, they fought the idea of expanding that segment.

However, early interviews in the Sioux Falls area indicated that the thirties were the area of interest most often referred to by the people. The second set of interviews revealed an educationally demanding aspect of that interest: everyone knew the Depression had happened and most had stories of its horrors, but few knew what a depression was and no one, even local bankers who had lived through it, knew why it had occurred. It seemed to people that the economic aspect of the thirties was as "causeless" and as unpredictable as the drought that turned the plains into the Dust Bowl. In spite of the confusion, there was still a sense of pride among people because they had survived—because they had been clever, resilient, or just plain tough enough to remain when so many others had left.

The Caravan decided to create a play that focused on survival, on the political and economic aspects of the Depression rather than on the sentimental side, as well as on the effects of the thirties on the people of the Great Plains. They decided that the texture of the script would be very important in delivering the message, and so the piece was conceived in terms of angles, of sharp and abrupt turns—or what Paterson has called "Guerilla ideology. Sort of hit and run. We do something [scary or risky]; then we run and do something safe" (interview). The goal of the play was to take people past their confusion about the decade: to show not only how people can lose their perspective on events, but also how they can see beyond those events to gain control.

> Ideologically, the statement [that the play makes against capitalism] was pretty strong—but we were very crafty. I think it's the most interesting of our plays....We did very difficult things in that play theatrically—not to cover what we were saying, but to do it in a way that they could hear. Because underneath all the conservatism that's in the area, there's also a stubborn streak of "I am an independent and I will think the way I want to think!" The Farmer-Labor movement came out of this area. And I think we were trying to reach that part of the people. (Glasser, interview).

As a result, *Dusting* is the least story-oriented of the Caravan's plays, and the most theme-centered. It describes the causes and effects of the Depression in relation to the Midwest by concentrating on three victims who try to find out what is happening around and to them: a small farmer, a store owner, and a school teacher, whose stories are interwoven with scenes of more general events of which the individual stories become types.

The first line of the body of the play, which follows a montage and music introduction, is spoken simultaneously by the three main characters: "What happened?" From that moment on, *Dusting Off the Thirties* attempts to provide a nearly two-hour, rapid-paced, nonstop answer. The scenes are not distinct as in the previous play, nor are there many direct addresses to the audience to set up episodes. Instead, scenes shift from reportage to present tense and from location to location through abrupt changes in character or focus, except for some notable changes of pace, each of which has been inserted for a particular effect.

The lives of the central characters connect with those of a series of minor characters who pass through the town and with the songs and comments of Homer, a ubiquitous Woody Guthrie–like hobo, who drifts somewhere between the characters and the audience in awareness and perception. By the end of the play, the picture of the Depression decade is complete, with the elements combining into a coherent whole according to a symbolic syntax that activates the audience's imagination.

Rollie, played by Doug Paterson, is a farmer with a family and a hired hand named Pete. (Pete, and all other minor characters, were played by Scott Glasser, who was introduced in the opening song as Jack [of all trades].) Rollie's early scenes concentrate on the effects of the Dust Bowl years on the farmers and trace the depletion of his prosperity and the devaluation of his labor. He attends a Farmer-Labor union meeting after which, in one of the only direct addresses in the play, he tells the audience: "Did you know that all along, rich folks that owned stock in the big companies that didn't go under got big dividends, right straight through. Here crops stagger to 17 cents because there's no money, and then come to find there's money all along. Just, it ain't ours, and it apparently ain't gonna be ours" (28-29). Determined to find out what caused the Depression, Rollie goes to Helen, a young school teacher. During a theatrically risky scene, she sits Rollie at a table and explains the economics of floating wealth, rampant speculation, overproduction, and the removal of money from the pockets of the workers and farmers, who could then no longer purchase the goods they produced. Instead of a direct lecture, however, she uses the analogy of a baseball team with a great pitcher. The "change of pace" scene is clear, short, and static yet theatrical, and it serves as an indictment of capitalism that the audience might not accept were it couched in any other terms.

Helen, who was played by Robyn Sue Schmidt, is laid off from her job but, after many difficulties, opens an alternative school for Native Americans and marries a writer. In all Helen's scenes there is clear development of a theme: the right of self-fulfillment, of an opportunity to fulfill one's own potential. (Even the casting of Helen, the love interest, ends up as political statement. Schmidt is a large woman who would probably never be given a romantic role in commercial theatre. The role of Helen, however, was the type of challenge she needed to progress as an actress, and casting against type was a challenge that the audience needed in order to outgrow its sexist stereotyping.) Her discussions of wartime prosperity, racism, and media-event history all point to repression and exploitation.

Edith (who was played by Mary Patton), is the third focal character. Edith owns a small store which she loses during the course of the play. In a rather poignant scene, she "decides" to accept relief money to support her family, dispelling the myth that people who take assistance are always selfish or lazy. The minor character with whom she appears in her scenes is Stu, an alcoholic hobo, whose image of the Depression provides an example of the type of period humor with which this play is peppered. He tells Edith: "It was like this guy he knew hitched his mule up to a wagon and the mule sat down right there and wouldn't budge. So, to remedy the situation, he got some straw, put it under the mule, and set it on fire. Well, the mule gets up, walks a few steps, sits down again, and the whole wagon burnt up" (37). Stu's tale stands in sharp contrast to Edith's recounting during a clever card-table montage later in the play, of the woes of hunger, of trying to explain the difficulties to her children, and of escape from her troubles by going to the movies.

The play contains other montages and a number of songs (most of them written by Dan Gilson) that are used more for thematic purposes than for plot movement (as in *Roads*). Three "Dusting Ballads" use the refrain "It's only life" to reveal the way in which the people saw the Depression, but the final verse of ballad three begins "How can we say it's only life/When we learn the reasons why?" There are songs that recount dust storms, the exodus to California, and work for the Works Progress Administration (WPA). "I'll See You in My Dreams" and "Happy Days are Here Again" are used for ironic commentary, and at one point the play practically stops for an abstract tap dance by a hobo to Homer's "Rich Guy," a song about how it is "mahv'lous to be of the wealthy breed." The total effect is one of rapidly shifting rhythms and moods, each developing a particular theme or motif and punctuated by the "slap-in-the-face" effect that is achieved when reality has to be confronted again at the end of each song.

The script is far more sophisticated than that of *Dakota Roads*, and it reveals growth in several areas. The monologues in *Dusting* are much more stageworthy and are constructed to emphasize sharper images. In fact, the dialogue of the entire play becomes almost a natural Midwest poetry—certainly more emotionally charged than everyday speech, but familiar and acceptable at the same time. The play, in spite of its purposeful breaks, is more coherent as well. This seems due partly to the consistent focus on fewer characters and partly to a greater clarity of thematic purpose.

The play also has a sharper sense of history. The connections between past and present—even past as present—are clear, and the use of factual information as commentary on the society that is contemporary to both characters and audience enhances this sharpness. Nevertheless, the play manages to be concentrated on stage more than *Roads*, to set up a multidimensional world in which typical, yet strongly individuated characters, can live fuller lives in front of the audience.

A final aspect of this on-stage life is the integration of much more of the exposition into the fabric of the play, and the trust that this reveals in the audience's ability to participate in what semiotician Anne Übersfeld called the "pleasure of '*bricolage*,'" of putting the picture together bit by bit during a performance from signs and images that are "ever in flight...In the work of staging a play there is perhaps a dialectic between the wealth of signs and the perceptive capacities of the spectator; if the spectator drowns, his pleasure stops" (131). The Dakota Theatre Caravan, which becomes so much a part of the community for which it performs, showed in *Dusting* that it was able to judge accurately the perceptive needs and patterns of the spectators.

The only point when the play does not remain tightly controlled—when it violates the semantics of its own structure—is near the end when an attempt is made to tie up all the loose ends in a positive fashion. In the scene between Helen and her fiancé, for example, he makes a 180-degree emotional turn as soon as Helen mentions that the WPA has a writers' project. As in *Dakota Roads*, the Caravan seems unable to make moments of relative happiness work theatrically.

Part of the difficulty could be due to the story-gathering procedure used by the Caravan. First of all, people have a propensity to remember and retell tales of "bad times" better than those of good times. Second, the Caravan is devoted to, and quite good at, fictionalizing the stories of the people, but the positive speculation at the end of the play is more or less completely invented. Finally, because of the circumstances in which we live, we have developed many ways of describing despair but have only a weak language of joy.

Another possibility is that the thematic message—that the people will go on regardless of what the system tries to do to them—was, to the members of the Caravan at this point, important enough to be articulated directly in spite of the need for obvious contrivance. "We're not miracle workers. We don't think that we have created the best theatre in the world. And we don't think that our theatre is perfect, or that it is great. We know that we do some playwriting that's too obvious, where the mechanics of the writing is very obvious[,]...but we've made choices, and there are reasons that the theatre is that way and the plays are that way. [Choices are made] partly [because of] our perception of the audience and partly [because of] our perception of ourselves (Glasser, interview).

Audiences and critics are less harsh in their judgments. Critics praised the play's accuracy in its portrayal of the people and the times, and many alluded to the positive sections of the script (those with which I took exception). Lawrence Christon wrote in the Los Angeles Times that "the Caravan has overlooked nothing of what people suffered...but it also shows us what they dreamed," and Midg Docken called the balance of hope and despair, of humor and hardship, "part of the *wonder* of this production. It portrays real people who worked and starved and tried to make light of their troubles while they waited for a better day." The response in the small towns around the country was even more positive. Few, however, noted the play's political statement.

It seems as if with *Dusting Off the Thirties*, the Caravan had accomplished several goals. They had created a piece of sophisticated and high quality theatre with general appeal, that still played well for the specific audience that was the source of the stories. The production made many demands on, while simultaneously pleasing and entertaining, audience members, yet it presented harsh criticisms of some of their widely accepted assumptions. Moreover, the Dakota Theatre Caravan had become an active part of the cultural life of the people of South Dakota. "This continuity with a people is especially important when we realize that at this stage people's theatres are by and large not 'chosen' by the people, and that we are, objectively, self-appointed representatives, and become true representatives only by our deeds" (Paterson, "Playmaking" 8).

SUMMER REAFFIRMATION—1981–1982

The Caravan was again offered a major grant from the South Dakota Arts Council and the Affiliated State Arts Agencies to do a tour of the upper Midwest during summer 1981. On June 1, the three continuing members, Joe Nelson (whom Glasser had seen perform in Minneapolis, auditioned, and then interviewed about his political concerns), and Jeannie Zeck (brought into the company in much the same way) met in Miller, South Dakota to do two things: create a new play and generate interest in the arts in order to promote the development of arts councils for the Rural Audience Development Project of the SDAC.

On July 3, 1981, the Caravan opened *Welcome Home*, a new play about living in a small, Great Plains town, in the Miller town park. Four hundred people attended, and by the third night the crowd had swelled to a thousand. That summer, with the assistance of a project director provided by the SDAC, the company toured widely. This time there was greater expense for each sponsor and certain aspects of the tour were much more structured.[4] The company took advantage of this, not financially but socially, taking time to reestablish contact with the members of each community where they performed.

Part of this change in touring procedure helped give the Caravan an image that more accurately represented what it was and did. Much of the publicity packet that was sent to sponsors stressed professionalism. Even the biographies of the company members in the programs concentrated on training and performance experience. In one way this was only fair to the Caravan, giving these workers recognition for their work. Politically, the message was that it is not necessary for the people of rural towns to go to a city to find high-quality theatre and that professional theatre does not have to perpetuate the mythology of a cultural model that denigrates the value of rural life. In other words, the Caravan's explanation of itself challenged the "South Dakota Complex": the assumption that the region's own material is neither significant nor "culture."

The other image-clarifying sections of the packet stressed the concepts of people's theatre and collectivism. The first concept was defined by stressing the connections of the company's plays to the stories of the people of the region and by noting that the company avoids any divisive elements in style or content. Collectivism was defined in terms of the responsibility of each member for all aspects of the work, the value of each member to the whole, and the sharing of decision-making power.

It is typical of the Caravan's ability to be relatively clear without being offensive that in spite of this publicity, DTC was not seen as a political theatre by its rural audiences. Some of the members found this frustrating, sometimes feeling that the message was not getting across or, worse, that the wrong messages were being heard, but everyone recognized the value of the Caravan's work and responded to the challenge to be cautious and the danger of leaving the city and theatre worlds, where anything can be said in any way the company might desire.

There may be a great deal of power in a nonpolitical identity, however; the power of what Friedrich Engels called "objective partisanship," which reveals a partisan view of reality without the direct expression of a political or subjective perspective. For one, DTC can raise questions in nonconfrontational ways, thereby penetrating preconceptions by sidestepping the audience's tendency to be defensive.

In addition, this image allows the Caravan to reappropriate the theatre and thus return to the people of the Midwest a means of expressing the vitality of their own culture. Just by presenting rural life as content it can validate positive concepts about that life, though the danger of reifying negative ones is ever present. The Caravan's active search for a new audience is in itself a political reorientation. Perhaps most significant, the company has the power of agenda setting: of presenting topics to the communities in which it performs for consideration and discussion.

The remainder of the publicity packet established procedures that the sponsors must follow, including checklists for local organizers and a list of company needs, including a required dinner time if food was to be provided and a note that two of the company members cannot eat sugar. All this eased the burden on the performers and involved the town as an active participant in the production.

While in Miller, the company gave a variety of workshops designed both to teach specific theatre skills and to demystify the profession of acting and the art of the theatre, what Nelson called "breaking down the conventions" (interview) of relationships. There was, however, some disagreement among the company members as to the value of these workshops in terms of political and social goals. Part of the difficulty was that the Caravan only taught the workshops requested by each sponsor, and the most overtly political offerings were rarely chosen.

For example, the workshop titled "What's So Special about the Dakota Theatre Caravan" was designed to explain to sponsors the goals of the Caravan, the nature of people's theatre, and the meaning of collective organization. "The New York Syndrome Workshop" was structured to "discuss how difficult it is for the Midwest, particularly the rural areas, to maintain a sense of their own culture [including] some thoughts about the impact of mass media, corporate interests, and government programs on rural/small town USA" (DTC, "Workshop Offerings"). Neither of these workshops was ever requested. On the other hand, workshops on makeup and music (the latter of which is practically a performance rather than a sharing of information) were consistently requested.

The workshops that seemed to have the greatest impact all led, however indirectly, to participant empowerment. In the "Creative Dramatics" workshop, which some of the Caravan members believe is the most effective, self-determining individuality and nonsexism were stressed. The "Massage" workshop allowed for touching and contact in nonsexual ways that were completely new to most participants. This workshop, and the "Acting" sessions, were organized over a three-day period and allowed for a great deal of growth and reflection.

The "Acting" workshop begins with relaxation and imagination exercises, and moves through various means of physical exploration to the creation of a persona. The participants are asked to explore the concepts of "Molder, floater, and flier" (adopted from Michael Chekhov), opened and closed stances, placement of energy centers, and emotional self-evaluation. At the end of the third day, time is taken for a half-hour improvisation during which the characters that the participants have developed "visit" each other. The excitement when the workshop members grasp what they have done and realize that they are not shut out from this creative outlet because they have "no talent," is evidence of the Caravan members' ability to use the theatre and their training in it as a means to return to the people confidence in themselves as makers of culture.

In the workshop titled "Understanding Directing," the Caravan concentrated on the skills that a director in community theatre needs to practice and on the idea that collaboration, "giving [the actors] responsibility ultimately," creates care and quality (Glasser). The insistence that rural directors and performers not denigrate their own work or compare it to the performance level of people who work in theatre full time bolsters the confidence of participants.

For their 1982 summer tour (again sponsored by the same groups) the Caravan added a new workshop called "What's So Special about Your Community," which was called by the Caravan members the "oral history workshop." Because the 1982 tour included four one-week residencies in South

Dakota towns, the company felt there was a need to make the kind of contact with people that paralleled the contact they made during the creation of new plays. The oral history workshop was designed to accomplish this by replicating in miniature the collective creation method of the Caravan to develop a history/story-telling, readers, theatre performance given by members of the Caravan and interested townspeople. All Caravan members are present at every session of this workshop and as they take turns speaking and listening, the participants are made quite comfortable, involved in conversations, and included in project planning. The project is explained, interview procedures are taught, names are gathered, and interviewees are assigned during the first session. On the second and third days, information from the interviews is shared and the participants, inspired by the process, swap stories in a lively discussion that is as full of laughter as quiet reflection.

The Caravan meets after the third session to organize the material into meaningful sections and assign stories and lines to volunteer participants. On the fourth day there is a rehearsal, and the performance takes place on the following night immediately after the Caravan does its musical show. The music performance is entertaining and reveals the virtuosity of the cast, but it lacks any discernible organization or message and, unlike the way in which Esperanza uses its music, is without any underlying purpose. However, the workshop presentation is very moving and a touch nostalgic, allowing people to own their own lives, and supporting what Barbara Meyerhoff (in her description of a story-telling project she had done with elderly Jewish people in Los Angeles) called:

> the crucial role that can be played by the very act of story-telling in preserving cultural life. In a room with persons of similar experiences and backgrounds, these...people began for the first time to truly listen to each other, to hear the culture they indeed had in common. Story--telling became transformed from a simple act of transmission into a complex life-giving activity. While they were themselves the storehouses of their history, their stories made that history immediately real—not just storable, but remembered and affirmed with old feelings made fresh. (Paterson, "Living Story" 21).

The summer of 1982 also signaled another major change in the Caravan. Members of the company again became dissatisfied with the limitations imposed by summer-only work. Although the Affiliated Arts granting procedure allowed for relatively easy summer scheduling, the fact that the company's permanent residence was a post office box in a city that it rarely visited made it impossible for DTC to do any long-range planning. The absolute reliance on grant money was becoming more frightening as "Reaganomics" and the NEA refocused funds toward established cultural "palaces," and the Caravan members were becoming increasingly worried that it might step on the wrong toes or, even worse, have to compromise with funding sources to continue the company's existence.

In addition, the personal life of the Caravan members was complicated by the summer-only commitment. Acting positions had to be turned down during the rest of the year if there was any chance they would continue into the summer. Zeck and Nelson were expecting a child and needed a steadier income. Moreover, and somewhat ironically, the fact that the company members only came together in places where none of them lived prevented the kind of community attachment that can be the real mainstay of a people's theatre. Finally Doug Paterson had just established the first graduate emphasis in People's Theatre at any university in the country and felt he needed to concentrate more on full-time teaching. The decision was made to explore ways to become full-time again and to allow the Caravan, which was seemingly established enough to weather almost any storm, to continue the experiment that was started five years before.

Welcome Home

Fortunately, the company had had great success with its third play, *Welcome Home*, and could count on additional performances of the show in 1983 to provide a touring schedule. This play, which is far simpler in structure than *Dusting* and far smaller in scope than *Roads*, is the most finely wrought of the Caravan's scripts and has the broadest appeal. Although it presents a portrait of life in a small town in the rural Midwest, it provides a clear picture of the interrelatedness of any people and their society. Describing the performance of *Welcome Home* that ended the Gathering, critic John Rezmerski wrote: "The play makes an unabashed pitch for honesty in discussing cultural values and emotions and shows how inextricably they are linked. It treats sensitive issues with unfailing good taste, but without artistic or ethical compromise. When the closing song is over, the audience is immediately on its feet, clapping vigorously as if to say, '*This* is the play we came to see!'" (30).

When the company members met in Miller, however, they did not have any plans for such a work. They knew only that they wanted to write a play about life in a small town during the present day. The interviews revealed certain common threads, including descriptions of the town as friendly, safe, boring, busy, gossipy, school-centered, athletic-centered, and "like a fishbowl." They also discovered that there had been a tragedy in the town that everyone had shared, and that there were stories that needed retelling. Most important for the structure of this play, however, was the way in which certain character types were easily discernible.

The choice was made to create a "typical" small town, but one that "would not be a generalized town. In the play's world, it would be very specific, real, and accurately represented so that people in any small town could see features of their lives in the play" (Paterson, "Theatre for a People" 12). It was important, as well, that the people of Miller not be exploited or displayed. The plot evolved from the need to have this picture develop through incidents that were necessitated more by character interaction than by the kind of historical pressure that was evident in the other two plays. The play is the least musical, most character-oriented, and most direct of the three.

The device that keeps the episodic structure tied together is the return of Curtis Daily, a reporter from the big-city *News Nation* magazine, to Welcome, the town where he was born, to cover its centennial as a human interest feature. His research uncovers all the positive and negative aspects of small-town life, as it reveals the human and individual side of public tragedy and divisive attitudes. In one sense, Daily represents the Caravan itself, discovering that the people have a story that is worth telling. In another, the device is so transparently and genially contrived that it almost remains on the outskirts of the play, providing a frame for the portrait of Welcome and its people.

The play opens with the creation of the atmosphere of New York City through the rapid movement and dialogue of five very animated actors. On cue they freeze and Curtis delivers the only expository monologue in the play. He not only announces the plot structure, but also reveals many typical urban misconceptions about the Midwest, mentioning, ironically, that he would "feel a lot safer staying in New York." The "Song of the Whistle Stops," a catalogue of town names in South Dakota, follows. We next see Curtis asking directions from a woman construction worker on the road. This scene introduces in a very delicate manner the theme of sexism, which plays a very important role throughout the play.

Curtis's first activity in Welcome is to be stared at by Fred, who gets very excited when he finds out why the stranger is in town and blurts out hints of major events about which Curtis will discover more later. Daily moves out into the street and begins to interview Betty. Others stop and interject their views, turning what could have been a dull conversation into an active and crowded barrage of information about attitudes in the town. There are forty-nine characters in *Welcome Home*, all performed by only five actors, and yet there is a sense throughout that there is constantly a great deal of activity on the stage and that the population of the town is going about its business as usual. The fullness of life on stage is a result of both careful construction in the dialogue and the versatility of the cast.

Curtis meets his old college friend Duffy, who is now a teacher and basketball coach in Welcome, and who takes Curtis on a tour. Duffy openly discusses the problems in the town, which include decreasing population, alcoholism, lack of privacy, limited activity, and economic dependency on crops and, therefore, on the weather. Curtis's urban misconceptions are questioned almost immediately. When Duffy mentions that movie attendance is decreasing, Curtis assumes it is because of "that moral majority stuff," to which Duffy replies: "Not really. We're actually more religious around here than moral" (11). The real reason is cable television.

The scene ends with an indication that Curtis will attend the town board meeting that night. Most scenes end like this, with an indication of where and when the next scene will take place integrated into the dialogue so that as soon as the actors enter, the scene can begin. This change from the previous plays allows the audience to concentrate on the nature of the events, but also forces them to figure out the roles of both actors and characters in town life. Because so many characters have different educational levels and occupations and because each has an indicative and appropriate idiom, character differentiation is made quite easy. In addition, many changes are made on stage by removing an appropriate hat or prop from a screen in full view of the audience and putting it over the basic costume. The pace is also kept up in this manner, and the changes can be made fast enough to allow actors to assume characters for interjections into scenes and then appear moments later as a different person.

The fifth scene introduces the "villain," Duane Decker, his son, Collin, and Hannah Shea, a school teacher and the emotional center of much of the play. The scene includes arguments over school closings, plans for the centennial celebration, and some very funny interjections and digressions by a farmer named Sam. The motif of the farmer is repeated throughout the play, although the theme is played differently each time, indicating that not all farmers are the same. Rather, we see them as activists, "starers," friendly conversationalists, busy people, and even drunks.

The remainder of the scenes are, for the most part, interviews presented in a variety of formats. In the first, Curtis interviews children at the library story hour. Not only is this scene very funny, but it reveals a great deal through the uninhibited comments of the children. The next scene takes place in a bar during an argument over the value of the 1971 basketball championship that Welcome won. Suddenly there is a reenactment of the final moments of the game complete with fans, cheerleaders, radio announcer, and Duane Decker berating his son for not being an athlete.

The next interview is with Claire, the niece of a teacher who was killed in the school fire: the tragedy to which everyone alludes at one time or another. This is followed by a montage in which the fact that Curtis talked to Claire on her porch is modified by rumormongers through a series of distortions into the belief that Curtis has set up a brothel. The gossip ends as Curtis enters the cafe the next morning and is slapped in the face. The theme of rumormongering is introduced comically through this rapid paced montage, but it is to become a much more serious topic later on. The device of introducing a theme subtly through chance comments or comic scenes and then letting it reverberate with varying degrees of seriousness is a particularly apt one for this play in which the unspoken is often the key to what is happening. It is this device that creates a richness of subtext not found in the earlier work of the Caravan.

In the cafe, Curtis interviews Jim, who has just returned from Panama where he was in the Peace Corps, and gets an international view of the town and its connections to Central American peasants, as well as to American people of color, because they are all "on the very bottom of the power structure." Curtis asks Jim about various people in town who appear to deliver speeches that are labeled "Portrait" in the script. They include a priest who gives a sermon in rhyme calling on people to join any church, a little girl whose parents yell at her at home, a drunk, a racist, and Barbara, the owner and editor of the local paper. It seems as if Duane Decker had planned to buy the paper and made slanderous insinuations about Barbara in order to make her seem unsuited for ownership. The women in the town held fund-raisers to help her buy it after the owner took exception to Decker's methods. Interestingly, this story is based partly on the actual acquisition of a radio station by a woman in Miller, and partly on an actual strike by church women against a doctrinaire priest, and is used to great advantage to bring together the themes of gossip, sexism, and greed. It is delivered in a short speech which includes all the essential facts and hints at the rest. This type of dramatic economy is another strength of *Welcome Home*. The scene ends with a discussion of racism between Curtis and Jim: a scene that is very direct and, although it reads poorly, works in performance because it provides such sharp contrast to the rapid pace of the previous scenes and serves as a needed resting point for the audience.

The tenth scene is again a series of interviews, each with a different structure. First Curtis discusses history and Native American relations with Hannah, but she rushes out when the school fire is mentioned. Curtis then turns his chair and is in the middle of an interview with Gary, who responds only "yea" or "I dunno" to his questions. The third interview in this scene is an antiphonic exchange between Duane and his son Collin. The men alternate answers as if they had been asked similar questions by Daily in two private interviews. The scene is simultaneously poignant and thematically clear, revealing the generational conflict and helping to explain it by indicating motivations, faulty though they may be, for Duane's behavior. This is an important political statement, tying reprehensible behavior to social causes, and is in direct opposition to mainstream media and theatre, which frequently present evil as an aberration that has little to do with social structures and systems. Duane Decker is revealed as a man who is driven to acquire because of a misunderstanding of his Depression-era poverty. He is overly competitive (athletics to him is a training ground for wresting control from others in the rest of life's activities), sexist, conservative, and ruthless. Colin, on the other hand, learned from Hannah to put his father's "old values" into historical perspective, even though he suffered the consequences of ostracism because he avoided sports.

Scene eleven presents a denial of Decker's assertions by Lucy, who literally pushes Curtis out the door to see Hannah. The twelfth scene is the completion of the portrait through a revelation of the truth behind the reticence of the other people. Hannah and Jessie, the teacher who died in the fire, were young widows sharing a house. When Hannah ran against Decker for a seat in the town Assembly, he spread the rumor that she and Jessie were lovers, ensuring Hannah would lose the election. When Jessie was killed saving children from the fire while Hannah and others watched, Hannah resolved not to cry in order to protect Jessie's name. She finally breaks down during the scene and, in only the third song in the play, sings about why she stayed in Welcome and about her love for and friendship with Jessie.

This scene is particularly delicate. It is the Caravan's intention to say that the rumor is bad, but Hannah's sexual preference, regardless of what it may be, is not. In the original version, Hannah called Decker's assertions a "malignant lie," and Hannah said to Curtis, "You can't deny such things." At one performance a lesbian in the audience pointed out that the implications of such language, especially to a rural audience that is likely to be homophobic in the first place, is that Hannah feels lesbianism is horrible. The Caravan changed "malignant lie" to "cold, calculated rumor" and "such things" to "rumor." Even Curtis's earlier response of a knowing verbalization was changed to just silent listening. It is important to note that Hannah's actual relationship to Jessie is completely irrelevant to the play and has been left up to the actress playing Hannah to decide. This is another example of the way in which the Caravan creates characters with functional places in the scheme of the action and then trusts each actor to give the character a life within the world of the play that will allow her or him to fulfill (or help account for) that function.

The final scene of the play is the actual centennial celebration. It begins with announcements, including comic errors, moves to a sometimes funny yet genuinely beautiful address by ninety-nine-year-old Oscar Hurlbutt, during which he tells a moving story about a Native American funeral for his mother, and continues through a montage of speeches in which one line of each speech is delivered in such a way as to make it connect to the next speech in a comic fashion, as if one were spinning a dial on a television. Daily tells the crowd that the story he writes will really be written by the people of the town; then there are four rapid responses to him by various characters and the play ends with a song. The scene is punctuated by the drunken Lyle complaining that his cat was sealed into the town's time capsule.

The celebration is upbeat but honest and does not fall prey to the kind of contrivance that earlier Caravan endings did. There is no attempt to resolve the conflicts or predict the future, but only to put the finishing touches on a portrait of a town in which "there is so much more to admire than despise." What is clear, however, is that these people will continue to live in the small town Welcome, not because they cannot do anything else, but because they want to: They like their lives, because the safety of small town life and the chance to have individual actions count for something are worth "gossip and little privacy and no big time excitement" (12).

Such a presentation is, in terms of commercial media's usual stereotyping, quite unconventional. The concept of the rural Midwest is, as Edward Hirsch says of early-twentieth-century Irish peasantry and the public reaction to John

Millington Synge's *Playboy of the Western World* (a play with which *Welcome Home* has several things in common), "encoded with political meaning," and to dramatize rural life in an accurate way, without denigration or idealization, is in itself a political act, "endowed with ideological significance" (86). To present rural people as sentient and able to change and react is empowering and makes the people of South Dakota "dangerous" (i.e., less easily exploitable). To the elite audiences for such plays as Sam Shepard's *Buried Child*, and to the urban audiences of such gross distortions in television sitcoms such as "Hee Haw" and "Green Acres," rural people exist only "as myths in both the social and political and the literary and cultural consciousness" (Hirsch 87). The Dakota Theatre Caravan's presentation of the truth of *Welcome Home* reappropriates that myth to rectify its inaccuracies, both positive and negative.

This is not to say that the play does not attempt to challenge the rural population as well, even though it calls for "simple" reforms and not systemic change. "The company found the people's own story and recast it in a form that would reveal to them both conscious and unconscious choices inherent in their lives; and invite them to use their power to change progressively" (Weinberg 6). The play raises questions in a way that is simultaneously respectful and delicate, yet attempts to be a call to personal action. Welcome is a microcosm more than just a typical small town, and the divisiveness that infects its life—that keeps people from becoming participants in the creation of their own history and culture—is endemic. The play claims there is a cure, however, and it begins with a recognition that there is a disease. *Welcome Home*, while never losing sight of the healthy parts of life, lets us know what we can do to make society better.

FINAL RESIDENCIES—1983–1989

During the off-season in 1982 and early 1983, the Caravan established two relationships that it hoped would allow it to become financially sound and have a home base from which it could operate as a full-time company. The first relationship was to be a purely commercial one. The town of Wall, South Dakota, is a tourist mecca, but people only stay for as long as it takes to wander through the famous Wall Drug store. In an effort to keep people in town overnight, the town organized the Badlands Western Musical Company which, in turn, hired the Dakota Theatre Caravan to stage *Dakota Roads* during the tourist season. When the Musical Company had difficulty raising the funds to build a performance space, the townspeople donated labor to help build an 1100-seat amphitheater on the slope of a ravine in the Badlands. The Caravan reworked *Roads* for a larger cast and a huge audience, and came together in August of 1983 to mount the show, somewhat naively relinquishing its collective process for what it hoped would be a way to serve an old audience, communicate to a new one, and earn enough money to operate more comfortably during the year.

The new *Dakota Roads* script contains a number of changes that were designed to play to larger audiences. Several expository monologues were replaced by active scenes or line changes, and some additional scenes and songs were added. Finally, there are a number of scenes in which the visual element is stressed to clarify both historical and emotional progress. For example, the scene on the train during which Eric and Christine discover that South Dakota is far less hospitable than they had been told is, in this version, done in a patter song that develops into an exchange between new and old settlers and in a large group song and procession. In a similar fashion, the brief scene in which Jonathan tells of his first wife's death is expanded into a mime-dance reenacting the events.

Several of the montages were modified or expanded to include more voices and to stress specific themes. Many of the problems of the expansion West are more clearly connected to the concept of manifest destiny. Native American genocide as an outrage is introduced much earlier in the play and is reiterated more forcefully later. "Who's to blame...?" the play asks, involving the audience as a whole, giving more force to later accusations because of questions about complicity, and pointing out the problems more clearly to a tourist audience. In this way, the play is more political because it is more clearly historical and analytical (a lesson the company learned in the creation of *Dusting*).

The play also contains a far stronger feminist message and is a clearer warning to farmers to moderate during times of apparent prosperity. The fifties montage presents an indictment of McCarthyism and the sixties are dealt with in an entirely new scene in which a new character, Patoulli, engages in rather witty banter with the now elderly Jonathan as they decorate the Anderson Christmas tree. This addition adds humor and an intimacy that is needed to refocus attention on the family, especially for a large audience in an amphitheater. It provides a recognition of the changes that took place in the sixties, reveals a level of family disagreement that adds dimensionality, and presents the Andersons as thoughtful and concerned people.

There is a vibrancy and a sense of originality in this script that are welcomed additions to the original, continuing the progress that the Caravan had made in playwriting. All the music is now original, "Who's on First" was replaced by a hilarious spoof of a radio serial called "The Creeper," and there is a sprightliness in the action that is enhanced by the addition of some well-chosen new characters. The coherence of the play reiterates a theme that must be made clear for the largely out-of-state audience: that there is a vibrancy, power, and continuity binding the past and present in the culture of South Dakota and its peoples. As a result, the tone is more celebratory than analytical and, though specific issues are clearer, the basis of analysis is not.

The five members of the Caravan hired twenty performers for the project and rehearsed the new play in much the same way that any commercial theatre would. Performances began on June 11 and ran six nights each week until August 28. Friday nights were taken up by variety shows that Caravan members and other participants in the project wrote.

The publicity was showy and expensive, but so were the tickets. There was much trepidation among company members about this arrangement and the ways in which it departed from previous ventures. In one way, the production was the opposite of earlier Caravan work: instead of bringing the people's own story to them, the Caravan attracted tourists who did not share the South Dakota experience.

A second difference was that many people were excluded because of the high ticket prices and because rural farmers cannot travel to see a play during planting and harvest season. Finally, the operation of the summer performing company was no longer completely collectivized because actors who had been brought in to play supporting roles were not considered part of the future of DTC. I got the sense from talking to Caravan members of a feeling that the Caravan's work and its relationship to the people of South Dakota was being "co-opted," exhibited rather than shared, and used by outside interests rather than serving its audiences. However, it was a compromise the Caravan believed it had to make in order to survive financially.

The 1983 summer in Wall was not as successful for the backers as they had hoped, although the performances were very well received by audiences, of which 80 percent were tourists. The venture did provide financial support that the Caravan needed, but was emotionally and physically draining. The company worked for ninety-five days straight, writing, rehearsing, and performing the weekly variety shows on top of the performances of *Dakota Roads*. Although the creative push was stimulating, the Caravan members remained isolated from their backers and fellow performers. The business people pressured them to make changes in the shows and personnel in order to raise revenues. There developed "an 'us and them' atmosphere which was disruptive. It is difficult to focus on stated objectives when the large majority of the company is outside the process. In the second year we made no distinction between long-time company members and new people. It was much less disruptive; the summer was more relaxed. [But] the project always had a sense of compromise about it" (Nelson, letter). The second summer, prices were lowered and a number of incentives were given to potential audience members. Although there was an increase of nearly 100 percent in attendance over the first year, the pressure from the investors continued. The Caravan decided not to renew its contract for a third season and was replaced in the summer of 1985 by "Las Vegas-like acts," something the company members regret.

The second attachment that was developed in 1982 was to the city of Sioux Falls and to the Sioux Falls Playhouse, a community theatre. The Caravan intended to conduct workshops for members of the theatre and the community at large (a grant obligation of the Playhouse), perform two shows a year in the theatre, and lend its prestigious name to the Playhouse. In exchange, DTC was going to share a two-person office staff—the first time that the company would even have anyone to receive mail all year—receive free rehearsal space, and have a way to make permanent connections with the community. Everyone in the company was excited about the prospect of a full-time residency even though the personnel changes would be drastic.

Nelson and Zeck did move to Sioux Falls in 1983 but, as in Wall, they were only able to sustain the new relationship for two years. For one thing, the Playhouse was not able to book the Caravan for enough performances to enable the company to make a living, and so the touring burden was not decreased. Second, the show that the company hoped would be a local commercial success, an adaptation by Jeannie Zeck of *A Christmas Carol* that used some of the stories the company had gathered, was very well received but lost money in both 1983 and 1984.

Finally, Nelson and Zeck, who had become the core of the Caravan and had kept the company going, barely scratching out a living for themselves while paying wages to forty-five different performers over three years, did not like living in Sioux Falls. Not only did Paterson leave when the Caravan went full-time, so did Glasser and Schmidt, both for professional reasons and without any animosity. Although they continued to work with previous members at times, only two people were, in a very real way, the Dakota Theatre Caravan. Even though they were able to do some local fund raising, the atmosphere in the city was not very supportive.

The years in Sioux Falls were not without success. *Prairie Tales*, a new script developed for performance in schools, toured to fourteen sites in South Dakota. The flexible script, an extension of the story-gathering workshop described above, contains ninety minutes of material, from which an appropriate forty-five is chosen for different age groups. It is a story-telling piece as well as a theatrical one.

The year 1983 included two major tours of *Welcome Home*. The company performed the play thirty times in West Germany under the auspices of the U.S. Department of Defense Tours (a fact that raises questions about the clarity of some of the play's messages, considering the blatant homophobia and sexism of the U.S. military) and then toured for two months in the Midwest. Audiences in both countries were still very enthusiastic and greatly appreciated the concern that the company showed for its characters. As of January 1986, *Welcome Home* had been performed over two hundred times, and bookings were still being requested, even by towns in which performances had been given previously. Although the old company members felt the productions had suffered because of the need to bring in contract performers, the play and characters were strong enough that audiences never complained.

Zeck and Nelson wanted to reestablish a structure based on the principles and working method used by the Caravan to develop their first three plays, but it was difficult to find new members who were willing to commit to DTC. Although they were able to find quality performers for individual tours, no-one became a long-term member. Some "feel uncomfortable being in a political theatre [or] working in any area that they don't consider their craft....Many don't like South Dakota....Ideally, we would like good performers, sensitive to issues, with enlightened points-of-view who like South Dakota who are willing to take great financial risk to work more than full time, can sing, write, act, play an instrument and are easy to get along with. They must also do workshops" (Nelson, letter). Tongue-in-cheek though this may be, the work of the Caravan is demanding and the necessary commitment is great indeed. The possibilities for forming a new company still existed, however. In 1985, Zeck and Nelson moved to Spearfish, on the edge of the Black Hills in South Dakota, to begin work on a new play and try to establish a base in a new community. Doug Paterson joined them for the summer and together they developed *In the Heart of the Hills*, a work "about how people are drawn to the Black Hills [which] includes elements of the mining issue and the contrast of those drawn for more spiritual reasons" (Nelson, letter). They toured the Midwest in the spring of 1986, but canceled the next year's tour because of dissatisfaction with the script and production quality.

Their hope was to find new company members in the Black Hills, where there is little work, but the residents stay because they love the hills. The problems faced in forming a new group are many, however, and sufficient time to integrate performers into a cohesive and creative unit of the same high quality as the collective that created *Welcome Home* was never found. Nelson and Zeck's experience, skills, and attitudes should have made them capable of forming a new collective or of leading a newly structured theatre that could sustain the mission of the DTC, "to discover what interests and moves its audiences, to learn from them, and to adjust so that our work will be more effective, more moving, and more connected to the lives and needs of the people" (DTC, "Dakota Theatre Caravan" 8).

Ironically, the more directly connected to their community the Caravan became, the less hospitably the company was received. Their direct involvement in fighting to prevent companies from mining around Spearfish, where unemployment was so high, created controversy that extended to their involvement in community projects. Because of this, as well as difficulties sustaining a company, Zeck and Nelson left South Dakota. Although they continued to do *Prairie Tales* projects (story gathering performances like the one in Wall described earlier), the Caravan became inactive. Because DTC's "community" of rural farmers and workers is so geographically diverse, the company could not move to a location where it could maintain its alliance with the people and still be a self-sustaining enterprise. Without such support, it could not go on.

NOTES

1. None of the Dakota Theatre Caravan's plays have been published. Page references are to unpublished manuscripts.

2. See her books *Theatre for the 98%* and *Time, Space, and Designs for Actors.*

3. D. Scott Glasser, "Letter of Agreement Proposal to the Actor's Equity Association (AEA)," 30 August 1979. The letter, asking for various exemptions from social security and unemployment insurance provisions of the AEA contract, presents a clear statement of the company's collective policy and is the most blatant, anticommercial political statement ever published by the Caravan. In it, D. Scott Glasser wrote: "I found most [of the companies I have worked for as an AEA member] to be administratively top-heavy. These were less acting companies than production factories whose actors were dispensable. The act of creating theatre for an audience was lost in the shuffle. I am a member of this company because it puts the focus where it should be: on the creative artists. I am a member of AEA because it believes theatre is a craft and occupation and works to help the creative artist survive with dignity."

4. $600 for a performance, $150 for a workshop, or $1,300 for a three-day residency (Dakota Theatre Caravan, publicity brochure). These figures represent the half of the total charges that the sponsor had to pay. The other half was covered by the state arts council.

5

The United Mime Workers

> I speak from experience when I say that one need never be frightened of putting bold and unaccustomed things before the proletariat, so long as they have to do with reality. There will always be educated persons, connoisseurs of the arts, who will step in with a "The people won't understand that." But the people impatiently shoves them aside and comes to terms directly with the artist. There is highly cultured stuff made for minorities, designed to form minorities: the two thousandth transformation of some old hat, the spicing-up of a venerable and now decomposing piece of meat. The proletariat rejects it ("they've got something to worry about") with an incredulous, somewhat reflective, shake of the head. It is not the spice that is being rejected, but the meat; not the two thousandth form, but the old hat.
>
> Bertolt Brecht, "A Short Organum for the Theatre"

Since its evolution out of a mime class at the University of Illinois in the spring of 1971, the United Mime Workers (UMW) has honed out of the world of performing arts a rather unusual niche for itself, one that has been both rewarding and difficult to maintain. Although their name includes the word *mime*, they use language as part of their performances. Although thoroughly collectivized, they rely on individual contributions during many stages of their work. Although they are clearly aligned with the very heart of the people's theatre movement in the United States, they are radically experimental. Moreover, although they are frankly political, they are more directly concerned with composition than content.

For the Mime Workers, the study and realization of form are the keys to the appropriate use of the theatre in a world of political change and struggle. According to UMW, artists have their greatest impact through their place as artists, but they often ignore their real strengths, miss their "leverage points," and jump too quickly to "modeling what they would like to see happen outside of theatre rather than making it happen in the theatre to begin with. [Artists] overlook the effectiveness they have available to them by doing that" (Glassman, interview). The UMW concentrates, instead, on developing the means to create an entirely new system of relationships between people and ideas, between actions and objects, and between the theatre and its elements of performance, and to present to an audience the results of manipulations guided by this newly created system. It is hoped that the audience will, through these presentations, be led to raise questions about its own perceptions and reposition itself on certain issues and assumptions.

To accomplish this task, UMW has developed a compositional method that relies on breadth of knowledge in a variety of media, an understanding of cybernetics, a willingness to study and contribute with individual intensity, and a commitment to the collective center as a meeting place for ideas. This process took an effort that was not anticipated when some interested, nontheatre people registered for a mime class with Claude Kipnis in the fall of 1970.

THE HARD CORE MIME TROUPE—1971–1972

Approximately twenty-five people began to study mime with Kipnis during his residency at the University of Illinois in Champaign (the home of the Mime Workers). A group of eleven people, of whom Bob Feldman and Jeff Glassman (half of the UMW company) were two, began to come to class an extra day each week to perfect their techniques and create skits. These hard-core class members formed the "Hard Core Mime Troupe" in the spring of 1971 to perform their work in coffeehouses and local student gatherings in and around Champaign. During the next semester, the company began to do major performances of full-length shows around the themes of Halloween, Christmas, and spring. These were collections of skits and technique demonstrations by performers in whiteface, typical of what most people who are familiar with Marcel Marceau's work consider the province of mime.

At the same time, Feldman and Glassman began to study Kabuki with Shozo Sato, who was also in residency at the university. They met Deb Langerman—the third performing member of UMW—in that group. She had been a member of Kipnis's performing company three years earlier but left acrimoniously because she felt Kipnis denied the value of company members' work. She was eager to perform, but had already developed definite views about the appropriate status of workers in a creative organization. Langerman joined the Hard Core Mime Troupe for the third show in 1971.

The group rapidly made a name for itself, and it was invited to become the full-time summer company at the Body Politic Theatre in Chicago in 1972. Only four of the company members (the three mentioned above and Nancy Gold) were willing to commit to an entire summer of performance. The summer proved to be very successful: performances attracted good-sized audiences and received positive reviews. In addition, the four performers were encouraged to begin experimentation in areas they had not explored during their early productions.

This is not to say that the troupe made radical changes. They still performed in whiteface and did mostly technique-oriented pieces. Nevertheless, they began in some skits to move into areas of social commentary. *The Psychiatrist*, a relatively traditional piece, "still solid in the so called 'dramatic element'" (Feldman, interview), began with three people (the patient's three personalities) sitting one behind the other on a bench, and a psychiatrist standing with his back to the audience. During the course of the skit, the three personalities answered the psychiatrist's questions (silently, of course) and simultaneously maneuvered him toward the couch. At the end of the piece, the opening positions were reversed and the psychiatrist was being questioned.

Evolution, a much more complex experiment with simultaneity and ensemble, was a transitional piece. It was performed with as many as seven company members who began by forming an amorphous "wave" out of which evolved progressively more complex organisms. Eventually, humans developed. They armed, went to war, and destroyed each other. The piece originally ended with the final person screaming, killing himself, and then becoming part of a reformed wave. The company became dissatisfied with this ending and began stopping the piece before the scream, explaining the original ending to the audience, and then asking for suggestions for a better one. The development of a political perspective and the challenge to the audience to make decisions about the performance continued to be mainstays of the work of UMW.

The final piece in the Hard Core's earliest repertoire was an experiment with form and a precursor of the types of productions that would precipitate the disbanding of the company. *Photo Finish* was a series of tableaux and scenes in which the company attempted to find a parallel on stage for the pan and zoom possibilities of film. The play consisted of two "advertisements," and three scenes, the central one of which was a 1971 news report about the killing of four students at Kent State University. In it, a metronome was used to time the turning on and off of lights. During each blackout the performers moved to a position that one would see through a lens if a camera had moved laterally. When the image reached the area on which they wanted to concentrate, their movements emulated a zoom lens by creating isolation and focus.

Although the productions were becoming more sophisticated, the company was splitting over issues that were to remain the focus of the UMW throughout its history. The central issue was political. Those who were to become the founders of UMW were concerned with the political import of the productions. It was not that they wanted an issue-oriented theatre, but they insisted that the political implications of their methods and performances be a focal point during composition.

That word, *composition*, was a second source of friction. Some members of the company wanted a story-oriented mime theatre that cleverly used the gestural language of mime to present more or less naturalistic events. The other members were concerned with formal experimentation and with using the techniques of mime to create works that operated according to compositional systems and not according to assumed causality in a set chronology (a concern not unlike that of Split Britches).

The group agreed to attempt a complex formal experiment. The result, *Les Mouton des Panurge* (The Sheep of Panurge), was a critical and aesthetic success (it was still in the UMW repertory thirteen years later), but exacerbated the divisions in the company. The piece is a movement analogy to music composed by Frederick Rzewski and performed by the Black Earth Percussion group. The score contains sixty-five notes; it begins with note one, repeats one and adds two, repeats one and two and adds three, and so on until the phrase includes all sixty-five notes. The score then indicates that the phrase is to be repeated beginning with note one and subtracting one note until the final phrase is only note sixty-five.

The movement piece is composed of sixty-five individual gestures added and subtracted in the same sequence as the notes in the score. It is not, however, a dance to the music. An audience can easily see that the pattern of movement shares something with the music, but it is not done in time to the musical performance. The gestures are, however, composed as notes so that "the meaning of each gesture, like notes, is dependent on the gesture prior to and after it" (Feldman, "Montage" 29). For example, at one point in the sixteen-minute performance, each of the three performers points his or her finger. Because of the linear context, the gesture means either hailing a bus, pressing an elevator button, or asking for a drink. The movement of a bent finger shuts off an alarm clock, hooks a coffee cup handle, types a letter, or deposits coins in a bus collection box. Even groups of gestures were modified according to relative positions; for example, talking on the telephone becomes talking to a bartender with a glass held beside one ear.

The piece makes conscious use of techniques with which mime and theatre are rarely directly concerned: counterpoint montage, repetition and variation, and dynamic modifications of audience expectations. The members of the Hard Core saw *Sheep of Panurge* as noncommercial, esoteric, and outside the traditional field of mime. The four people who became the United Mime Workers—Bob Feldman, Bruce Garrett, Jeff Glassman, and Deborah Langerman—saw it as a logical extension of the principles of mime and as a political statement about the relationship of new structures and forms to critical and social thinking: a challenge to the entire system of representation. Needless to say, this was the last piece created by the Hard Core Mime Troupe.

THE STUDENT YEARS—1972–1974

UMW formed, without a name, in 1972. The company's skill and audience appeal made it useful to the university's public programs, and the company's material needs made university support almost essential. During the second semester of the 1972/1973 school year, and for twelve months afterwards while they finished their degree work, the United Mime Workers toured extensively under the outreach and extension programs of the University of Illinois. In return for their performances as representatives of the university, they received free publicity, brochure printing, and booking services. At the same time, they developed a more fully integrated approach to composing and performing, one that had implications both artistic and political and that necessitated an evolution into collective creation.

The members of the company came under the influence of several people both in and outside theatre early in 1972. Although they stopped working with Kipnis, the technical mime skills they learned from him remained the mainstay of their performance approach. They extended the usual arena of mime, however, by adding objects to their work, by dropping whiteface and leotards, and by experimenting with relationships other than those of cause and effect.

From Shozo Sato they learned an exquisite sense of timing, and developed an appreciation for the art of Kabuki: the relationship of voice to movement, the use of the narrator, and the technique of *hikinuki*, "string pulling," to achieve an instantaneous change of costume. Attitudinal elements of Kabuki are still apparent in their mature work, and the Oriental artist's devotion to work and the perfection of technique have colored their performance stance.

The company began, as well, to study composition with Herbert Brün, a composer of computer music whose seminars promote experimentation, and cybernetics (the science of systems) with Heinz von Foerster, a neurophysiologist. Both these men have had a profound influence on UMW's work, and members of the company periodically attended Brün's seminar years later. Herbert Brün stressed the political significance of compositional methods. In "Infraudibles," a complex aesthetic discussion occasioned by the performance of a musical piece by the same name, he noted that there are two basic modes of composition. The first is to choose known sounds and search for a means to make and organize them; while the second is to "provide for a series of events to happen and then to discover the timbre of the sounds so generated" (117). In other words, one can either begin with known content and manipulate its elements by adhering to a predetermined (one may, I think, read traditional, conservative, or even coercive) system of prescribed possible relationships, or one may develop a set of rules that define a system and then explore permutations of that system before submitting elements of content. To Brün, "These are not only two different approaches to the composition of music, but also two different political attitudes" and the resulting compositions have different political significance (117).

One can see in the company's writings about its own work, as well as in its theoretical discussions, the influence of Brün's vision of the composer as one who provides input to, rather than output from, a society. To the United Mime Workers, the meaningful political act is not to develop a position or create an art work about an issue. Looking at an issue does not examine the underlying phenomena that produce the issue in the first place. Meaningful political change comes instead from challenging people's conception of form or upsetting their ways of seeing, and such challenge can only arise from the artist's response to the efforts of composition.

> When theatre workers apply themselves seriously to the problem of developing new techniques of presentation—instead of using old methods in hopes of *this time* finding *the* accurate reflection of life—the story line ceases to be the dominant focus of the work. Rather, the production process of the work and the cognitive processes of all involved (artist, audience, character and actor) become the central focus. When audience members present at a work of art arrive at a new understanding of the production process of the work they do, and their relation to it, this art functions in a revolutionary way. (Langerman, "Technique" 28)

In current terminology, the deconstruction of compositional and representational systems is the source of political impact, not just the information or content.

The company's study of cybernetics has led them to an examination of the ways in which the politics of systems function in fields as varied as logic, economics, mathematics, language, information theory, and media. The Mime Workers have discovered that the way in which they work best is to discard the systems that control daily perceptions, but to keep the pieces of daily life, and then to subject these pieces to the ramifications of newly created, artificial systems. In this way, their productions force viewers to question their own perceptive apparatus and to posit the possibility of organizational structures other than the ones they have come to regard as inevitable. UMW's work as artists is not descriptive: theatre is an intervention, not a reflection, or as Darko Suvin puts it, a *dynamo*: "an artistic and scenic vision which penetrates Nature's possibilities, which finds out the 'co-variant' laws of its processes, and makes it possible for critical understanding to intervene into them. This attitude attempts to raise art to an ontologically—or at least epistemologically—higher plane of creative significance than illusionism" (73–74).

Positions this radical and complex raise questions that cannot be immediately answered, leaving the audience somewhat discomforted, yet the United Mime Workers have been in demand to produce from the moment of their inception. During the summer of 1973 they were resident in Crested Butte, Colorado, at a small, tourist-attended theatre. They returned to Illinois as full-time professional performers, organized collectively, and determined to continue experiments that would produce works appealing to a variety of audiences. Their development into such a group was tentative, without real planning, administrative knowledge, or organizational goals. Jeff Glassman remembered, "We found that we were a collective and then we started realizing that that's a definite form of organization for a lot of people. But there wasn't any other way of doing things that would have made sense or been acceptable to all of us at the time" (interview).

Their next few pieces were transitional, progressing not toward a definable performance style, but as manifestations of a developing compositional method. *Is the Price Right* (created in 1973) is their most didactic piece. In it, a series of vignettes was performed during which either applause signs would light or a buzzer would sound. Applause indicated that the action was acceptable to "the system" and the performers were permitted to continue. The buzzer was a censor demanding that the scene change direction. Finally, the buzzer became continuous, indicating systemic repression, and the actors found and disconnected it.

During 1974 the company developed five new pieces, some exploratory and some successful enough to remain in the repertoire. *The Bubble* was an experiment in light, shadow, and distortion that took place inside a three-piece, Visqueen (translucent flexible plastic), clover-shaped chamber, with leaves twelve feet high and thirty feet in circumference, which was supported by an external "spider web" suspension system. *Zounds* was an experiment with the technique of "dislocation." In it, sounds were changed or removed from their normal associations. The sound of a nail clipper became that of opening a purse, a person "shhhing" another became the spray of a perfume bottle, and a variety of actions and sounds blended to create a train leaving a station.

Self, a Distinct Relation to Others was the first of UMW's compositions to examine the nature of identity, a theme central to their last play, which was composed nearly a decade later. It was also a technically innovative work that made rather novel use of slide projections. The company took slides of themselves and choreographed movement so that the slides could be projected back onto the performers. As the actors moved from isolation into contact with each other, their slides and projected environments changed as well, until all four met. At that point, they began to slip into each others' slides, an identity confusion heightened by the projection of easily confused personal pronouns on each performer. *Self* "demonstrated observation and self-observation through the cybernetic ideas of feedback. Each actor was connected to a slide projector by the advance/reverse control wire" and his or her identity was determined by projections more than by physical presence.[1]

Two other compositions, *Chaos and Order* and *Implication*, were performed for years by the company. *Chaos and Order* is one of the earliest UMW pieces to make use of an actual scene. It explored relationships in the workplace through the example of a restaurant and four characters: a cook/boss, a waitress, a consumer, and a janitor/busboy. In it the cycle of movement of a bowl from the cook to the other characters and back to the cook begins to be regularized and controlled by the subtle permeation of Muzak into the scene. The actors' movements are influenced, and order is maintained. However, one by one, the characters break free of the music's control and sit at the table, thereby forcing the other actors to do more work and go out of synch with the music. When all three are seated, they conspire against the cook, who (until a revision in 1980) was invited to sit with them. The piece ended when all four rose and began doing new tasks cooperatively.

This easy programmatic ending was challenged as being politically inaccurate and naive, and was eventually dropped. In the new ending there is a "take-over," new roles are taken by three characters, and the boss is given the check for the food he eats. He leaves without paying. The clear use of Muzak to represent any number of external systems by which our perceptions and actions are controlled is particularly appropriate in a movement piece where the cycles of food preparation, serving, and consumption already have a rhythmic base. Work relationships are also a system: as imposed, insidious, and unavoidable as Muzak.

Implication, the most exciting and theoretically challenging of the pieces, again makes use of projections, but this time to examine the nature of mundane relationships in terms of the objectification of language and people. In this piece a couple carries on a "conversation" as they have breakfast and the husband leaves for work. The same conversation and gestures are used in reverse when he returns. The set consists of a black backdrop behind the actors; the objects and furniture are all completely white. The stage is illuminated by the light from slide projectors. Whenever an actor moves a white object through an area where words are being projected (which are invisible on the backdrop), the words appear in black on the object. What is created is a conversation suspended in air, existing without references, and made readable as a result of the choreography.

The dialogue moves from the center of the stage to the edges and back again. The gestures are performed forward and then in reverse order, but the syntax of the movement and language makes sense in both directions. The cliché string has a slightly altered meaning in reverse, however. As they drink coffee, read the newspaper, clean up, and go to work, the couple "discusses" the state of the world and their place in it ("Honey, you can't change human nature" and "We can't complain"), dismissing all problems as unchangeable and inevitable: "That's life." But the conversation remains, somewhere in the air, with its own reality, speakable by anyone, usable as a definitive statement, yet attached to no reality other than itself, and "meaningful" in either direction.[2]

THE FULL-TIME COMPANY—1974–1975

The company was working too hard to maintain its creative focus only avocationally. By the end of 1974, its members (although some of them had to take other part-time jobs during particularly lean years) were full-time professional theatre makers. Throughout the early period, the company had begun to explore techniques, or, more accurately, technical problems that raised the questions that would come to focus in their first long composition. They were, as well, touring, spending part of the summer of 1974 in Colorado and much of the fall on the road. They were frequently asked to perform for schools and youth groups, where they basically did mime demonstrations. In early 1975 it became apparent that performances for children would be their prime source of income and that their political integrity was not being bolstered by such apolitical work. They developed, therefore, a somewhat more progressive children's show: *The President's New Clothes.*

An entire performance of this show takes seventy minutes. The first forty are an introduction during which the Mime Workers do some demonstration and then work with children in a highly cooperative fashion. The play itself uses impersonations of the current president and his cabinet, but is not about party politics or individual vanity. It is more about the blindness of those in any hierarchy whose positions become more important than their functions. The familiarity of the characters, combined with the remoteness of the pantomime technique, helps even young children examine the event critically on some level. When the play is performed for junior high school students, the *Sheep of Panurge* is also done, and a discussion follows the show.

In the fall of 1975, the company members went to Indiana to see a performance of Tomashevski's Polish Mime Ballet Theatre. At a reception (into which they had to sneak) they met the director of a pantomime camp/workshop in Poland, who invited them to attend. Bruce Garrett had recently left the company and had been replaced by Linda Holmes. The foursome put together the skeleton of a European tour which they hoped to flesh out while they were overseas, and in September they left for Poland. During the next six months, the company toured extensively in Europe, learning how a variety of audiences responded to their work. In Poland they experimented further with the technique of separating scenes or actions into their component parts and recombining the parts so that the newly created action was not one of the original events, but rather the result of the dialectic inherent in the juxtapositions. In many ways, UMW's concern with the capabilities of film and film director Sergei Eisenstein's concept of montage were coming together in a concept of theatre that mirrored their anticapitalist political leanings and their belief in the compositional power of the dialectic.

One of the newest pieces they took to Poland already made fuller use of the technique of dislocations. *Myra's Birthday*, a play that was accidentally named when Glassman jotted a reminder to himself about his sister's birthday on the top of the script just before it was to be reproduced, was subtitled "A Trio for Actors and Objects." In it, three performers sat on chairs facing the audience, next to tables heaped with objects. The objects were manipulated as if in response to each other, but were always directed straight out at the audience. The play opens with an offer of coffee by Jeff (most UMW scripts indicate the performer rather than character name). Deborah accepts and holds out her cup, as Bob proffers the sugar bowl. Jeff pours coffee on the floor directly in front of his chair, Bob spoons sugar in front of his chair, and Deb stirs and drinks as if her cup had been filled.

The actions were further complicated as movements became disassociated from their original purpose. At one point in the play, Jeff and Deborah simultaneously fold napkins, using identical gestures. Later in the performance, they repeat these gestures, but this time Deborah is folding a magazine and Jeff is squeezing toothpaste (onto the floor, of course, while Bob holds out his toothbrush). Later, gestures pass from one person to another while the objects remain with the originator. This results in a misuse of objects, such as Jeff using a cigarette to wipe a table while Bob smokes a napkin. Such an examination of the syntax of relationships between action and action, action and object, or movement and change contains no political message. In fact, this is the last play that the company did that lacked a discernible political content. Nevertheless, the play had a definite effect on audience perceptions, clarifying the fact for them that apparent chaos is really a set of relationships that are not easily discernible from a position inside a system that denies those relationships and claims exclusivity and necessity. This is a Brechtian notion of "making the familiar strange," and the troupe openly acknowledges its debt to Brecht's theories, even though their actualization of them is unlike any work of Brecht or his emulators in this country (compare Esperanza's very different application of Brechtian techniques). The piece, like most of their others, is very funny.

The company was, as well, making attachments to the mime world that would serve it well over the next ten years, during which, because of its unusual performances, theatre people were not inclined to accept its work. And yet, UMW was discovering that its political concerns were not shared by most mimes, who saw their own work to be involved with a set of "universal" gestures that expressed clearly understood stories unencumbered by objects or speech. Even though the United Mime Workers had been invited to festivals of mimes around the country and became accepted as innovators in the form, they still found it necessary to explain the political nature of their work to other artists in the field.

The company had, as well, begun to combine its influences and concerns into a working methodology that would allow it to produce more complex and demanding, longer pieces that would make fuller use of the ideas hinted at in earlier works. A crisis developed, however, that had the potential to disrupt the work of the collective. Because she lacked the extensive training of the other three performers, and because she had not shared their long hours on stage, Linda Holmes was unable to become a totally successful member of the performing company. She and Feldman had a personal relationship, however, and it became difficult at best to remove her from the performance group. When she left immediately after the return from Europe, the decision was made to limit the performance company to Feldman, Glassman, and Langerman but to share all other responsibilities with a new fourth member. The attempt to have one level of company membership, yet two levels of artistic activity, is unlike that made by any other company. Those with clearly defined administrative staffs, such as Split Britches and Esperanza, do not involve the office people fully in the creative process; while those without them, such as DTC, do not split the group functionally for the performance part of the process.

THE METHOD

The creative method of the United Mime Workers cannot be as easily described as those of the previous two companies because of its complexity, which is due not to a particular desire for difficulty, but to the nature of the material with which the company works and the political focus that the company takes. According to the Mime Workers, "When new formal structures are used in theatre to find new ways to articulate the political concerns of the people for which it is performed, the audience is given new perceptual tools for use in life outside the theatre" (Langerman, "Theatre" 31). The difficulty arises from the need to use the material from the life of the audience, so that spectators can recognize not only what is, but also what can be, and to develop forms that manipulate that material in ways that are simultaneously theatrical, accessible, and challenging to the audience.

The actual process can be described as a compositional, rather than a script-oriented or improvisational, approach. Composition, "the putting together of a thing or event that does something that's never been done before, that creates alternatives that just didn't exist previously" (Glassman, interview), requires that the process begin not with material that will be used as the "stuff" of the play, and not with a preconceived notion about the types of structures that can communicate with an audience, but with the statement of what the UMW calls "legitimate problems," problems to which "we don't know the solutions;...we know what we're trying to do, but we don't know how to do it or what the answers to the questions are" (Langerman, interview). In fact, it seems as if the definition of the questions requires more effort than the creation of the answers.

The Mime Workers speak of the process metaphorically as bridge building. There is always a "distance" between the composer and the composition, not in terms of time or space, but in terms of resistance to the achievement of the goal of creation. (The distance between New York and Chicago, approximately 800 miles, or eighteen driving hours, becomes $238, the cost of a plane ticket.) The distance between the composer and the composition is, in many ways, unknown. What is known is that steps may be taken between the *is* and the *desired*; in other words, a bridge may be built. The compositional method of the United Mime Workers is an attempt to build a bridge "as soon as how to build it is known" and to count on the bridge to lead to a composed destination, so that the content of the piece can be taken across. "Composing as if the world exists, or as if the world is imaginary, is futile. Composing a movement from one to the other is not futile" (Glassman, notes).

The actual process of group creation begins with meetings at which three types of discussions occur more or less separately. The primary set of discussions at the early stages are concerned with *form*, which is defined by various company members as "techniques—both theatrical and as ways of examining a problem," "compositional systems," "technical ideas about experimental theatre," and "ideas without images yet tied to them."[3] It is the goal of the company at this point to define a system without having to use examples to describe what it looks like. Examples tend to be given an authority, to modify the system before it is fully developed, if they are introduced too early in the creative process. For discussion purposes, the form itself "has a sort of pictorial existence. [It describes] a set of relationships which, because they're relationships, are abstract at the same time, not yet applied to anything, not yet put into effect or used to operate on anything where the results of the operation are visible. So it's really a structure in the strictest sense. It's not in the form of an example of itself" (Glassman, interview). An attempt is made to keep this form separate from any content as long as possible so that the implications of the system discovered can be tested without any restrictions other than those necessitated by the limitations of the system itself.

The second area of discussion is *content*, what it is the company wants to examine in society and that which the company wants to imbed in the form. The content is usually discovered by making a list or lists of specific problems that members of the company are particularly interested in exploring. From these lists, a general systemic or widely applicable category of issues is discovered. The attempt is then made to discern particularly vulnerable points in the existing social system where problems are most apparent and where, therefore, the system seems weakest.

In general, though, the broadly social orientation of the Mime Workers dictated a certain perspective that led them toward mundane, work- and home-related subject matter, rather than toward particular issue choices. They envisioned a society restructured so that the useful, humane, and supportive values of current social systems are not lost; but one in which power is not wielded merely because of the ownership of property. They were, therefore, frequently led to choose a content that examines work relationships: the relationships most clearly dominated by those who own property.

Second, the company is committed to analyzing social systems rather than individual reactions, perceptions rather than emotions, and restructuring rather than coping. This necessitates that they choose to present on stage relationships about which people have made decisions that seem incontrovertible. "The more rational, productive, technical, and total the repressive administration of society becomes," wrote Marcuse, "the more unimaginable the means and ways by which the administered individuals might break their servitude and seize their own liberation" (*One-Dimensional Man* 6-7). The Mime Workers desire not only to make those ways and means imaginable, but to present actual manifestations of choices made in systems different than the ones the audience may now consider inevitable. "Only artificial systems will clearly show that they have been elected by choice, thus implying the intended rejection of other, equally possible, yes, even equally reasonable systems" (Brün, 117).

This does not mean that the productions of the United Mime Workers illustrate what the world will look like after other "correct" choices have been made, nor that they show changes that occur in the lives of those who find ways to live relatively happily within the current system. In fact, UMW's plays have been criticized for being negative, for not showing the worker-hero overcoming adversity or gaining awareness: that is, for being without hope.

This suits the Mime Workers quite well. They argue, first of all, that an audience does not change merely by seeing a character on stage alter her or his perceptions. The model—the "sugar-coated pill" theory—is not necessarily productive. The important change does not occur on stage, but in the audience; and this change is achieved only through the dialectic approach that reveals contradictions in an idea or event, and not through one that holds out a glimmer of hope. On the contrary, hope is a mechanism for not making choices, for not working hard to achieve change. "The act of hoping prevents the act that would achieve that which is hoped for" (Langerman, "Hopeless" 30).

Second, they maintain that hope apologizes for society. It is tied to the future, preventing identification with the work needed in, and the problems of, the present. It denies the argument which maintains that the ability to hope or criticize proves that the current system is not so bad after all. Such a view, they argue, is tied to the past, to traditions that, when unquestioned, perpetuate current problems. Moreover, it is tied to previously accepted, usually didactic, forms of what has come to be called (and summarily rejected as) political theatre.

> Since this type of political theatre relies on popular forms (i.e., melodrama, commedia dell'arte, circus, popular music, science fiction, etc.), whether or not it undermines or changes the cultural values of society is questionable; the vicious circle being that if a form is recognizably popular, it has already been incorporated into the culture of the society and is representative of its cultural values. Whether an audience is sympathetic with the point of view of the piece is a moot point, in terms of the political function of this type of theatre. One either agrees with what one has seen presented, or one doesn't. The political effect of this type of theatre is limited....What I'm getting at is the fact that what we popularly refer to as political theatre generally does not help to change anything, simply because it is our popular notion of what political theatre is. (Langerman, "Theatre" 30)

In other words, it reifies the forms, and hence the apparatus, of oppression in its very approach to the complaint.

The third topic of discussions is *perceptions*. Consideration is given not only to ways of seeing in general, that is, to "how people look at things and what they call it when they see them, to cognition" (Langerman, interview), but also to what a particular audience sees on stage. The company assumes that neither the content nor the form carries a clear or definitive message, but that the meaning received by any individual, although related to form and content, is ascribed during the process of experiencing a production (a belief objectified in *Implication*, which was described above). Far from being concerned about "accuracy," the company fosters diversity of opinion in its audience. In discussions that follow each performance, company members often refuse to divulge intent and ask, instead, what the individual audience member saw. It is the Mime Workers' hope that in this way they can, at minimum, reveal to an audience the variety of approaches one can take to a perceived event and the variety of ideologies that others can see as "given" in the world.

They do hint that the world should move in a certain general direction and that there is a set of general problems with which society must confront itself, but they do not demand particular solutions. In early discussions they did not even insist that there was any interpretation that was more or less valid than any other. This is, in my opinion, quite dangerous. It is one thing to invite the audience members to be collaborators in the analysis of a work, but it is quite another to deny artistic responsibility by seeming to claim that the work has no intended meaning beyond what a particular audience member sees in it. The nature of audience discussion does not necessarily result in even remotely accurate understanding. In later years, the company members became more direct in their statements about their intention when talking to audiences.

On the other hand, if the Mime Workers are more concerned with revealing the political nature of perceptions and systems that determine the limits of perceptions than with a particular progressive approach to social problems, then they must not interfere too much in the free exchange of ideas in an audience. Their desire is to raise questions, "throw curves, and pull rugs out from under people on the idea of what is normal, what is inevitable, what is daily life and is that desirable....I hope we provide a process for the audience to think critically, to examine what forces are contained in a particular problem and how there's no easy solution to anything" (Feldman, interview). The discussion is an extension into postperformance activity of a compositional position that Walter Benjamin, in his essays (such as "Conversations with Brecht"), called a new social relationship between artist and audience, in which usual processes are disrupted and the spectator becomes collaborator—shocked into insight by the apparent discontinuity (almost anarchy) of the experience.

The company, in its own work, seeks alternatives to the traditional processes of play creation, rejecting the "easy solution" or the known quantity, and examining alternatives in much the same way that it would like to have its audiences do. "Alternatives mean a lot of different things to a lot of different people. Presenting an alternative on stage when the alternative doesn't yet exist in society, on a scale that you would want, often reduces it to the form of a cliche, or the form of hope or optimism....The alternatives we present are in ways of examining what one sees (Feldman, interview).

Their own process of examination through discussion continues until the script has been written. There are, however, other steps that take place either concurrently with, or between, group meetings. One of these is research. The group members read widely, studying systems in general, particular compositional ideas, and specific aspects of suggested content. Another is non-script-oriented creative work, such as writing dialogues that are attempts to use or illustrate formal ideas, or developing scenes that can be manipulated in ways that are consistent with the systems being explored by the group.

It is important to note that this work is individual in a way that is unique among collectives. Members either choose what interests them from a particular discussion or are assigned work in particular areas at meetings. In either case, until near the end of the process, the subsequent work is done by the individual in almost any way he or she sees fit. Part of this may be due to the highly cerebral nature of the early discussions and the need of each individual to spend time considering the implications of ideas in solitude. Part may be due to the highly abstract nature of much of the work and the need for individuals to gain personal understanding of ideas.

Part may be due, as well, to the recognition by every member of the company that each other member has particular strengths, the output of which must be evaluated and modified by the group, but the exercise of which can happen most efficiently outside meetings. Jeff Glassman is adept at developing compositional and notational systems that enable the unusual presentation style of the company to be actualized. Deb Langerman provides the political voice of the group and is particularly skilled at discovering appropriate content and at doing research. She is also an articulate spokesperson for the group to the public and can make particularly abstract notions rather clear. Candace Walworth has considerable ability as a dialogue and text writer, while Bob Feldman, who holds an unusual degree in movement and psychology, is able to create or discover physical examples of formal concepts.

Another reason for such individual effort is the nature of "legitimate problems," part of which is that the steps that need to be taken to solve them are as unknown as the solution. Each meeting either examines the current step in the process or generates an idea for the next step that must be taken outside or after the meeting which has discovered it. Each member acts, in a way, as a tentacle of the analytical body, stretching out to test and bring in what it feels the body needs, but not making decisions about whether to actually ingest those ideas or how to assimilate them once they are part of the center. Such a process provides little sense of stability for some group members, because it changes for each production and each problem, while others "would feel extremely uncomfortable and unhappy were there a predictable set of steps" that led to a predictable outcome (Walworth, letter). Unlike the previous two groups that were examined, the Mime Workers are never certain where they stand. "We don't have a set of steps we follow like the Dakota Theatre Caravan. That's another reason why the work makes me so nervous all the time; because I never know what the next step is and we're constantly talking about what the next step is" (Langerman, interview). And yet every person in the company indicated that the compositional process is extremely rewarding.

Perhaps causes for being "nervous" are inherent not only in the process of creation, but in the topics of examination as well. The work of the United Mime Workers is analytical, intellectual, and, in a way, cold, while being, at the same time, highly stimulating. In addition, the group is examining "how people think and look at things in the society, and not necessarily how they feel about them" (Langerman, interview). In other words, neither the form nor the content provides the same level of emotional support or outlet for all company members (quite the opposite of Split Britches, whose creative method resembles that of UMW). It seemed to me that there was a recognizable split in the company along attitudinal lines in this area, which was similar to that between the theatrical voice and the political voice in Esperanza's work. Although this, too, can be seen as complementary, it made demands on the group to assist members who were not fully supported by the work to have fuller lives outside the company, a difficult task for a touring group. While Esperanza has specific mechanisms for handling personal needs, UMW had none, and this may have been a contributing factor in the group's decision to disband in 1986.

In spite of this tension there was never a question about the value of exploration in the work. The company not only is devoted politically to their process, but they are convinced that it results in a mode of representation that has the potential to affect a general audience and to disrupt its notions about society and social problems. Other companies, in their desire to "accurately depict the lives of working people, work, and its problems [choose old, familiar forms. The United Mime Workers] propose that the question of accurate portrayal is answered in the very process of trying to develop new techniques for the stage, and this process may even render the question [of accuracy] irrelevant. Using theatre to represent the work of others is a mistake, when separated from the understanding that artistic production is, itself, work (Langerman, "Technique" 27).

The work does, indeed, continue for a long period, as company members continue to meet to present individual developments, split up to continue investigations, and meet again. The tenor of these meetings is much less frenetic than rehearsals of many other companies. The attitude may almost be called cogitational. Things are, of course, not always on such an even keel and personal agendas, emotions, and squabbles often cause disruptions, but at the meetings I attended, no one interrupted anyone else's presentation except for carefully worded questions to clarify a point or define a term. Sometimes the company members took notes on each other's statements and, after long periods of silence, asked perhaps what the presenter meant by a certain statement or if the presenter meant to imply or realized the implications of a particular point. Such a slow and deliberate Socratic method does not lead one company member or another to take a position, but rather has the effect of forcing ideas to be developed as they are being explained.

Much reference is made to past meetings as well as to current proposals, and every member of the group appears able to recall what to most people would seem arcane conversations from the distant past. The three areas of discussion are clearly different, yet they weave together and affect each other. Although decisions did not seem to be necessary at the meetings I attended, choices are subtly made and areas of concentration are either clarified or rejected. The procedure is clearly consensual.

For the earlier productions by the company, the next step would have been script creation. However, because of the length and complexity of their more recent pieces, the Mime Workers had to develop a new step, the creation of the bridge that will tie form and content. This takes the form of a notational system that allows the group to test permutations of the chosen compositional system and to keep track of phenomenally complex and exacting movements of objects and people on stage. The result is a "score," a two-dimensional rendering using symbols to describe movement in a four-dimensional performance. What was discovered after the company had developed the system for ordering and reordering the elements of performance in *Mime Is No Object*, their next composition, was that testing the results of each permutation by moving bodies and objects on stage was prohibitively time-consuming. There were literally thousands of possible combinations, most of which were neither illustrative of the point of the play nor theatrically viable. The notation, then, became

> the computational device, in a way. And afterwards it becomes the record for the piece. So it has a dual function. And it's not only the record of the piece; it becomes a work of art in itself. It's the set of relationships played out in a different medium...and somebody could take that score and apply values to the various colors and the various line segments or dots and whether something moves left or right and do it according to the time line that moves down the page...and write music using that as the score. (Langerman, interview)

What has happened is that the company's mature method has come full circle, rediscovering what can be seen in their earliest composition, *The Sheep of Panurge*, that a compositional device independent of content can be used for any art form that makes use of a finite number of elements with an infinite number of possible combinations.

It is this fact that has made much of what might seem esoteric work by

UMW easily accessible to a broad range of audiences. Computer programmers respond to the seeming parallel between the Mime Workers's creative method and programming, people in the medical profession recognize the score's analytical function and compare it to electrocardiogram readouts, line workers understand the sequencing device in terms of flow charts for their own work, and many recognize for the first time that social and economic systems can be charted and implemented just like more narrowly applicable systems—and can be modified, restructured, or replaced. Without any hard political line to accept or reject, audiences are led to believe that there are new ways to think about their social and political environment.

This does not mean that all performances meet with universal acceptance. The images that any artist creates will be rejected by some, but the fear of rejection of experimental forms does not worry the Mime Workers. Deborah Langerman wrote:

> I wish, on the contrary, that I could instill the fear that people *will* accept "accurate" and "objective" portrayals of life on stage (as they already do with television programming) without analyzing or understanding how and why things got to be the way they are. The danger of this blind and enthusiastic acceptance is increased when well-meaning theatre groups, wishing to portray workers in the best possible light, glorify the workers' victimization. This can happen easily in a theatre piece which plays on the audience's emotions and sympathy with any "heroic" worker who transcends or overcomes his situation. (Langerman, "Hopeless" 44)

The company, then, is free to follow any system to whatever conclusions it may lead, without consideration for prescribed political lines or representational conventions.

The next step in the process is the result of that freedom. The company writes the script for the play by choosing a content both in terms of idea and situation, and tests what happens when the stage elements that are motivated or necessitated by that content are subject to manipulations according to the system notated in the score. Dialogue is created where necessary, the set and costumes are designed in accordance with the needs of the developing piece, and the actions are choreographed on a time line of the score.

The script may be written by an individual member, pieces may be created by various members, or the notational system may dictate specific events or activities. In any case, the script is developed and handed out to all members at a rehearsal to begin the fifth step, that of filling out the bare bones of the composition. The Mime Workers do not note what the acting elements should look like in their scripts. There are very few indications of performer or character attitude or of the emotional tenor of specific physical activities, in short, of how that which the script indicates is to be done.

The members of the troupe take turns walking through the script. At this point all four perform, frequently taking roles that they will not play so that each performer can sit out to serve as directorial eye. The actors suggest facial expression, body position, attitude, visual focus, and so forth, and it is up to the group as a whole to agree on what works best. The demands on the outside eye are great here, particularly after each performer settles into the roles she or he will create fully. It is up to the person who is sitting out (Candace Walworth since 1980) to determine if the will of the group is being carried out by each performer, if any decisions still need to be made, and if there is a consistency of performance style.

After walking through the script, the company members begin another round of discussions, this time focusing on the text. Action at this point varies from making minor modifications to a sequence to accepting the idea but throwing out all the specifics suggested by the writer. The on-stage rehearsal process is repeated and followed by more discussion until everything that can be notated in the score has been agreed on.

The cast again moves to the stage, this time with each person developing the roles he or she will play. The concentration at this point is on developing the acting elements fully and on getting the complex actions and timing exact. As soon as they feel they have the beginnings of a set production, the Mime Workers invite one or two friends from a close circle of supporters to critique the work. In this way the company tests its suppositions about audience reception even before the final composition is established. If the criticism from these friends seems appropriate, the company modifies the performance accordingly. They even, on one occasion, laid aside an entire project when the criticism was particularly harsh and, after consideration, seemed accurate.

The final part of the process is, as with most other collectives, gathering information from audiences after performances and, if necessary, modifying the production to respond to audience reaction. The Mime Workers consider after-performance discussions as part of the bill of fare. The chance for audience members to analyze the play and debate, share, or compare reactions is essential to the promotion of critical thinking.

This basic process is quite flexible; it is kept that way to accommodate the variety of solutions that may be found to compositional questions and to allow for any next step to be taken as soon as that step is defined for the particular production. Langerman uses a cooking analogy to explain the possibilities for variation in the process. The United Mime Workers have a system (an analytical method) for doing things, but they do not have a formula: they have the tools and knowledge of the chef, but do not have any recipes. They can determine the relationships between elements, use a system of measurements for each ingredient, cooking temperature, and so on, "but all the elements that [we] will be using will be different with each recipe or formula and the end result, the product, is completely different" (Langerman, interview).

The difficulty with the process, though, is that there is no product in sight, or even known, in the beginning, and so there is no easy way to know when it is time to choose specific elements or ingredients. It is possible for discussions to go on endlessly, raising questions about the developing system, and then searching for the next unknown step. It is the responsibility of one or more members to push for a limitation of the area of examination and demand that a particular part of the work be used to create the performance piece. The sense I got from watching the work was that Langerman frequently presses for solidification while Glassman is often willing to continue searching. This was confirmed when two company members in separate interviews reported an incident in which the decision was made that a dialogue would be needed to examine a particular process. When Langerman said she was certain she could create one, Glassman replied, "If you know you can do something, don't do it." Obviously, doing something when one has the answer removes the question's "legitimacy," but exploring only what one does not know prevents one from ever using anything one has discovered.[4]

When asked to briefly describe their method of creating a performance, the Mime Workers wrote:

> In our experiments for the stage we have attempted to find ways of presenting pieces which come directly out of our studies in logic, economics, language, cybernetics, information theory, and mathematics. Through the use of tools and techniques found in other art forms (i.e., music, photography, film, dance, and graphics) we try to find a realization for the stage of the product of the process of inquiry we have gone through, using mundane gestures, language, images and situations as the basic building materials. (questionnaire response)

The two longest compositions they have created have managed to be both realizations of the process and vital performance pieces, and have been received well by audiences around the country.

INTERNATIONAL RECOGNITION—1975–1980

The company returned from Europe with new energy, knowledge, and methods. They had performed in Poland, Austria, Switzerland, Rumania, Germany, and Denmark and studied at the Studio Pantomimy Workshop in Poland. They began, in the spring of 1976, an unusual residency that would give them the opportunity to use much of what they had learned. On the campus of the University of Illinois there was an open "live and learn" dormitory that came to be called "Unit 1." UMW was invited to spend first three weeks and then the full semester as artists in residence there.

Their first task was to rewrite all possible pieces for three performers. They succeeded with all but *Chaos and Order*, for which they invited any one of a number of friends to fill in or, when on tour, hired a technical person who would be expected to perform that piece. Next, they needed to find a fourth person to take, it was hoped, most of the nonperformance responsibility and to become part of the compositional process in the collective. Bob Rebitzer, a man who shared the political and analytical bent of the three members, but was not a performer, joined to replace Linda Holmes.

Rebitzer was able to provide the kind of support the group needed at that time. He fulfilled all its business demands, was adept at arranging bookings, served as road manager, rapidly became a participant in script creation, and had an eye for detail that made him an excellent "audience" during the rehearsal period. It was during his tenure with the company that UMW matured as a creative unit and at the same time became a leader in community arts development, to which UMW devoted much of its energy.

UMW's first community activity at Unit 1 was performance-oriented. While in Denmark they had learned the technique of "action theatre" from the Solwaagen Theatre of Copenhagen. Action theatre, like guerrilla theatre, was to be performed in nontraditional settings without any indication to the audience that it is involved in a theatre piece. "In this type of theatre action, people are forced to analyze their own actions, values, and notions, rather than judge whether or not a group performing for them has a correct analysis" (Langerman, "Theatre" 30). Frequently these are pieces created by a group of people with the assistance of theatre professionals.

While their first piece, performed by UMW and Unit 1 students on National Food Day, was a rather simple parody of the McDonald's hamburger jingle sung by a group dressed in facsimile uniforms, after which they handed out a fact sheet about food policy to McDonald's customers, the second piece was much wittier. UMW and a number of students included a handout they had written with the regular handouts that were picked up by more than five hundred premed students in a large lecture hall. Their multiple-choice "Examination for Entrance to Medical School" included questions that had answers which were not only not mutually exclusive, but not even related. The lettering of answer choices spilled over from one "question" to another, and the implication was that the kind of right/wrong, impersonal process of medical education was less than appropriate for a doctor. During the lecture, plants in the audience stood and dressed as surgeons, then sat and took notes. When the professor asked them to leave, they conferred in the center of the room and then left. The goal had not been to disrupt the class, but rather to disrupt the thought process that allowed the class to progress in a manner not questioned by those attending it.

Action theatre, although very different from anything else UMW has done stylistically, maintained the same political focus. Other experiments with forms that were unusual for UMW were undertaken while at Unit 1 as well. Glassman wrote two dialogues that UMW performed. The first, "A Buck Apiece," is a rather funny conversation in which one character tries to sell tickets for the second half of a concert to another character who already has better tickets than those for sale, and then, perhaps, tries to buy them back. The organization of the dialogue is musical, building rhythmically, through repetition and variation, on the "buck apiece" theme.

As the concertgoers bicker over the basis for setting price (number of pieces left in the concert, percentage of the concert remaining, number of musicians), the meaning of the word *piece* constantly fluctuates. The mathematics remain logical, but the process becomes progressively more absurd.

...Give ya a buck apiece.
That's three bucks.
That's two bucks.
Three bucks: three pieces, buck a piece, three bucks.
Tickets, stupid. Two tickets, buck apiece, two bucks (2).

The resolution, "five pieces down, three to go, no intermission left, no drinks, each musician two pieces apiece....I'll give you five bucks and I won't listen to the flute" (3), is somehow the inevitable result of systems of language and mathematics imposed on simple information. What appears to be a light comic exchange raises serious questions about the relationship of systems to truth.

A second text, "Good Piece," appears to be two monologues spoken by a male and female character who, although speaking to the audience, alternate speeches. Without any context, the monologues are ambiguous; they could be talking about a concert that has just finished, about a love affair (either between them or with two other people), or about some other relationship. The script uses the techniques of montage to create a dialectic between speeches that operates on language just as Eisensteinian montage operates on visual images. Each monologue segment seems to have its own meaning, but is modified by the other person's monologue because of the juxtapositions. The real "text" is what the audience perceives between the two monologues.

Once again, the Mime Workers are exploring rhetorical systems and the consequences of their syntax, which become very apparent when contextual relationships do not clarify meaning. The script seems to raise the question of meaning in another way as well. The woman is very exact and her diction is relatively precise, while the man is emotionally inarticulate in a way quite common in the 1960s. Nevertheless, he is no more or less clear than she is. Words, the play seems to be saying, are not clear signifiers, but are rather more like objects whose significance arises from the system by which they are manipulated. This topic would surface again in later works.

Champaign County Consortium for Cultural Arts (CCCCA)

In addition, while at Unit 1, the company began a different type of community arts project that would consume a great deal of their energy for the next four years and decrease their output of new theatre pieces considerably. In 1976, with the aid of CETA grant money, the UMW helped found the CCCCA "to bring cultural activities to people who have the least opportunity to directly experience performances and workshops" (Feldman, "Rise" 3). The organization was run by a board, organized collectively, and composed of an equal number of black and white artists and community workers who were committed to active participation in the arts. The goal of the organization was to act as an umbrella group for funding so that artists could be hired to serve the community.

The first CCCCA project took place in the summer of 1976. Twenty-seven local artists were hired to teach forty unemployed youths (who were CETA-salaried) in arts skills. In 1977, only ten artists were employed, but they taught fifty young people skills in "creative writing, mime, dance, vocal and instrumental music, drama, crafts, and video production" (Feldman, "Rise" 4). The effort was rather successful, bringing new funds into the community and involving all-too-often isolated artists with a racially mixed group of young people. The group published *Young Voices*, a creative writing anthology, and documented the training process on videotape and in text for broader dissemination.

In the third year, funding decreased. CETA funding, which had to be renewed each year, demanded much paper work and a supervisory structure that imposed a hierarchy on the group. As the administration became too time-consuming, the creative output of CCCCA workers, and of the Mime Workers, decreased as well. That year, seven artists provided free cultural services (training, performances, and so on) to public service agencies with limited funds.

What seemed most logical after that was to restructure the organization to create an Arts Advocates Network, representing the concerns of the Mime Workers and making demands on its members much like UMW makes on itself. The hope was to create a network of community agencies sharing the services of the organization. Fifteen community arts advocates were hired. Each was an artist whose charge was to work with a community agency to provide services and meet functions *not previously defined* that would support the agency and its goals. It was the responsibility of each artist, then, to create his or her own job and then to do it.

There was some success. Prairie Air Radio, which was founded to produce programs and provide open access to community groups, was given new potential when CCCCA provided its first paid staff person. The station got its license and is still on the air. Members of the Community Access Center were trained to create videos. The center had programs on the local cable channel and ran a television issues program for quite a while. Other groups organized field trips, assisted with changes in libraries, and organized community arts festivals. Artists were placed with health care and recycling centers as well as with arts organizations and were given the chance to work. CCCCA sponsored touring groups, opened a pottery shop, provided graphics services to eligible organizations, and even assisted in grant writing.

However, the project was too difficult to manage. The lack of long-term funding inhibited many groups. Many of the advocates were unable to define their jobs and so did little or nothing. Each group that did work became so involved in its own projects that the network never developed. By June 1980, there was no longer enough support to maintain the consortium. The Arts Advocate project was an admirable experiment that attempted to reconnect artists to their communities and to make their work part of community life: to bring the questions raised and answers proposed by artists to various endeavors.

Unfortunately, the Mime Workers expectations were too high. It is not that the community is unable to understand what an artist can provide. It is just that the kind of study and definition it takes to define one's own role is foreign to the members of this society, and UMW, assuming that because it does certain things everyone else will do them when necessary, overextended the people on whom it counted. UMW provided all the right questions but not enough of the answers.

While it was attempting to hold the consortium together, the troupe was also trying to maintain a performance and workshop schedule and create new compositions. It is a testament to their devotion to their work that all members of the company held on for so long. During the spring of 1977, the company toured the East Coast with a bill of short mime pieces, the children's play, and a variety of workshops. Whenever possible, the group selected "the format of community oriented residencies in which performances and workshops for adults and children are scheduled throughout the community using a theatre or university as the center of operations" (UMW History). The residencies range from two-and-a-half days to several weeks. The East Coast tour moved the company around a good deal, but helped it establish a number of contacts in the mime and dance worlds that were helpful later in festival bookings.

The company committed, as well, to a major West Coast tour the following year, and had to have new material. *Mime Is No Object: The Reproduction of the Working Day*, the composition that was to become the mainstay of the company for the next four years, now became the focus of the its efforts.

Mime Is No Object: The Reproduction of the Working Day

Mime is No Object (*MINO*) is the result of combining a rather clear area of subject matter with a formal idea that is simple to state, yet complex to actualize. When the group began to discuss the structure of this piece, they decided to extend the techniques used in *Myra's Birthday*, to break down actions into separate elements and to recombine "patterns that could be derived from any observed behavior...of any given instance of human interaction" (Glassman, interview). They decided as well to experiment with two film techniques: "split screen" and parallel montage, in which the significance of two scenes or actions is determined by the comparison of one with the other.

The group was particularly attracted to the work of M. C. Escher, an artist in Holland. They read *The Magic Mirror of M. C. Escher* and were excited enough to send pages of the book to a friend who was imprisoned in Spain as encouragement. In a letter accompanying the pages, Jeff Glassman wrote that

Escher "is especially interested in the 2-dimensional representation of what in 3-dimensions is impossible. In our work now, we attempt to represent in a theatrical frame what in the 'real' world is impossible, or not yet possible. Escher does this on paper with such techniques as 'wrong connections' or 'impossible connections.' We do this in the time and space of the stage by breaking ordinary activity into parts, then rearranging the parts using a different set of rules than is expected (letter).

The subject matter was chosen early in the content discussions. All the issues that the company was interested in examining at the time were concerned with economics. The pool of subject matter centered around work, especially in service areas, and in the relation of the workers to the work process. In addition, the company was concerned with "how people's daily lives are organized in order to accommodate their working lives, and how the two are organizationally extensions of the same sort of economic system."[5]

UMW's concern with disruptive personal and vocational interaction led them to seek images, symbols, and actions that could be used in the play to create a mini-economic system both "at home" and "at work" that would illustrate the macroeconomy of capitalism. Very early in the compositional phase, then, the group was able to choose a waitress as a central character, because her home activity can be made to duplicate her work activity very easily. This choice allowed them to modify for human actors the Kabuki technique of *hikinuki*: locations were changed instantaneously by a quick change of costume. The two locations, and the work oriented subject matter, dictated two sets of characters: a pair of workers with "normal" domestic and workplace relationships, and characters who represent intruding structures, institutions, and processes ("middleman" characters). The specific activities came much later in the process, though, because they could not be chosen until structural considerations had been met.

The company did extensive and eclectic research. They examined Frederick Taylor's techniques of time-motion study and the resulting dehumanization of the worker. They did Marxist analyses of economic systems, reread the plays of Bertolt Brecht, and returned to the techniques of Herbert Brün for inspiration. When they perform *MINO*, they display the books they read in the lobby area and distribute bibliographies. Audiences seem to respect the kind of work the Mime Workers did to create the play and so appreciate in one more way the alternative perspectives on social systems.

Most important, it seems (though rarely mentioned by company members when they discuss their creative process), is their reassessment of the technique of mime itself according to their political vision of the work of the artist/composer and their extrapolation from these techniques to a unique presentational format. In an article prepared in 1982, Langerman noted that classical mime techniques require the audience to imagine what is not there and describe what it sees, and thus make the audience members active participants in the creative process. Most classical mime pieces, however, deny the individuality of these descriptions by merely being showcases for technical skills "which have been thought of as tools for expressing 'universal themes.' Mime has also been called the 'universal language'" (Langerman, "United" 175).

The implication of this is that there is one common set of human interactions and relations and one clear set of gestures for describing those interactions that will be perceived and understood by everyone in the same way. However, most performances generate questions about what people saw and how they would describe it. "If the use of certain techniques can trigger a process of inquiry, why use them for the purpose of supporting the assumptions that some ideas are universal, understood by all, and need not be questioned?" (Langerman, "United" 176).

What the United Mime Workers do is to use the essence of mime, the "slicing" off of objects and language, but leave those elements of experience on stage. A minor change in the expected cycle of any one element creates a circulation of objects (or language in the company's final play) independent of the control of the characters on stage, and raises questions about the relationships of people to objects and to the language they use to describe the processes by which those relationships are made manifest. In this way, the relative arbitrariness of any system is revealed through the obviously imposed nature of the system being examined on stage.

For example, in *MINO*, the husband holds out his cup and the wife fills it with coffee. At one point in the performance the relative location of these two elements is thrown off and the coffee is poured on the floor. If the husband or wife noticed this, they would move one or the other object to successfully pour the coffee. However, this would disrupt the perfect system that was established earlier in the play. The objective of a full coffee cup would be achieved, but change would appear, from the perspective of the system, to be chaos. Without change, however, there is failure; in other words, the apparently ordered system leads to absurd results.

What began to happen in rehearsal was that this chaos became readily apparent. The company developed a base scene, the elements of which would be recombined in the remainder of the composition. In it, Bob Feldman enters, puts his cap on a shelf from which he takes a newspaper, sits at a table which he pulls toward him, and begins to read. Deborah Langerman enters, sometimes in housecoat and sometimes in waitress uniform, fills Feldman's cup with coffee, and puts a slice of bread on a plate beside him. Feldman drinks, the two characters grin at each other, and Langerman leaves. Feldman bites the bread, puts the cup on the plate with the bread, and pushes the dishes away. He rises, stops, removes a dollar bill from his wallet which he proudly shows the audience, and sets the bill (tip or allowance?) on the table. He taps it once, puts the newspaper back on the shelf, puts on his hat, and leaves. Langerman returns with another cup which she puts on the shelves where the hat was. She moves the shelves, frowns as she wipes a spot from the floor, picks up the dishes and tip/allowance (about which she is none too happy), crumples a napkin, throws it into a wastebasket, and exits. This scene is repeated, with modifications, several times during the play.

This three-minute scene was broken down into its specific elements, which were then recombined in a variety of ways by performers on stage. It was rapidly discovered that it took a very long time to explore the ramifications of even one change, let alone the variety of differences induced when the third character entered and purposely distorted the sequence. The decision was made to develop a notational device for testing possibilities on paper. The result was a score using dots, lines, and colors to indicate the movements of objects around the set. Each character's manipulation of objects was written on a twenty-foot role of plastic. When the three sheets were overlaid, it was immediately apparent what would happen when a particular object was shifted because of time or purposeful change. The three sheets were then placed over a time grid that helped coordinate activities. When the actors returned to the stage with their actions dictated by the score, they found that everything that they thought would work, did. They had much difficulty tracing back to errors, but when they were accurate, the expected (for them; it was the unexpected for the audience) occurred.

The set that developed used three screens, each four feet wide and located three feet apart and six feet from the front of the performance area. The effect was to "divide the stage space into two sections: the general action in front, and two 'windows' in-between the screens which can isolate two scenes of action in a different time and space from the front. In the windows, actions can happen in two different areas of the same space...and also in two different spaces" (Feldman, "Montage" 23). For example, at one point in the play, Langerman is hanging wash on a clothesline in one window, and Feldman is hanging clothes on a display rack in the other. The two are doing the same actions, but it is obvious that he is getting paid for his while her labor is given no value. It is hoped that the audience will compare the two. This is an example of parallel montage.

At another point, actions happen in two different areas of the same space, but what should be separated by time is not. The screen in the center allows Feldman in the left window to stack bread on shelves (unseen behind the screen) while Langerman, in the right window, removes them instantly from a place three feet away. Once Feldman's arm seems to stretch the entire space, and later when Langerman rejects an item as too expensive, it inexplicably leaps off the shelf at Feldman. It is obvious that the third actor is behind the screen manipulating the objects. He serves in this capacity the role of stage manager, literally of middle-man, in a position analogous to a film editor making cuts between shots in the two windows.

The score only represents what happens in the front area. It indicates which objects are moved, by whom, and from what coordinate to what other. The area is divided into 130 imaginary "nodes." There are five height levels, two depth levels, and thirteen horizontal levels. Each object has an absolute relationship to this grid and a relative relationship to every other object on stage. For example, a crumpled napkin thrown into the wastepaper basket moves from one node to another, but also changes its position relative to the basket, so that when the basket is moved, so is the napkin. Objects can move around stage apparently of their own accord because they are moved in conjunction with other objects or can be deliberately manipulated. Although each character's time frame slips a bit, each maintains his or her activity within the strictures of his or her own timed sequence. Not only is coffee poured on the floor, but Feldman reads his cup, drinks from his hat, eats a dollar bill, and leaves bread on the table which Langerman treats as her tip.

It is the function of Glassman, the third actor, to perform the more nefarious manipulations. Dressed variously as judge, clergyman, professor, army general, and rich old codger, Glassman makes minor changes in the positions of objects which have already become askew because of miscoordinated timing between the scene. Each shift is calculated to allow him to remove money from the other two characters. He gains time to exchange the bill for a quarter at one point, to remove it from the wastebasket at another, and even to exchange it for a Bible. He receives the tip and, at the end, when it seems he will have the bread and coffee as well, he is left seated stage center, without any chair and too far from the table to reach the food. He is framed by the other actors, who are each in work clothes, holding mops and looking, for the first time in the play, *knowingly* at each other.

> This is all done in a very tightly controlled choreography that looks in some ways like a music composition. The activities of the husband and wife have many repetitions, such that there is a certain level of predictability. Yet the changes in how the husband and wife *connect*, as a result of the changes in how they are related in *time*, are not at all predictable to the audience. So you have surprise in the form of repetition that asks you to look at large patterns rather than isolated moments. We try to broaden the *frame* of individual action, to the level where individual activity only makes sense in the context of social activity (Glassman, letter).

The result is a very funny play that challenges the audience's perceptions and raises a number of questions. The piece is "making humor out of the mundane, rather than exaggerating what's already exaggerated" (Kramer 3) and its naturalistic (although somewhat emotionless) acting style makes it resemble a silent movie, in the style of Charlie Chaplin more than Abbott and Costello or Dean Martin and Jerry Lewis.

The performance is followed by a discussion (which frequently takes longer than the forty minute play) in which perceptions are discussed, interpretations debated, and questions asked out loud.[6] Inevitably some of the discussion is critical in nature, although most of the comments are positive. Some people say that *MINO* is difficult to understand; yet when questions about what they saw are asked of them, it is clear that there is in the audience a general understanding of what happened on stage. This may lead to some self-congratulation, but it also leaves some audience members convinced that the Mime Workers are politically or artistically irresponsible, because they are unwilling to be clear. It is important to note that it is rarely the working class members of the audience who complain about clarity. This is even true of professional critics: while Deborah Jowitt, in a mixed review in the *Village Voice*, questioned the direction of the group's social criticism, and Jack Anderson (in a rather negative review that did praise the company for raising serious questions, "something that the often genial art of mime only rarely attempts to do") claimed that the production was "too vague." Pamela Mincey, writing in the *Daily World*, a workers' paper, called the play "a true work of genius" and praised it for its clarity of perception and presentation.

A seeming lack of clarity is inherent in the company's belief that differences of interpretation are desirable and foster the kind of discussion in which real political discoveries can be made.

> Our main effectiveness politically is to try to develop a critical audience and to present events in a different or new way to an audience so that they can reflect, hopefully critically, on their own lives and how they look at the system in which we live. And if we present things formally in kind of an unusual way, an unusual format, that takes away a lot of preconceptions about theatre, at least people will have to question their preconceptions about theatre in order to watch, understand, and enjoy (and think about) what we do—and that's a beginning. (Feldman, interview)

One still may argue (with some validity, I feel) that the company would have done well to take some more responsibility for interpretation; something they did during discussions following their next play by carefully structuring questions and by directly stating their intentions when audience interpretations went too far astray.[7]

Another criticism raised by audiences and critics alike, particularly those on the left, is that *MINO* is an unintentionally negative presentation of working-class people, and of working women in particular. Some call it nihilistic, while others have said that it is a condemnation of work rather than of *this* system. The lack of heroism is clearly the company's intention; nihilism is not. According to Deborah Langerman, the company is not interested in examining ways of coping with or existing in the system. Showing the happy, clever worker only perpetuates this system, while showing the drudgery and exploitation implies that things can never get better until the system is changed. "To give people a way to deal with the system is, in a way, giving people defensive tools; but it's not giving them offensive tools" (Langerman, interview). It is interesting to note that Esperanza sees itself as fulfilling the same function, critical challenge, even though its plays are formally much different than UMW's and much more emotionally charged. The similarity, however, lies in their failing protagonists: Sammy in *La Victima* and Manuel in *Hijos*.

The kind of criticism mentioned above provides, in itself, an example of the kind of narrow, "one-dimensional thought," that the company is trying to combat. It is not necessary for a work to have certain "signature" attributes to be political, and, in fact, those plays that do have them may be relatively ineffective because of those very attributes.

However, some other criticism is, I feel, somewhat more valid. The first complaint concerns pacing. While the pace needs to be relatively slow to allow the audience to follow the machinations of the system and to guess, usually wrongly, what will next happen, it does not necessarily have to be unvarying, as it is in *MINO. This* problem can be attributed to the notational system, which needs a regular time grid to be clear, and to the lack of a certain directorial perspective. It seems as if by the time on stage rehearsal begins, the "director" is often concentrating on whether the performers are fulfilling the requirements of the score and not if they are making viable theatrical choices.

The second criticism centers on the acting, and is again, I feel, symptomatic of the relative weakness of the company's directorial eye. The characters lack a consistent awareness of the changes occurring in the system on stage. The original conception was to have each reenactment of the basic scene be just that, a reenactment with a different perspective or variation. Shortly after performances began, it was discovered that audiences inevitably saw the repetitions as a progression. The problem is, I feel, that the company was never able to figure out how to change the acting elements so that they could incorporate the audience's perception into the performance. The characters' lack of awareness contributes to the sense of negative portrayal that some audiences mention, and the partial awareness of some characters at times can be very confusing.

Nevertheless, the piece remains highly entertaining as "the three weave their way through a series of basically repetitious sets of actions, varying them slightly with split-second coordination that is mind-boggling, to create funny and significant malfunctions of the basic system" (Lewis 1). Not only does it remain an extremely effective piece of experimental theatre, but it fulfills in many ways its political function. *MINO* has been performed hundreds of times for a wider variety of audiences than that reached by almost any other theatre company, political or otherwise. Performance sponsors have included mime and theatre festivals, schools, factories and unions, foreign governments, and even the Center for Popular Economics, where the company studied economics and taught through performance. The discussions thus generated form the seeds of political change, and the sheer pleasure derived from watching the play has led many to consider the theatre as a useful tool in their work.

The 1978 West Coast tour of *MINO* and *The President's New Clothes* was a great success. The company generated so much attention that it was invited to the Eleventh World Festival of Youth and Students in Havana, Cuba. It was the only mime company to be invited to the event, which included over 20,000 people from 140 nations, a recognition of the political nature of its plays and analytical methods. And yet, the company was able to return to perform at the Illinois State Fair, proof that it is able to reach the broadest variety of audiences.

The Mime Workers spent the remainder of 1978 and 1979 touring extensively. Although *MINO* was the centerpiece of their compositions, their children's play was to remain the major source of income until after 1980. In 1978 they were invited to the Festival of American Mime in Milwaukee, where their leadership in (ironically, because of their departure from) the world of mime was critically acclaimed. "Of the companies performing at the festival, only one, the United Mime Workers, seems to be working in a style that is not derivative. That they also work with ideas and a humanistic theme, successfully fusing form and content, is amazing. That they are also entertaining and excellent theatre is a miracle. This troupe, which was trained in pantomime, has grown beyond its limitations, forcing one to ask, 'why haven't the others?'" (Robinson 2).

The company entered 1980 riding a wave of critical acclaim and successful performances around the country. Most of their performances were part of residencies during which workshops, another tool of the company for modifying and expanding perceptions, could be used. Their workshops are extremely challenging to participants because they both explain and use complex techniques, and because they are concerned with problems of composition, broader than specific problems of a particular medium or genre. Because the exercises are investigations into techniques, and because they are balanced among group, pair, and individual work, they simultaneously teach control (particularly of the self), a specific technique, and how to use that technique to create and examine results. "The group activities are especially important since they are designed to help people understand conceptual problems through movement activities" (UMW Cover Letter).

Specific workshop activities are modified depending on participants and on the work in which the company is involved at the time. In Poland, for example, while they were experimenting with the disassociation and montage techniques later to be used in *MINO*, one workshop exercise explored dialectic by choosing two scenes created by groups in the workshop, dividing the scenes into movements, and then performing the first movement of scene one followed by the first movement of scene two, the second movement of scene one, then the second of two, an so on. The goal was not only to discover what would occur, but to generate a third scene, "the collection of movements we need to travel between the first and the second" (Glassman, letter 2). During that same workshop the company led improvisations with a live band, only doing the opposite of what one might expect. Instead of the musician and actor working together, each moved or played only when the partner in the other medium to which he or she was assigned was still or silent. Each actor was connected to the instrument, not to its sound.

At other times UMW has led workshops assisting groups that wish to use theatrical techniques to support their own political or community efforts. One such workshop examines techniques by which the participants can create illustrative or exemplary scenes. The exercises begin with a theme, and examine ways of developing that theme in action. At one workshop, for example, the participants began examining the themes of competition and control. They eventually developed a scene in which three events, each using the same physical actions, were used to trace the life of one character. In the first event, a baseball game, program booklets were distributed and the coach gave hand signals. During the war episode, propaganda booklets were distributed, and the signals came from a general; while in the funeral scene, prayer books were handed out while a priest gesticulated.[8]

Their brochure advertising a five-day workshop at Parkland College listed seven areas of work in which interested participants could be involved. These included warm up techniques from Yoga and T'ai Chi, mime and acting techniques, application of techniques for nontheatre classrooms, and a discussion of the function of performance in society. As would be expected, the workshops were expansive, emphasizing "relations between theatre, other media (such as film, music, and graphic arts) and performance in everyday life" (UMW, "Parkland Brochure").

The group remained involved in other nonperformance political and community activity as well. In 1980 they arranged the tour of a Cuban mime company in the United States and became very active in the Neighborhood Arts Programs National Organizing Committee. Since NAPNOC has become the Alliance for Cultural Democracy, a group without a paid staff, UMW members have continued to support its work by organizing regional meetings and serving on the board of directors.

Another attempt to broaden their impact was a project designed to create theatre groups in communities as defined by workplace, union affiliation, and so forth. The Workplace-Oriented Theatre Groups project would have, had it been funded, included a series of residencies by the Mime Workers during which they would give a performance, conduct workshops, and then lead the participants in the creation and performance of a piece of their own. UMW would then move on to the next residency, but would make periodic follow-up visits to assist the worker group in continued creation.

In the grant proposal for the project, they were clear about their political orientation as *animateurs*, insisting that the grantors recognize that most people's connection to culture is just through "the consumption of the product of the various culture industries" (Rebitzer 3). Not only did they maintain the alienation of people from culture, but they maintained that of culture from people, the evidence for which is an "absence of imagery that accurately reflects upon our lives and our work. Since a function of culture is to allow us to see ourselves, we are faced with a situation where large numbers of people are made invisible to society at large. This is especially true of working people" (Rebitzer 3).

The devotion of the United Mime Workers as workers to workers has remained a constant throughout their history. They have continued, in spite of a devotion to experimentation that has led other groups to ever narrower audiences, to stay in contact with working people throughout the United States. Much of this is due to their collective process, in which the value of individual and group effort is maximized in the development of new techniques for accomplishing changing tasks, rather than in the maintenance of an institution or hierarchy. In 1980, however, personnel changes again strained the collective cohesion and created a rift that still cast shadows that were apparent three years later.

FINAL PROJECTS—THE 1980s

In 1980, the United Mime Workers were invited to tour Mexico as part of the International Festival of Mime and to perform in New York in the New Mime Series. Before either of these commitments could be prepared for, Bob Rebitzer left the company to return to school. For the past three years he had managed almost all administrative affairs and had been an active contributor to *MINO*. The company felt the work was too great for three and invited someone with business expertise to replace Rebitzer. When that person declined, Candace Walworth, a playwright associate of the groups from Herbert Brün's seminars, and a teacher at an alternative school, was invited, although she made it clear from the beginning that she was uncomfortable with business. She went to Mexico with the company as a "trial attempt" and did everything on tour except performing. She was, in her words, able to "elbow in," and the stage management tasks for which her effort was required were relatively easy. That first trip was, for her, "a matter of figuring out in what way I could contribute something to the group that wouldn't be there if I wasn't there, because the essential tasks were pretty much taken care of. I'm still finding those things" (Walworth, interview).

During the composition of the company's next play, Walworth's writing skills became one of "those things," but on the return from Mexico, she was still looking for a way to contribute. Earlier in 1980 the company decided to work very quickly to produce a new children's show to take on tour. They had experimented with all-night or several day sessions before when necessary, but this time the push was to be sustained enough to create a complete piece. They invited a friend, Susan Perenti, to write with them, another break from their norm, but the process did not produce anything.

After the tour, Walworth collaborated with a writer outside the collective on a new children's piece, an adaptation of the story "Stone Soup." The situation is difficult for anyone entering a collective, particularly a small, long-lived one, but the problems were exacerbated in this case by restrictions placed on the membership of the fourth person: she would not be able to perform. She did not, therefore, have the rehearsal route that provides an inroad for many new members in collective theatres, nor did she seem to want to learn slowly what lies somewhere between a social entity's "shared knowledge" and what Walworth called in a letter to me, "the slowly accumulated habits, prejudices, and blind spots" of the group (letter).

The Mime Workers and their closer associates knew that the company's compositional method led them to "make up its rules as it goes along." Walworth stated that she entered knowing that once a compositional approach has been decided upon, "there are very definite rules established...and the rules last as long as they apply to a situation; and I did not assume that there were already rules set up that I had to learn to obey in the group" (interview). After a long pause, she added, "I did consider that there were certain unspoken norms that I had to learn...and either accept or [learn] ways to change [them]" (interview). Rules regulating composition are clearly stipulated; those regulating interpersonal interaction are not. This is not a unique problem, but in this case it was amplified by the change in creative process necessitated by the new approach to the children's piece.

There was some disagreement between company members as well. Both Glassman and Feldman were glad to relinquish control of the children's piece and have someone else write it. Langerman had disagreed and wanted to work with Walworth on the project, but Walworth had reservations about that. The play was submitted to the company and went through the remainder of the process as usual. In the summer of 1981 the company did a performance for a small group of friends, but although the criticism was mixed, they decided to scrap the script "because of interpersonal hostilities that seemed irreparable and certainly not conducive for creative conspiracies" (Walworth, letter). To Langerman, though, it "*seemed* like a step backward."[9]

However, as the focus of the group's creative efforts turned toward a new adult composition, Walworth was able to use her writing skills to make a more integrated contribution to the group. She continued to maintain other outlets for her own desires as a performer, and it seemed to me, though there was still some resentment, that all members acknowledged her full participation in the company and her influence in its growth. When I asked her what part she had played in the early experiments that led to *Shadows Beyond the Benefit of a Doubt*, the company's last piece, she said she had contributed the beginnings of what had become scenes. The group was responsible for the scenes; she only synthesized them as "the liaison between that particular cluster of ideas and the troupe" (Walworth, interview). At the meeting I attended she was obviously as involved as anyone else in the compositional stage, and she was the sole writer of several scenes during the scripting.

In 1981 and 1982 the company continued to expand its performance schedule, giving sixty performances, most with workshops, teaching, and discussions, during that season. They continued to be participate in festivals, performing at the Whole Art Festival in Michigan and the People's Theatre Festival in San Francisco in the summer of 1982. They were the only group from the latter to be asked to perform at a non-theatre function. Nevertheless, it was becoming harder to find bookings for *MINO*, a piece they had been doing for four years, at the same time that it was becoming financially more necessary to tour. In addition, a major European tour had to be canceled because the festival that was going to pay for their transportation had lost its funding. The company desperately needed a new piece, and an invitation to the Politics and Performance Festival in New York in August of 1982 provided the impetus.

Their goal for the new piece was not only to create a play, but to develop a compositional method that could be used to create a number of pieces, unlike the process for creating and notating *MINO*, which they felt was unique to that piece. They also hoped to use this technique to create a performance that would not be such a clear illustration of the technique itself.

Shadows Beyond the Benefit of a Doubt: Matters of Fact or Friction [sic]

Shadows is both a continuation of the early work of the Mime Workers and a significant departure. For one thing, it is the first piece to rely heavily on dialogue. Prior to this, except for the two short dialogues described above, all pieces had been performed in silence. When language was important, as in *Implication*, it was projected or printed. The performance of pieces was scored, but not scripted. *Shadows* has a script, a multicolored score, and a short, rather cryptic, description of "Ten Episodes" which are parts of the play.

Because of this, it is the first piece to be able to examine the perceptions of *characters on stage*, presenting clearly a fuller range of social interactions and contradictions. While earlier pieces have concentrated on pared down scenes or short activity sequences, *Shadows* includes a myriad of details as it moves freely from one scene to the next or presents up to three scenes simultaneously.

Finally, unlike other UMW pieces, this composition makes demands on the actors outside the areas of technical training in movement and gesture. The nature of the piece requires that actors change roles, or maintain the same roles but change attitude, physical or emotional direction, or even time, without any transition; in order to perform what company members call a "pivot." It is in this activity that the company's development of a completely new performance system, a "set of gestural, vocal and manual techniques for performing sequences of pivots [that] is as fully a set of techniques as is that of classical mime or pantomime" (UMW, "Artistic Statement") can be seen.

However, this search for a more generally applicable performance and compositional system was not based on a completely new set of performance assumptions. On the contrary, it was a logical step in the growth of the company as a composing unit, and was based on the explorations made in earlier work:

particularly in mime's "slicing" off of language and objects, leaving only the performer to create what has been removed. In *Shadows* UMW slices not only objects and dialogue, but even character and time sequence, from the actor, yet it does not remove them from the stage. The play juggles each of these independently so that as the performers move through the linear sequence of the score and script, they are jumping from one place, time, and character to another in front of the audience.

The composition continues as well to explore the use of film techniques in live performance. To the Mime Workers, filmmakers,

> as technologists of culture...had at their disposal the possibility of not only reproducing the temporal and spatial continuities of the stage, but also the ability to subject those conventions of continuity to practically limitless sub-divisions, extensions, contractions, displacements, subversions, parallelisms, distortions and all new modes of abstraction unfurling not from the time and space of the subject material, but from the qualities of the new medium itself, the time and space of its montage....Theatre remains bounded within acts, within scenes, entrances and exits, signs and symbols of passing time and changing place—all adequate for most purposes, yet crude by the standards of cinema. *The single most outstanding problem we have set ourselves to solve is this: Invent a method for the creation of theatre which departs from the conventions of time and space illusion in film in as fruitful a way as film initially departed from the conventions of theater* [author's emphasis]. (UMW, "Artistic Statement)

One of the great successes of *Shadows* is the way in which it uses film techniques, but modifies them to make them into stage devices.

Finally, this piece continues to study cybernetics, logic, and perception. It is, in some scenes, like an Escher drawing in which one has been trapped, so that it feels, as one audience member put it during a discussion, "Like I just finished climbing up stairs and find I've gotten to the bottom." Each scene "confuses" the audience, not by breaking or ignoring logic, but rather by following a strict logic in which expectations are established and then radically unfulfilled. A simple example will illustrate one application of this technique. At one point in the play, Jeff and Bob are rotating their upper bodies as if to begin putting on jackets to go out, but the movement and the dialogue suddenly reverses itself so that it is apparent that they have just finished removing their jackets after coming in. Not only that, but the conversation indicates that a significant, but indefinite, amount of time has elapsed.

This technique is called a "pivot," which is:

> accomplished conceptually and in practice when the actor arrives at a composed juncture of his two roles [either the same character in different times or situations, or two different characters]: a moment that occurs identically in both scenes, in the same spot on stage and with the actor's

> body passing through identical positions in both roles. The one moment and the one position satisfy both roles. When he continues on from this juncture into the time and space of his other role, when he occupies its 'body,' we say she [sic] has pivoted. (UMW, "Artistic Statement)

Pivots do not only occur in movement, however, but also in dialogue and in ideology or attitude. At one point in the play, one of the characters, who is unemployed after his business has failed, is berating people for taking public assistance and complaining it is not enough. The script contains the dialogue in the form that follows:

> I'd never take any welfare. Those people just want things handed/
> me
> a check at the unemployment office and I know/
> way can I afford to live on these benefits (6).

The character has not only leaped ahead in time, but has also changed attitudes radically, yet the elapsed time on stage is only three or four seconds. One is reminded of the technique of *jump cuts* used by filmmakers like Jean-Luc Godard to skip from one significant moment to the next, while the visuals remain relatively constant. The audience either fills in the gap or senses that the character is, at each moment, in a present that is only vaguely related to a specific past or future. Each moment, and the characters, objects, actions, and words in it, are thereby objectified; each exists on a separate "track" that can be moved independently of the other. Time and context can be manipulated so that those things by which we comfortably define the world are in a new relationship to each other, and each can be examined and questioned.

The original impetus for the content of this piece was the Iranian "hostage situation." The Mime Workers began to question the relationship between what people are shown, what they see, and what is really happening. They noticed, as well, that a number of emotionally loaded words were used with equal claim by both sides to define and justify what they were doing: Words such as *freedom, choice, democracy*, and *liberty* are used by the entire spectrum of political ideologies. "Freedom of choice," a right claimed by all, is limited by one's sources of information, and it seemed to UMW that the television as a sole source was far more limiting than liberating.

As the company began examining freedom, it soon discovered that choices are further limited by "national priorities"; in this case, by militarization. In addition, choices are limited by what each person sees as possible, and further by the language that each person can use to describe the range of possibilities. "Sometimes," says Bob Feldman, "in any political debate someone will say 'at least we're free,' and that's the end of the conversation. We want to examine what that means" (interview).

The production itself appears, in many ways, to an be extremely complex examination of and performance about these issues. It is, however, a simplification of "real-life" pivoting and inexact language, of the disparity between what we say, perceive, and do in our daily lives. By actually decreasing the number of contradictions in each scene on stage, and by making the contradictions more exaggerated, the play emphasizes the disparity inherent in our lives, our social interactions, and the ways in which the public and private intrude upon one another to create the illusion of freely chosen paths through life.

The play begins with a crowded, though unpopulated, set. Coffee is percolating, the toaster is popping, a cigarette is burning, and the furniture and shelves are cluttered with books and blenders, a television and vacuum cleaner, dishes, papers, and a basket of laundry. Bob Feldman enters, pours coffee into two cups on the table, prepares to use the vacuum cleaner, and starts the machine by pulling the chain on the floor lamp. Jeff Glassman enters, ready but unable to shave until Bob starts his electric razor with the blender switch. The telephone, which operates as expected at all other times, turns on the blender.

When Jeff enters, he does not appear either to ignore nor acknowledge Bob. It is as if they are, although on the same set in front of the audience, in different places. Throughout the play this technique is used periodically. Characters are aware only of what is in their own environment, thereby enabling three people to be on stage who are, in the context of the play, occupying two or three different environments.

Bob turns on the television as Jeff turns off the razor, but the razor sound continues from the television set. Deborah Langerman enters, but her lines come from the television Bob responds live. The three sit down to breakfast as their conversation and that of the characters on television mix. But the conversations are erratic and do not cohere. Sometimes an actor begins a line in response to his or her own television voice. At one point the two men seem to lose their own identities as Bob claims, "I wasn't saying that really, I was quoting someone else" (2). Private and media reality become blended and confused.

Action or dialogue scenes continue, sometimes changing abruptly, but often connected by transitions in which pivots occur every three to five seconds. At times it is time itself that seems to be dislocated, as in the third scene in which the dialogue is progressing as the actors are passing a beer can and coffee cup between them while moving about the stage in such a way as to make it appear that each character is always right in the middle of using the object. In other words, it is as if while a piece of one scene is being performed, another scene is progressing somewhere else. At each pivot, the performers step from the on stage scene into the "other" one, although it seems to be the scenes which are "changing locations" and not the actors.

The piece makes extensive use of montage, as defined by Walter Benjamin: The "principle of interruption...the superimposed element disrupts the context in which it is inserted."[10] At some points meaning and language are dissociated. In one sequence television voices play a soap-opera love scene while live actors use the same dialogue to discuss nuclear arms policy. In other segments, actions lead to unexpected consequences, discovery creates further confusion, and "help" from the outside (media, government, and telephone calls) creates limitations more often than it fulfills potentials. The challenge to the audience to reassess its perceptions is tied to an explicit attack on so-called free market capitalism, media distortion, and militarization, yet the play never compromises technique for thematic clarity. It is extremely clever and entertaining with performances that are marked both by technical virtuosity and emotional clarity.

Although some of the politics are relatively overt, and some of the ways in which the play twists perceptions and expectations can be frustrating, there is enough here to keep everyone responding. Almost as if to check on that, during the seventh scene, all three actors turn to the audience in a manner reminiscent of the way they did when responding to the television voices in the first scene. This time, however, it is not clear where the focus lies. Bob asks, half indicating the television set, "Is anybody still listening to this?" Although the line makes perfectly good sense in the context of the scene, the sense of direct address is rather shocking and confusing. (Glassman called it a "clearly specified ambiguity. We come to the border of things, but we don't exactly cross"; taped discussion.) It serves as a reminder that any system can be broken, that any performance is cognizant of its audience, and that perceptions of art or work or life are subject to a variety of conscious and unconscious manipulations. It gives, in an interesting way, permission to the audience to reject the work at that point. However, no one does.

The establishment's critical response was, however, mixed after the premier in New York. Mel Gussow, in the *New York Times*, found it at times "imprecise, but *Shadows* remains a clever social commentary on the depersonalization of humanity in a mechanized society." Barbara Garson, who demands didactic specificity in all political work, hated the lack of clarity and what she perceived as the negative portrayal of people. The production was very well received by the audience at the Politics and Performance festival, as it has been all over the country by those very people who are supposedly negatively presented.

Once again, as with *MINO*, the company exhibited the score and a bibliography after the performance. The score for this piece is deceptively simple. It contains one column for each actor, vertical lines indicating pivots, angled lines pointing to the person who picks up the second half of the pivot change, and dark lines charting object movement from one person to another. Each change of scene or context is indicated by a change of color in the actor's column. The simplicity of the notational system, compared to the complexity of the one's used in earlier work, seems to indicate that the system it charts is far more flexible than the earlier ones.

Unfortunately, that flexibility will never be exercised by the United Mime Workers. Although the new piece opened new venues for the company, and their bookings increased from approximately sixty during the 1981-1982 season to seventy the next season and over eighty in the next two, and although UMW continued to be invited to perform by groups not normally involved with theatre and to receive national recognition (they were one of only fifty-three companies to tour under the Dance Touring Program of the NEA in 1982–1983), the 1986 season was their last. The reasons for the dissolution are many; some are very much like those given by other groups, and some are unique to UMW. Perhaps the best way to examine the company's dissolution is to explore the structure that kept it together for so many years.

ORGANIZATION

As is true of the company's compositional process, its organizational structure changed to reflect particular problems as they arose, particularly those of personnel. Since Bob Rebitzer left the company in 1980, however, the administration has remained the same. Basically, Bob Feldman took care of all business aspects of the collective and shared grant writing and publicity work with other company members.

The Mime Workers have always been on shaky financial ground. In spite of the fact that they earned a higher percentage of their budget than most groups doing socially conscious theatre (60 to 70 percent), members were rarely paid a decent living wage. In the early years, when a check from a sponsor came in, expenses were subtracted, out-of-pocket expenditures reimbursed, a little was taken out for company expenses such as publicity and supplies, and the remainder was divided by four. During the early 1980s it sometimes became necessary to borrow from some private funds of one of the members to pay for company needs. Not only was this an added financial burden on the member, but it was "uncomfortable" for the group not to be self-sufficient. It is difficult enough to take a position outside the mainstream of the socioeconomic structure; to be unable to succeed financially as a model of collective organization and people's artistic endeavors is most disheartening.

After 1981 the company tried to meet a self-imposed monthly payroll for tax and accounting purposes. The fact that it has been more or less successful helps account for the steadiness of the group's membership. Previous fourth members cited finances as a contributing factor in their departure.

Some difficulty arose because of a decline in grant money that affected not only the theatre but its sponsors as well. The NEA had been the company's major granting source since its inception, but that money had always been supplemented by other grants. In 1979, for example, the Mime Workers received $4,800 from the Illinois State Arts Council. In 1981 they had to fight to get half as much. The Arts Council at first refused to fund the group at all. For one thing, UMW has always applied for grants from the dance panel, but in 1981 the panel decided the company's compositions were too close to theatre. The complaint was also made that they had not produced any new work. Although this was true, the panel did not take into consideration the consortium and the consulting work that UMW had been doing for other arts groups. The real complaint, though, was that the company's work was "too dogmatic": This is somewhat ironic when one considers that the most frequent complaint that the troupe gets from political artists is that they are not didactic enough. The Mime Workers protested because political stance is specifically prohibited as a criteria for funding. Although they won their battle, UMW was assured that the next year there would be little for them, and there would probably be nothing after that.

This meant the group had to tour a great deal, certainly a factor in the difficulties faced by any political theatre. For one, travel time leaves little time for composition, and it is frustrating to be unable to actualize ideas for new work. It also leaves little time for family. After Feldman's marriage, he wanted to spend more time near Urbana, Illinois. Walworth's long-term relationship had to bear the burden of long separations. Langerman and Glassman had been married for many years, but the theatre work prevented their lives from being as settled as Langerman might have liked. They did not have time to plan to meet both their needs, and it has resulted in the dissolution of their relationship and is partly responsible for the company's cessation.

This is not at all unusual. Groups like Teatro de la Esperanza which have managed to develop a structure for familial support are rare, and they can only operate collectively if the members agree to serve as an extended family for significant others and children while maintaining a collective, nonfamilial, working relationship. For a group as small as UMW, this is almost impossible. For one thing, if Langerman had had a child, she would have had to take a leave from the company, effectively stopping performances for some time. The company's decision to limit the performing group to three specific individuals was rather inhibiting. Nevertheless, when I spent time with company members in 1982, some were talking about how they would manage if the couple had a child. It seemed to me at the time as if the decision to press on regardless had been made. In 1985, however, they still did not have children: a source of great frustration and anger for Langerman and, because the couple's personal difficulties could not be kept out of meetings, for the rest of the group as well.

I mention these personal details as an illustration of the difficulty a collective can face. Once a group establishes itself in the way UMW has, it is very difficult for it to cope with any major disruption of its normal operating procedures. In recognition of this, the three performers insulated themselves from such disruptions on stage, but at the same time created tremendous pressure on themselves to maintain an unchanging and almost absolute level of commitment, a difficulty that the three-member Split Britches collective has faced much more successfully (see Chapter 6).

The Mime Workers either did not realize how such pressure could build or did not feel the need in earlier years to establish any mechanism for handling resulting emotional disruptions. It is as if, because the collective structure of the company emerged without planning, the group felt that there was no need to consciously create specific mechanisms for circumstances that were not directly related to composition. Unlike the early collectives, which may have spent too much time on planning for personal relations, UMW spent next to none. As Langerman put it, this made "some things come out in 'undesirable ways'" (telephone conversation with author).

However, the company was able to maintain its artistic integrity throughout everything. UMW was so totally committed to its work, and so convinced of the political efficacity of its efforts, that it was able to persevere for almost fifteen years, producing ever more sophisticated and challenging works for a wide range of audiences. It still, in spite of personal difficulties, worked full time, and it began 1986 with an eight-week residency at an Illinois college. Much of this was due to the group's public and private images. The Mime Workers have always felt, and made clear to their audiences, that the goal of their compositions is not merely to be seen by an audience, but to involve that audience in the creative and critical process of which the composition is only one possible manifestation. While the company is not openly socialist in its productions, it has always let audiences know in one way or another that worker exploitation is a facet of the current system and that the workers themselves are the only group that can (once they realize the possibility for new visions) apply those visions to a new social order.

The troupe's publicity and grant applications concentrated on its nontraditional organization and its unusual touring range, noting members' functions as teachers, tourers, and performers, and stressing its collective organization and longevity. The very fact that the group received grants not only from national funding sources, but also from local business and community service organizations in the Champaign-Urbana area, and that it had been invited by schools, unions, and political organizations to perform, indicates its popularity and image as a public service theatre, in spite of the fact that some sponsors would not agree with the members' political philosophies.

This can be explained by the company's concentration on an examination of "paradigms of thought rather than issues" (Feldman, "Montage"). The focus has allowed the group to play for a wide variety of audiences, stimulating people critically first and then allowing them to apply that mode of thought to their own issues during discussion. This focus helps account, as well, for the group's lack of concern with organization. Interpersonal difficulties, or personal dissatisfactions, are issues that lie outside the pall of critical detachment, and therefore outside the concern of the group's compositional activities. In other words, the group as a unit failed to answer questions about the responsibilities associated with the highly personal side of political and work-related activities, a criticism sometimes inaccurately leveled at their plays, but this time evidenced in their inability to continue as a creative unit.

The loss of the United Mime Workers will be felt by theatre makers, mime performers, and politically conscious artists in all fields. Their work has bridged the gaps between composers and creators in a variety of media and has helped to reestablish the connection between labor and socially conscious theatre, a connection that has been beneficial to both. They have explored the theatre in ways no other group has, and have left a legacy of creative vision that can influence groups in the future. Their attachment to their community serves as a model for people's theatres, and their efforts at home have borne practical fruit for the groups with whom they have worked.

NOTES

1. Feldman, "Montage" 33. It is fascinating to see how Split Britches has purposely chosen a "low-tech" mode, a development of theatre-based techniques rather than of elements brought into the theatre, for some of the same types of explorations.

2. The script, which was told to me during an interview, follows. The objects in parentheses are those on which the projections appeared.

SHE: It's late. (Coffee pot)
HE: Yes. (Cup)
HE: They'll never stop killing people. (Newspaper)
SHE: Honey, you can't change human nature. (Apron)
HE: People are starving. (Newspaper)
SHE: We can't complain. (Garbage can)
HE: But (Hat)
SHE: That's life. (Tray)
HE: Work Work Work (Attaché case)

3. Deborah Langerman, Bob Feldman, Bob Rebitzer, and Jeff Glassman respectively. Rebitzer is quoted in Hodgson 5. The other three are quoted from interviews by the author.

4. Both Deborah Langerman and Bob Feldman mentioned this incident in interviews by the author. It was an emotionally charged moment that raised issues of final decision making power and of the need for establishing, somewhere in the process of composition for each production, a ground. Decisions remained consensual, taking into account the degree of commitment to a particular choice, and the pressure of booking deadlines made the second issue moot. It seemed to me, however, to be a particularly telling moment during which the emotional needs of one company member were not made part of the process of the work.

5. Jeff Glassman interview. It is rather ironic that one of the reasons why that there was some tension in the group was because Deborah Langerman, for whom children and family are an important part of a fulfilling life, was not satisfied with the organization of her personal life around work needs. As with so many socially concerned artists, the company members were sacrificing the very rights they were hoping to vitalize in society. The tensions that marital problems and interpersonal difficulties brought to meetings also caused all four company members to suffer. Many collectives plan for some of these personal difficulties and have a mechanism for allowing tensions to surface and be resolved in a controlled manner. The failure of UMW to have such a mechanism had much to do with the dissolution of the company.

6. During the discussion after the performance of *MINO* at the Gathering, one local resident began to analyze the actions on stage in terms of his own supportive view of the capitalist system in the United States. By the time he had finished, he had equated much government activity with thievery and, when he realized what he had said, his shock generated a gasp, laughter, and then applause from the audience.

7. The company members sometimes also use a vocabulary during discussions that is the result of their research and their attachment to a university community, and that may not be as clear as they would like it to be to an audience with less formal education.

8. This workshop and others are described by Bob Feldman in the "Montage" manuscript.

9. Deborah Langerman, quotation noted in my journal from the People's Theatre Festival in San Francisco, 25 June 1982. At a meeting at which groups discussed problems associated with continued survival, Langerman spoke quite openly about the difficulties UMW has had over the years with fourth members, and about the problems she had accepting Walworth. The men, it seems, stayed out of the controversy: a stance that has caused some resentment.

10. "The Author as Producer," in *Reflections: Essays, Aphorisms, Autobiographical Writings*, p. 234. In fact, the politics of the group as a whole resemble Benjamin's rather unique mix of Marxism, anarchy, spiritualism, and a more-or-less pervasive aesthetic sensibility.

6

Split Britches

The question I should like to ask is what can a laugh, a song, and a dance contribute to this problem? The answer, I think, is quite a lot, if you are laughing at the right things, singing the right songs, and dancing well enough--and if your drama is meaning something to the right people, penetrating the right mystique in a dialectical manner.

John McGrath, "The Theory and Practice of Political Theatre"

You have paid to see me. You will not get your money back. Your money does not pay me for my work. I work alwayS...Do you like...to tell stories? Do you get paid for your stories? Do you get paid what you are worth for your work? Am I worth five dollars? Would you like more room to watch me in, a bigger theatre, more comfortable seats? Are you willing to pay for that? Or would you like to pay for a more comfortable show? I'm a mother, a good mother. Are you willing to pay to see a good lesbian mother?...Would you like to see my legs?

Mother Goddam in *Upwardly Mobile Home*

Since its founding in 1981, Split Britches has challenged audiences and analysts alike with its gender-bending, lesbio-centered, multilayered, celebratory, and frequently hilarious productions. The three-woman company, with a collective sensibility arising "at the overlapping point of Sapphic poetry, Mad Magazine, and the Talmud" (press release) has been hailed by some feminist theorists for being on the cutting edge of the postmodern deconstruction of the representation of woman on stage, and derided by others for not being politically coherent or stridently feminist. Reference to their productions has at times become a weapon in a battle the company itself does not seem to want to fight.

Yet it is somehow natural that Split Britches, which came into being almost by accident, acknowledging and embracing diversity at each point in its development, and creating productions known for "eclectic combinations of fastidious attention to realistic detail with bizarre flights of surrealistic fancy" (Dolan, "Dynamics" 168), should be available to audience members with almost any agenda.

COMING TOGETHER AND GETTING A NAME—1975–1982

When Lois Weaver graduated Radford University, not far from her home in the Blue Ridge Mountains in Virginia in 1972, she had a degree in theatre, a background in Method acting, experience as a performer in a small college, and a sense that she wanted to use what she knew in a politically significant way. After spending time doing political work in Baltimore, where she studied with former members of the Open Theatre, she made her way to New York. In 1975 she helped found the Spiderwoman Theatre Company. Originally formed as a workshop/discussion/consciousness-raising group, the members developed a story-weaving project, and began to tell stories about women's lives that "had to do with those parts of us that had been overlooked and forgotten and sometimes denied, and for me that was the supreme political statement...turning our lives into viable theatrical material" (Weaver). Spiderwoman became an internationally respected performing company of women of various ages, races, and ethnic backgrounds who made exciting theatre out of the material of their own lives.

At the same time, Peggy Shaw, an artist-become-social-worker, was living in New York. Not long after her daughter was born in 1969, Shaw came out as a lesbian. Dissatisfied with her painting and work life, she became entranced with a street theatre company of drag queens called Hot Peaches. In 1974 she gave away all she had and, with her daughter in tow, went to London to work for, but not perform with, this highly political and rather outrageous cabaret. That same year, though, she went on stage in *The Divas of Sheridan Square* and, while performing in Amsterdam, met Spiderwoman.

Shaw was ready to be with other women and out of the highly competitive and confrontational drag performance milieu, so when the opportunity arose in 1978 she joined Spiderwoman to work on *An Evening of Disgusting Songs and Pukey Images*. Weaver also was ready for changes both personal and artistic. She and Shaw fell in love. Additionally, Weaver had been interviewing her family about two aunts and a great-aunt who had lived together in an old farmhouse in Virginia. She began to develop a play called *Split Britches* (named after the garments worn by women in the fields to facilitate urinating while standing up), in which Shaw would perform.

At the same time, she and Shaw had begun to fantasize about a festival at which some of the theatre produced by women that they had seen in Europe could be performed in New York. Their May, 1980 dream became an October reality called the Women's One World (WOW) Festival at which *Split Britches: A True Story* premiered as a work-in-progress under the auspices of Spiderwoman. The play continued to be developed in workshop with Spiderwoman in late 1980 and early 1981, but Weaver's desire to direct and clashes with the group members over relationships and emotional work led to a difficult split. Shaw and Weaver had hidden their relationship for a year, marginalized by a group whose stated purpose was to speak for marginalized women. Their work in the future was to challenge such marginalization not by focussing on it, but by simply assuming lesbian desire, making a battle over acceptability meaningless.

Deborah Margolin, a fan of Spiderwoman, was invited by a friend to see *Split Britches* when it was remounted in the spring of 1981. She had seen the original, but had not gotten any sense of how it might develop. Although she had no experience in the theatre, she had done some writing and was asked to help with the "connective tissue" of the script. She told of composing madly while in isolation in Boston, being tormented by a mosquito (an event that provided a significant image in the written text), but thrilled by the discovery that writing for the theatre was "the most human-like place I could apply my desire to use language" (interview). Shaw and Weaver used her contributions immediately, and shortly after, Margolin replaced Pamela Verge as Emma in the cast. The version of the play that the three women developed was well received at the Boston Women's Festival and by the end of the second WOW Festival the company of Split Britches, (briefly called Shirley, Goodness and Mercy) had been formed, with what has come to be regarded as a classic piece of women's theatre already to its credit.

Weaver and Shaw had produced, in only two years, thirty-five performances from eight different countries in five different spaces during the WOW festivals. Audience response indicated that there needed to be a permanent space in New York where women could gather and perform. As they have continued to do in their productions since, they reacted to their audience and, in 1982, they founded the WOW Cafe, a venue which is credited with revitalizing East Village performance.[1] On an eight-by-eight-foot stage as many as thirteen women performed simultaneously, took risks in front of one another, and generated excitement that both fed the community and gave Split Britches a safe place to develop its work in front of an audience (a practice the group still maintains).

Split Britches soon began developing a new piece, and preparing for a tour that would take them to Baltimore, Copenhagen for the Fool's Fest, the Netherlands, England, Italy, Germany, Scotland, back to the WOW, and even off-Broadway for a run at the Nat Horne Theatre. Wherever they went in Europe and the United States their performances were well received by audiences, while garnering a revealing mix of published reviews. In this country alone, they were praised by papers as disparate in view as the *New York Post*, the *Village Voice*, and the *Christian Science Monitor*, whose male reviewer called the play "a tiny masterpiece" (Swan). However, though audiences of both sexes responded positively to the production, male reviewers were often unwilling to appreciate the play's dynamic. They complained that it went nowhere, that nothing happened, and that "even Shakespeare knew better than to put three women on stage for over an hour without men" (Weaver, interview). In spite of, or perhaps because of, the company's nonconfrontational performance stance in *Split Britches*, traditional male critics rejected their challenge to both commercial and accepted alternative representational practices.

Split Britches

Nonnarrative in form, and structured much like a piece of chamber music, *Split Britches: A True Story* encapsulates the lives of its three characters, Cora Gearhart (Weaver), the youngest sister, who is "slow" and out of touch with time; Della (Shaw), the older sister, who buries her lesbian desire in the running of the farm; and Emma (Margolin), the nearly senile aunt, whose head swims with barely coherent imagery. The play repeats and defines the boundaries within which these women lived and the fantasies into which they channeled their desires like motifs, drawing multileveled portraits through detail, and developing a fuller sense of lives lived than a rush of narrative events would have allowed. Although begun by Weaver before the company was formed, and less comic and frantic than the pieces developed through their fully collectivized methodology, *Split Britches* is certainly the work of all three company members, and it remains representative of the style and concerns of the theatre for which it has become a signature piece and by whom it is still performed.

And, like music, it is designed to be experienced more than once. Split Britches' productions, because they do not rely on suspense and narrative, are not what Weaver calls "consumable theatre....I didn't understand why once somebody saw a play they felt they had seen it; whereas if they went to hear music they would go back more than once [as they do to art galleries and long retained dance repertoires]. I wanted theatre to be more like that, both in its form and content. Our pieces are...dense, and there are things to be gotten the second time around that you wouldn't get the first time. I like that" (interview).

Split Britches begins with a monologue: Lois Weaver-as-Cora Gearhart-as-Narrator explains the background of the play and the genealogy of herself and the characters. The audience is immediately engaged through the "blurring of the boundaries between person, writer, narrator, and character that will continue throughout the piece" (Petraka 61). The introduction is followed by a series of three-person tableaux, lighted by a slide projector, out of which Cora speaks describing the "slides" or, when the theatre lights come up, from which all characters move into the functions they have established for themselves in their farmhouse in the 1930s. However, even these characters and the space they inhabit are unstable. They improvise their lives, repeating almost ritualized vaudeville turns, suddenly breaking into song or exchanging roles, complaining that they cannot leave their constructed reality and then suddenly walking off stage, and periodically erupting into flights of fantasy—flights which may be memory, or dreams, or only the ramblings of a retarded young or senile old woman.

The script is unified through patterns of repetition and variation and the elaboration through images of themes that would find their way into the company's later plays: the affirmation and celebration of the lives and eccentricities of marginalized women, the fluidity and complexity of identity as a challenge to male-dictated gender ideology, and the mode of theatrical representation of both character and situation that deconstructs (although *explodes* might be a more accurate word) the closed system of narrative continuity with its reification of the dominant social structure. The multilevel richness of their work is often pointed to and intensified by the company's assumption of lesbian desire and identity, although, ironically, this has often led critics to miss many of the work's broader implications by leading them to assume that the challenges to traditional forms and ideologies of representation arise exclusively from an agenda based on sexuality.

It is important to note immediately that the company does not usually begin with a particular thematic area to explore and then structure a play to examine that area. Themes arise, however, from their desire for honest portrayals of what they see as truth. "My political beliefs," said Margolin, "come, like anybody's, from having been hurt, having been discriminated against, having been treated with disrespect in a way that has to do with sex, ethnic background....[I have an] intense commitment to feminism [and] to civil rights" for lesbians (interview). Their flexible collective creation method (discussed later in the chapter) is a way of ensuring that these concerns will be foregrounded theatrically. "Their conception of 'trueness' lies in its playing with narrativity, in its insistent theatricalizing and shifts in perspective that locate these invisible women [in *Split Britches*] in an unstable space of representation revealed in a flickering way on stage" (Petraka 62).

The company's conception of truth denies illusionism, opting instead for the simultaneous display of the characters, the performers, and the theatrical apparatus that binds them. The "meaning" of such a performance lies in the theatre as "event, as a relationship between the company and the audience through the performance" (Buenaventura 47). For political actors that relationship is multilevel. "Above and below fiction, they are making anti-fiction. The affirmation and negation of fiction is a kind of dialectical fundamental relationship with the public" (Buenaventura 50). To Split Britches, realism exists in the actuality of the image in its performance; the event itself functions as metaphor. For example, for Shaw and Weaver, who often appear in butch and femme roles that parody gender conventions, performance on and off stage is a reclaiming of power over "real" identity and over a fictionalized representation that disenfranchises those who challenge dominant patterns of behavior.[2]

In the play *Split Britches*, the concern for the living truth of marginalized women is revealed not only in the choice of characters, but also in the way in which they are elaborated. Rather than focus on the narrative thrust of their story, *Split Britches* examines the details by which people actually create their own histories and communities. Much is made of Cora's ritualized drinking of imaginary tea out of a child's toy teacup—an image that defines her relationship to the world around her—of Emma's pipe lighting, and most significantly, of Della's baking and her refusal to allow her biscuits to be eaten with jam.[3]

Another central issue in Split Britches' work is the ostracism of lesbians in the theatre as well as society at large. Most history and its fictionalization in the theatre assumes that all characters are heterosexual. In this play the company assumed that Della was homosexual: an assumption that allowed Shaw to make use of her own experiences in creating the character, but also allowed the play to work on the audience in an unusual way. Rather than foreground lesbianism as an issue, the play presents a loving portrait of a character that the audience will certainly "identify with and like, and then realize that this is a lesbian....You know, 'This is nice, this is nice; Oh my God, I like a lesbian.'...We create likeable characters working on a lot of levels other than their sexual identity. And then we deal with the sexual identity" (Blair).

Their multifaceted and protean characters raise the issue of the fluidity and constructedness of identity. In a culture that does not permit the open expression of same-sex desire, a lesbian often seems forced to create a series of fantasies which, paradoxically, allow her to be her "real" self—not the masquerading other that society demands. Early in the play, Della refuses to allow Cora to sell her share of the land, insisting that she (Della) makes all the decisions, "Remember?" That word leads Emma to sing "Remember the wings of Gabriel," which introduces Della's pilot fantasy:

> Yeah, wings. They're trying to steal your land, Cora Jane, and I ain't ever comin down...I ain't ever comin' down. You should have seen'em, Emma, you should have seen'em. They were all down there waitin' for me to sign that piece of paper, they were all down there in their city suits waitin' for me. Well when I decided to go down there I walked up them steps and into that office and I opened the door and they were all lookin' at me and what I had on. Well I paid them no mind. I walked into that room and they all stepped back against the wall and when I got in the middle of the room I could feel the sun on my face. I could feel my scarf brush against my cheek. I could hear my leather jacket as I turned and got into that plane. And I took that plane down the runway. And took off up into the sky. And I kept on goin' higher and higher in the sky....I left all the crowds behind me....The sun was gettin' brighter and brighter.[4]

After a brief interruption to hand Emma a fly-swatter, Della continues but this time changes "I" to "she." Later the pilot fantasy resolves itself more fully as Della describes her moment of honest contact with life: when she went to a dance in drag and, unrecognized, danced with all the girls. She dances with Cora and plays an almost stereotypical war pilot's farewell to "his girl." The boundaries of identity dissolve as we realize that the adopted persona is the one that Della plays all the time: Her reality is more a masquerade than her fantasies or "dress up."

Dressing up and undressing is another device used in nearly all Split Britches' plays to indicate multilevel identities and to challenge any diminution of the human spirit, especially that imposed by gender ideology. In *Split Britches* Della removes her layers of clothes, indicating from what threat each piece provides protection or to what oppressive event it is a memorial. Wearing only long underwear, she sings "BD Women," a moment of desperate joy wrenched from the stultifying routines of identity creation with which these women fill their daily lives.

One of the most shocking aspects of the characters' rapid transformations in this play is the sudden realization we have that *they* are aware of what they are doing: They are not merely retarded or senile, but have made conscious adaptations. During a very funny singing-in-the-round of "Hey Diddle Diddle," the characters change places and voices, parodying each others' identities. Significantly, however, although they can occupy each others' spaces, they cannot perform each others' functions: Cora cannot make biscuits and Della can not light Emma's pipe. The characters return to their places, ready to repeat the rituals of the sick cow, of foot washing, of questions about dinner.

There is a certain level of change that would permit escape, but such escape would mean a return to a hostile society. The construction of the world of this play is circular: Even the logic used to decide who should go for help when the cow is sick is designed, much like Abbot and Costello's "Who's on first" routine, to create questions with answers that lead nowhere. Moreover, when it appears as if it is logical for them all to leave, Della uses the fire, for which Emma has been bringing in wood throughout the play, as an excuse to stay: the fire that threatens daily the fragile structure in which these women survive.

> I feel like that farmhouse...and dry. And that fire can make ashes out of me if I ain't careful. Once I had a fire in my pocket. I put my hand in and I pulled it our real quick, and I said, why'd I do that. And I looked in my pocket, and there was the fire, lookin' up at me just cute and sweet as a pretty girl....But then it starts to hurt. So you got to beat it. You got to put it out." (95)

It is the fire of repressed energy, especially repressed sexuality, that threatens to destroy these women and at the same time drives them on.

Interestingly, the other intrusion with which we are presented is through Cora's description of the man who came to the window while she was visiting Blanche, leaving his footprints in the snow, trying to ruin her reputation. Cora protected herself by obliterating the evidence, stamping out the footprints with her own, thus denying the outside, male-dominated freeze as much as Della denies her inner fire.

The play continues, doubling back on itself and interrupting its own development with "slides" that blur the distinctions between creator and created. The women continually reiterate and reinvent the "logic" of their own entrapment: arguing about coming and going until Cora and Della can only stamp and huff at each other; wresting a moment of ironic pleasure in the three-part harmony of "My Man's Gone;" or performing forbidden acts like dancing to hymns, until the final tableau from which Weaver and Margolin describe their own characters' deaths while Shaw/Della delivers the speech quoted above about the fire in her pocket.

The story does not end, however. There has been no climax and no denouement. The sense is more like one might view while watching an artist paint a portrait. The likeness is now there for us to look at, and we are amazed at how much it resembles the subject and how much it reveals. But more than that, we are shocked at how the chaos of individual brush strokes has resolved itself into a whole, and the movement of the artist's hand remains as much a part of the experience as the finished representation.

Those movements, like the speech noted above or any monologue in the play, and like each "slide" as well, could resolve itself in any direction. A case in point is Emma's story of the blind turkey whose relation to the world is defined by his misunderstanding, yet whose body, when cut open, reveals a furnished place to live that is clean and bug-free. The fact that the monologues twist as they do results in part from the creation and acting methods of Split Britches, which echo the challenge to rigidity that is so prevalent in their plays.

Early Performance Style

The acting method, which Weaver calls "multiple choice" acting or impulse acting, is based on her work with Mark Samuels, Muriel Miguel, and others, grounded in "Sound and Movement" techniques developed by Chaikin's Open Theatre in the late sixties, and is guided by the simple dictum that was a principle of Spiderwoman's work: you can be and do anything you want on stage.

Weaver, who has functioned in many ways as the acting tutor for the group, realized that she had never directly applied the actor training techniques used by the Open to either the creation of a text or onstage performance. Sound and movement requires that the actor respond to the impulse: "somewhere between the moment when something occurs and the action; in between that lies the truth. It's not when the action becomes an idea; but somewhere in that moment between when you start to get up and then get up lies the truth" (Weaver, interview). The focus of their acting work is to respond to the moment, thereby challenging the psychological basis of the Method and the causal basis of narrative structure, both of which claim that all action is somehow the result of a logically developed cause, defined either in terms of psychological motivation or situational necessity. In other words, the very acting style of the company deconstructs the notion of inevitability and makes apparent the construction of identity in moments of choice.

Besides, as Weaver noted, "There's a value to not knowing" (Blair) that is attractive to the audience and performers because it is genuinely unpredictable—and the company members' performances *are* exciting. Even the rhythms of the production, "repetitive dialogue and long pauses, suddenly interrupted by bursts of energy and narrative color" (Dolan, "Dynamics" 169), depend on the moments when the pressure of the performance demands a new beat.

This is not to say that their productions are only "accidentally" political, nor that they are haphazardly improvised, but that the generative impulse is performative and theatrical (and far more personal) rather than one engendered by a preconceived notion about how the work on stage should illustrate an idea. "I guess we just try to be honest to our own imagery and our own impulses and how that's informed by how we'd like to see the world" (Weaver, interview). Their reliance on individual choice in the moment, in defiance of the demands of a system, denies inevitability in almost a mirror image of the work of the United Mime Workers, whose productions insist that the need for power *in* the system dominates individual decisions, but the choice *of* system is infinitely variable, based on human needs and desires. In both cases, the apparatuses of coercion and choice are made a subject of the plays through challenges to theatrical systems and their imbedded ideology of representation.

Such an approach implies a deconstruction of the dominant modes of performance. Denial of the conventions of realism and narrative, which "are implicated in relation to patriarchal ideology," is simultaneously a disruption of "the theatrical institution, with its accretions of cultural convention and inscription of a dominant system of representation [which] operates to inhibit radicality (e.g., feminism) in service of the ideology which informs its tradition" (Forte 115). Even their collective process, which builds a performance (and the script before that) from the small up to the large, denies any metanarrative and subverts predetermined interpretations, instead opening up "the negotiation of meaning to contradictions, circularity, and multiple viewpoints" (Forte 117) related to gender, class, race, sexuality, age, etc.

In addition, the highly theatricalized presentation of character as construction, which is in many ways the most striking feature of the company's later productions, provides a challenge to both Method acting's psychological determinism (dominated by the blatant misogyny of Freud) and the atheatrical, or perhaps antitheatrical, "assumption behind much of the experimental theatre and performance of the 1960's...that because the presence of the actor as one living human being before others is spiritually and psychologically liberating, pure presentation of performer to audience is the best means available to the theatre to make a radical spiritual/political statement" (Auslander, "Toward" 24). This performance definition remains part of the concept of presence in the ritualistic performances of cultural feminist companies.[5] Split Britches' approach to representation, however, is materialist and Brechtian. "Naturalism is never enough for me. I wanted to do the character and comment on it at the same time. I sometimes think [that desire] comes from growing up in the mountains. The way the foothills grow into the mountains grow into the trees and then double back on each other" (Weaver, interview).

When, during the work on their next production, *Beauty and the Beast*, this acting approach became infused by the company's developing collective method, by Shaw's flair for the fabulous and Margolin's flair for language, by the group's love of vaudevillian turns, and by a clearer articulation of the members' political sensibilities, the signature elements of the company's performance mode, delicately outlined in *Split Britches*, became a recognizable style, providing a flexible and expanding paradigm for their approach to performance since 1982.

THE METHOD

Split Britches' collective creation process is in part a result of its members' individual backgrounds and in part accident, but mostly it came about because of the ways in which their desire to make theatre and the condition of women in the traditional theatre hierarchy are incompatible. While their work is consciously radical, it is not merely an attempt to articulate a political stand nor agitate for programmatic concerns. It is thoroughly grounded in theatricality and in an understanding of the relationship of the performer to the audience. "A lot of groups starting doing theatre for political reasons rather than theatrical reasons. Because we are theatre people...we'd be doing theatre even if everything was fine in the world. We'd still be doing theatre and trying to make it funny" (Weaver, interview).[6] The three, somewhat bizarre, yet highly responsive sensibilities that form this company have found a way to combine their predilections into a process that relies more fully than any of the other collectives so far described on the metaphoric "center," and yet has much in common with other groups for whom form and representation dominate concerns over reception.

Their task-oriented work begins with a period of unstructured "gripe" sessions during which company members bring the events and pressures of their lives into direct contact with each other. It is instructive to note how these early meetings were described by each performer. Peggy Shaw, who is acknowledged to be the most physical and action-oriented of the company, said "We hold things inside, burning thing....All the garbage that's been stored in our physical bodies since we made the last show just comes throwing up into the rehearsal process and the writing process" (interview). Lois Weaver, who is counted on to have the clearest sense of the piece being created as a whole, noted that themes, related ideas, and stories are discussed in the early work; while the person with the most responsibility for scripting, Deborah Margolin, said that the decision to do a new piece "puts a certain tenderness in everybody's thoughts and a certain receptiveness to any weird observations and fantasies they may have" (interview). Regardless of early ways of approaching conversations, it is clear from all company members that talking is the key to the early work. Like the United Mime Workers and the Dakota Theatre Caravan, Split Britches finds that the life of the group begins in the ways in which members share what they have to offer and the staged mediation does not start until ideas are being generated from the center.

As is every rehearsal, these early meetings are "scribed": a notebook of every idea, image, impulse is kept as a source for a "charting" procedure later in the process. Meanwhile, company members begin to create lists under headings of those things that seem to warrant further consideration: for example, themes, songs, things that disgust us (the starting place for *Little Women*), or things we would like to do or see others do on stage (an important part of the development of *Beauty and the Beast*).

The talk in this and all stages is uncensored and in-depth. This is a gathering process, and the relevance of any particular image or story is not a consideration: It will, if the idea is appropriate, become apparent later. Much of the work that appears on stage comes from this process of eclectic gathering. Company members bring in any material that they want: moments of significance from other activities, written work they find, odd items that point to human eccentricities gathered at Salvation Army stores, and "accidental imagery" that occurs in the impulse and image work that the company does on its feet (usually after a focal idea is discovered; it is responsible, for example, for the binoculars scene at the beginning of *Little Women*).

It is important to note that two elements of structure are important here: imagery (with its attendant elements of fantasy and desire), and narrative, the latter of which is conspicuous by its absence. Choices are based on association and discovery in the moment rather than on the demands of illusionism and linear narration, and the entire process is informed by the assertion of the company members (all women, two lesbian) that the hierarchical, heterosexual, and male-dominated structures of traditional theatre practice cannot dictate the limits of possibility to them. There is a reclaiming of the process of creation that allows it to develop for the stage performances and characters who reconfigure in a highly theatrical manner real people/women, in direct opposition to the fictional representation of class and gender that pervades the conventions of the realistic narrative. The aim is to allow the stage to be peopled with characters who are true *because of* their theatricalization, to create an art that has, as part of its content, its relationship to dominant ideology and is therefore held within it, but consciously. In French Marxist Louis Althusser's terms, it "manages to distance itself from it, to the point where it permits us to 'feel' and 'perceive' the ideology from which it springs" (Eagleton 18). Margolin uses the image of "ideas that just get thrown up in the air and as they fall, they fall in the form of dialogues or monologues....They fall into the deep place that people need to speak from even though the lines may be abstracted from the situation in which they [originally] appeared" (Margolin,interview).

The process of list making and talking continues at the same time that the parameters for focus on a particular idea are being drawn. It is during this period that musical numbers, a defining element in the company's burlesque approach, are chosen and the process of learning them begins with Margolin at the piano. The company, which is without what would be called a strong singer in commercial circles, performs close harmonies that are not only well executed, but also sonorous. Music becomes another theatrical form of address, disrupting yet commenting on the action, demanding a response, and providing an element of pure fun.

The scripting, staging, designing, and rehearsal take place almost simultaneously from this point on. Although Margolin is usually responsible for scripting, all members of the company have written at some point. Although Shaw is nominally the designer, the restrictions caused by the need for touring and the ways in which the images and language resolve themselves in the first place often dictate design directions. And, while Weaver is the resident director and acting coach, performances and staging are often more closely related to scene and image development than directorial "concept."

Characters are chosen about three-fourths of the way through the process. Split Britches tries to find eccentric characters because, according to Shaw, they are more "real" than the stage representations that are so often seen. The company members make it clear that they want to be able to do anything they want on stage, but their actions are tempered by a respect for the truth behind the characters', and their own, lives. Shaw traces this desire to her "working class ethic—our premise for the group, our real desire...is to love our characters, even if they're evil people, or bad people, or religious people, or whatever they are; we don't see the purpose of portraying them unless we love them" (interview). The impetus comes not only from Shaw's working class background (until the late eighties she was a stone mason, painter, and wall paperer), but from her knowledge that the working class people with whom she feels most at home (both as characters and audience) are the very people who would "be the first to punch me in the face for being a lesbian" (interview). By treating their characters with love and respect at the same time that they comment on their foibles, the actors are educating their audiences to the human values that allow people to escape from fear and prejudice, from homophobia and anti-Semitism.

This multifaceted goal necessitates the inclusion of monologues, during which characters are developed in front of the audience, but more important, the relationships between character and performer and audience are reconfigured. For example, in the monologue quoted at the beginning of this chapter, Shaw addresses the audience, noting the actual performance situation (they are indeed in a small theatre watching a lesbian mother), but without dropping the performative elements of her character (accent, movement style, and attitude). In *Little Women* Weaver takes questions from the audience about the performance and performers, but mixes the answers to them with answers to unheard questions "asked" of Louisa May Alcott, without differentiating between the terms of actor and character address. These challenges to the objectification of performer and performed are often built on images from the lives of the company members in and out of the theatre, which were tossed into the center during the talking process before writing.

The writing process focuses on small pieces, as scenes are written before connective tissue is discussed. Margolin functions as conduit for the group's ideas ("Scenes begin to get written" she said in an interview). Her task, as she sees it, is to take the images "from the person and put them back into the mouth of the character, so that the writing style goes with the acting style. Lois teaches a very layered method so that you have many many things under the line you say. You're not left alone with just you, your beating heart, and the line of text" (interview). It is important to note that the group does not stage its process, although much of the development of the finished product happens in front of an audience, nor does it stage its members' lives, although much of the impetus for their work is very personal and experiential. Split Britches presents a product for which it takes full responsibility, justified by the members' assumption that they can trust their own lives to be representative of their audience's confrontations with the world. "I'm able to offer people back their own lives in a way that doesn't have to do with the way I initially found out about them" (Margolin, interview).

In most instances, Margolin writes scenes that are brought to the rest of the group for changes through discussion and rehearsal. She describes her writing as the skill to *say* the things that the collective *saw*, and shows no sense of ownership or pride of authorship in the written work. Shaw also writes and (it seemed to me as I watched the company work with students on a performance development project at Hampshire College) has a wonderful ear for the way in which language works as sound. Weaver frequently functions as editor, actually talking over a scene with Margolin while she is sitting at the typewriter, and thus directing and scripting occur simultaneously. At other times Weaver's vision of the completed project, which is arrived at in part by charting the flow of ideas and images from the notebooks of discussions, will lead her to ask for specific written support, particularly after the company has begun discussing the connective tissue that will tie the scenes together. For example, during the later work on *Upwardly Mobile Home*, she asked for an "eating scene," which Margolin wrote by elaborating on images in the notebook, using her own life experiences "to augment or decorate any idea I wish" (Margolin, interview) and her own vision of absurdity to make it funny.

While it sounds as if Margolin has a great degree of autonomy once the scripting begins, what she feels she has is an understanding of the core of the company members' desires and a facility for translating those desires into language. As Shaw put it, "her writing comes from our hearts" (interview). When scenes are brought to meetings, they are the subject of much discussion; issues are usually resolved by talking (although Shaw noted that as opening approaches, "If someone has an idea, I tend to jump up and do it") and the group only reluctantly gets on its feet.

And only reluctantly do they put a piece in front of an audience. Although the process as I have described it seems to be constantly moving toward development of a performance, it really focuses on the development of a desire that can be scripted and performed. While the interaction between company members is loving and supportive, it is also brutally honest and, because the process is cumulative, it can appear never-ending. A show is usually mounted (put "literally on its knees") in front of an audience because the company has committed to a date and provided a title. First performances are usually review-like, skeletal, and without much of the connective tissue that will unify the piece when it is fully developed—after six months to a year of performances. This is not to say that Split Britches has little to offer during early performances, but that the nature of the piece is clearly "work-in-progress" and that its potential is certainly part of the experience.

The pressure as the company nears the last steps of the development process is striking. Shaw explained that before every opening, "We almost break. It's like putting your guts on the stage all the time. It's very exhausting." "Agonizing" is the way Weaver described the end of the process; it "makes you want to die, throw up, and cry all the time" while Margolin said that getting to the root of what the company wants to say "is very painful sometimes; it's disgusting, actually. It seems to have no end; it's like hell sometimes," but she went on to note that the actual scripting is relatively easy. (interviews)

Personal issues begin to affect the working relationships, and frequently, the first hour of rehearsals is devoted to "personal agony." While this sounds destructive, it is not. This time provides a pressure valve that allows for task-focused concentration later. Such a dynamic of interaction style seems to come with the territory. Michelene Wandor, who was studying British groups working in some of the same areas as Split Britches, wrote, "In all groups, the collective process of control over a product which in itself contained a radical approach to sexual politics, directly affected the working relations within the groups" (10). Split Britches' procedures mitigate against this effect by supporting company members' artistic projects outside the collective. Actually, the rhythm of coming together and separating developed by the company accounts for its ability to stay together in spite of some of the same interpersonal issues that have caused ruptures in other groups. As a side benefit, their work alone and in other venues generates experiences that fertilize the collective work.

A great deal of the work of development continues in performance, much the same way that a stand-up comic (a performance style with which Split Britches work has much in common) hones routines. Plays usually open in front of responsive audiences (often at WOW) who know the company and participate in its off-stage life. In a reversal of the commercial theatre tactic, the shows open and are developed in New York before they go on the road. Scenes continue to be written, bits are refined or discarded (*Beauty and the Beast* was a two and a half hour review when it first opened) and the piece both shapes and is shaped by the responses of its audiences. The performers do not watch videotapes, nor do they seek out "educated" theatre voices. Rather, they work in known venues until they sense that it is time to set and rehearse the script.

Not one of the company members could describe clearly the staging process. Although it seems to be, in part, a traditional process, with Weaver moving bodies around the set for maximum effect, there is a prestaging process that provides a collectively developed guide for the blocking work. During a rehearsal for the Alcestis Project (at Hampshire College) which occurred at the point when workshops were ending but rehearsal had not clearly begun yet, Shaw and Weaver were developing an image-as-impulse into an exploration of circling (which defined the relationship of characters clearly at this stage of development). Margolin sat out, calling for extensions of what she saw developing on stage, and pushing the performers toward an elaboration of the image. While there was no directing of the action, it was clear that the image would resolve itself physically (as well as in Margolin's script) and would become more-or-less ready to be put on stage. Clearly their method maintains its basis in theatricality and leads to the creation of a performance text more than a written one.

Even after the work has been on the boards for long enough to write and polish all scenes, the company does not consider it to exist in the form of ink on paper. Since pieces stay in repertory once they are developed and are returned to from a distance, sometimes ongoing workshops or training are needed to keep a piece alive: "to return to the deep place from which a piece came, to rediscover the reasons why we're doing a piece and the impulses that lie underneath it" (Margolin, interview). So much of what is constructed is based on a theatrical attitude that they do not feel the scripted work presents any clear guide for a performer or any real indication of how the performance is designed to appeal to an audience.

For example, many observers of their performances comment on the fact that "feminism and lesbianism appear in the shows not as issues but as givens... drawn from the women's lives" (Solomon, "WOW" 100). Because of this, the performance ambiance becomes part of the dismantling of the conventions of representation, thereby forcing the audience to "read" the performance text from a new perspective. Jonathan Culler's development of reception theory, which "locates the organizing principle of textual interpretation not in the reader but in the institutions that teach readers to read" (Davy, "Constructing" 44), helps explain the inadequacy of Split Britches' written texts to elicit the response they seek through performance. Since the institutions that teach most audiences are based on the assumption of heterosexual and male dominated cultural norms, readers of the written text will almost assuredly assume these constructs to be guiding principles. However, when an audience is presented with on stage action that assumes a different "axis of categorization," then the conventions associated with the ideological assumptions and their manifestations in popular forms are foregrounded. Therefore, when "lesbianism is assumed[,]...the conventions of popular forms become startling instead" (Dolan, "Dynamics" 167).

In other words, the assumption of a feminist subject can only be made manifest in performance where its presentation can challenge the assumptions of a genderized subject. It is unfortunate that many critics seem to assume that the audience must *enter* the theatre denying the "normalcy" of heterosexuality to clearly see the implications of Split Britches' performances. Their theatre is not exclusively for lesbians just because it is performed by women of whom two are lesbian, any more than it is for Jews because one of the members of the company is Jewish, nor do its audiences have to be lesbian or Jewish to be challenged by the productions. If they did, then any chance of initiating change or teaching would be lost in the need to preach to the converted, and the company insists on its desire to effect change in perceptions. Split Britches does not separate art and politics, yet no one in the company articulates any political philosophy as a starting place except feminism. "We're a stridently feminist company. I'm not saying our politics aren't important; they're critical, but they're not exclusive....We don't slam the door, and we probably never will" (Margolin, interview).

In spite of their theatrical focus, the charge levelled against many collectives, even by their apologists, that their scripts are "inelegant [and] strategically vague," even if engaging (Keyssar, "Feminist" 168), would be inappropriate here. The music and humor of the company's sensibility charges the dialogue of each script. The monologues quoted above are both functional and viable as dramatic literature. Margolin's macaronic Shakespearean prose for the play-within-a-play in *Beauty and the Beast* is both literate and hilarious, while the flow of the language in *Little Women* is funny, challenging, and often as shocking as, to borrow an image from one of their own pieces, eating a bowl of mirror fragments for breakfast.

Their work ultimately denies the distinction between written text and performance text, denying by implication the ideologically encumbered prescriptions for organization behind acceptable play structures and, further, denying the standards by which the canon of "great plays" has been defined.

THE "DISCOVERY" OF VAUDEVILLE—THE EARLY 1980s

Buoyed by success at the Boston Women's and second WOW festivals, Split Britches began work almost immediately on a new piece. "We really had a good time together [doing *Split Britches*]. Then we heard Debbie played the piano and we wanted to do a cabaret and before we knew it we had this other show" (Shaw, interview). The show, *Beauty and the Beast*, premiered in March 1982 at WOW.

Although the play was over two-and-a-half hours long and less than fully developed, the company took it on tour with *Split Britches* during the spring of that year. Beginning at the Fool's Festival in Amsterdam, continuing through Europe, (establishing contacts in Great Britain that are still important), and returning to the United States, the company toured almost constantly until the spring of the following year. After particularly good reviews in the *Village Voice* of performances at the Open Gate theatre, *Split Britches* moved to theatre row.

During periods in New York, the company was also involved in a "story-telling mode" adaptation of the novel *Patience and Sarah* for performances at WOW. Aimed at a lesbian audience, the play adapts in a relatively naturalistic manner the narrative of the lesbian love story. There was "nothing obscure or abstract. [It was] a piece of popular theatre. It was our community theatre. It was not *our* work, but it was satisfying work that reached a community of women—a straight lesbian audience—that we otherwise wouldn't reach" (Weaver, interview).

Even though the company was only two years old, the amount of travel was already affecting the way in which its members felt about their participation. It is Split Britches' solution to the problem of different personal needs that has kept the company together and vibrant to the present. Basically, Weaver loves to tour while Margolin wants to stay in New York more often. In the summer of 1983, Weaver and Shaw took a production of *Patience and Sarah* to London while Margolin developed other performance work in New York. After their return, the piece was modified to include Margolin.

At the same time, the ideas that would lead to their next play, *Upwardly Mobile Home*, "began to ferment, because we were feeling very disillusioned. A lot of people we knew had stopped living an alternative life style and had started getting jobs on Wall Street...Friends were spending money on Broadway but not coming to see us. [We were] very disillusioned about the economic reality of our life style choices" (Weaver, interview). Although they were working "day jobs" to support themselves, Weaver "wanted to buy a van and be a gypsy and a vagrant" (interview). The differences between the members' desires is the root of the comic of tension from which much of the humor in *Upwardly Mobile Home* grows.

By March 1984 the company was performing regularly again, doing the new play in New York and taking it on a fall tour of Europe with *Patience and*

Sarah. At the same time there were increased demands on Shaw and Weaver at WOW, which had become a growing café, mounting full productions and involving a greater portion of the women's community, particularly lesbians, than ever before. When they returned to New York near the end of the year, the company members needed to focus on personal and political demands. Although they continued to work together, it was not until 1988 that their next fully collectivized creation was mounted.

Beauty and the Beast

However, the vibrancy of the company in front of an audience did not wane during those years because of the vibrancy of the material created earlier. *Beauty and the Beast*, the most politically direct of all their plays, was originally a series of vaudeville-like bits that the company maintains arose purely from the desire to do a vaudeville cabaret. That choice, though, is still a result of the deep-seated political sensibility of the company members and their assumption of power over their medium. Shaw talked about vaudeville's excitement and variety ("You can wait for the next bit if one fails"), but was quick to add that the form contains elements that communicate to working class audiences, that it is neither dated nor geographically dependent, and that it provides the performers with the opportunity to play roles that are free from those dependencies as well (interview).

In its initial stages, the three cast members played a series of roles in front of rather fully articulated sets. The company soon discovered the performance expediency and political efficacity of layering roles: of allowing a performer to play multiple roles simultaneously. The resulting play-within-a-play format presents a performance by a ragtag Salvation Army troupe (one of whom is a Hasidic rabbi) of "Beauty and the Beast" and of assorted oleo's (entr'actes), as a way to deliver the words of salvation to its audience. The two-level structure allows the company to play all the roles it wants in a shorter time (less than ninety minutes), but mostly it disrupts traditions of gender representation and narrative seamlessness to reveal the imbedded assumptions behind those traditions. As well, the juxtaposition of the fairy tale, songs, contemporary commentary, and entr'actes creates a montage that raises additional questions about the fluidity of identity and the meaning of performance. Besides, the piece is outrageously funny.

For example, Shaw plays troupe member Gussie Umburger, an eighty-four-year-old woman who thinks she is James Dean, is in love with Sergeant Ratledge (Weaver), and often can not tell the difference between one level of performance and the other—between her personal life and her character lives in "Beauty." When Beauty's father mentions a cup of tea, Gussie (who entered playing the role of messenger) drops her role to state that caffeine makes her nervous, and then continues to list her ailments while the others try to return to the play. Every time Beauty and her father (Margolin/Rabbi Hitchcock Rabin) express their devotion to each other, Gussie becomes jealous. Finally, during entr'actes, especially one in which Shaw lip-syncs Perry Como's "It's Impossible," the audience is not certain if it is watching Shaw as Como or Gussie as Como (Perry Como was introduced as a performer in the opening speech of the play), making explicit the third level: the performers whose image life is being created and simultaneously fictionalized in front of the audience.

The play begins as Weaver announces from off stage that the audience is about to see an "absurd drama of ridiculous people, out-dated morals, and watchwords and jokes for a nuclear age."[7] Carrying an accordion and garbed in a black skirt-suit with a superwoman emblem replacing the Salvation Army sign, Weaver introduces the company. Each actor is introduced more than once—Margolin, for example, is introduced first as ballerina Natasha Macaroni, even though she is wearing a yarmulke and rabbinical garb. She then pretends to be a ventriloquist's dummy, and finally is introduced as the rabbi. Questions about playing a role and assuming one are immediately raised, as they were in the opening monologue of *Split Britches.*

Also introduced is Patricia Nixon's cloth coat. Patricia, who "had a stroke and right after that she redid her floors," is greatly admired, though it is significant that her role as the epitome of righteous womanhood is represented by a nondescript costume item. Supposedly the head of the Nuclear Regulatory Commission is in the audience and is introduced as well.

The fairy-tale enactment, introduced by a sign which reads "Scene one. Scene them all," is clearly a critique of the patriarchal family in which women are "conditioned to equate dependence and self-sacrifice with femininity (and goodness)" (Margolis 77). Written in overblown Elizabethan style, the story follows the traditional narrative. Beauty's father, when he is about to leave on a business trip, asks Beauty what she desires as a souvenir gift upon his return. Gussie, as Beauty's sister, requests "an older woman, nuclear disarmament, passage of the ERA before I die," but Beauty asks only for a rose. Her father picks one of the Beast's roses, for which he is sentenced to imprisonment in the Beast's castle. Beauty volunteers to live with the Beast (Shaw in Gussie's dress overlaid with a regal cape) to fulfill her father's obligation (although the "volunteering" scene clearly indicates that the father is manipulating and that Weaver—or is it Rutledge?—is aware of what is going on, even if Beauty is not). She of course falls in love with the beast, and after saving him/her with a kiss, lives with Beast/Shaw happily ever after.

The performance of the fairy tale is interrupted frequently by the Salvation Army troupe itself, sometimes because they drop character to argue about lines or behavior, and other times because they perform oleos. It is significant that as the play progresses, what would have been interruptions in the narrative flow become parts of the fairy tale-as-play, pointing to the seduction of the patriarchal narrative and the clarity of role/function in it. For example, early songs like

"Kitty from Kansas City," performed by the cast wearing 1930s dresses hanging on loops around their necks, or routines like Hitchcock's desperately unfunny stand-up comedy monologue and Rutledge's dramatic reading of Lady Macbeth's "unsex me here" speech (during which she discovers the orgasmic pleasure of hatred), are clearly outside the internal play. Later, though, "Heard It through the Grapevine" is part of the internal play, and "routines" like the interwoven monologues of Shaw/Gussie/Beast as James Dean and Weaver/Rutledge/Beauty as Katherine Hepburn seem to be intertwined with all levels. Gussie's warning to the audience in the middle of the Beast's near-death scene not to be fooled by death scenes (or assassination attempts on Reagan, or even faked film footage of men walking on the moon) dismantles the already ridiculed emotional power of story.

The Dean-Hepburn segment is occasioned when Beast, trying to convince Beauty to marry him, says she will be Tracey to Beauty's Hepburn. It is comic, poignant, and thematically clear as it traces role-playing in lesbian affairs and the discovery of lesbian love. Based as it is on elements of the performers' lives, it is a superb example of the way in which the company uses images in a theatrical context.

> This willingness on the part of lesbian playwrights to locate their work in theatre conventions, rather than in the illusionless documentation of most cultural feminist performance art, allows for the use of fantasy to imagine different realities. Gender roles, for example, are reimagined along an expanded continuum. Sexuality and desire, as opposed to being banished as problematic taboos, are continually present as subtext in these performances. The presence of lesbian desire, in fact, helps to refashion the manner in which gender and sexual roles are played in both performance and reality. Basing their work in the conventions of theatre also allows these performers to comment on and manipulate the traditional gender-coded performance apparatus. (Dolan, "Dynamics" 169–70)

Although not specifically about Split Britches, the passage above certainly is applicable to their work, except for the fact that Margolin, who does most of the scripting, is not lesbian (Weaver and Shaw refer to her as "heterosexual, but not straight"). As noted earlier, pointing to the significance of the company's theatricality and multilayered performances for lesbians is only a partial recognition of their implications. For example, the contributions to the script of Margolin's love-hate relationship with her character, and the moment during which the woman-as-rabbi vehemently denies her own sex to the seeming horror and confusion of the other performers, are as important a challenge to traditional gender/sex role assignments, valuation, and desire as is the elaboration of the butch/femme sensibility. The assumption of lesbian desire in the play foregrounds the apparatus that marginalizes lesbians more than it is a performance of lesbian desire for public consumption.

Split Britches creates a parody of the type of burlesque reviews in which women usually appear as elaborately decorated objects. "Through the use of deliberately naive sets [note: the original sets were replaced by small drops], props and costumes, the performers turn the conventions inside-out, revealing the way social order works against the best interest of women" (Margolis 76). The irony of a rabbi, who had just portrayed Beauty's manipulative father, suddenly donning a tutu over his religious garb to dance as Beauty in a ballet, only to be lifted by the Beast and suddenly assuming the role of foul-mouthed ventriloquist's dummy railing against the sexist comments that men make to women in the street, provides a striking example.

Significant as well is the way in that the somewhat anarchic form of *Beauty and the Beast*, with its rejection of an Aristotelian sense of order (and its coercive limitations), parallels the development of the company's collective method, with its rejection of hierarchical and one-directional models. The performance seems to embody the associative structure of the "center" which gives life to images without the limitations of individual ownership or assumptions about (particularly gender) propriety; in other words, without a predetermined subject position. "What is the difference between an actor, a celebrity, a social role, or a self-conscious system of gestures? Which character is the owner of the play, the protagonist, the 'lead,' the subject of the drama? If there is something like a subject position in this kind of performance, it is that of a collective subject" (Jenkins 313). The impulse work, and the development of scenes without narrative demands for linear character development, promote a "deliberate player/role discontinuity [which] replaces the aura of inevitability in player/role pairings (whether in theatre or in society) with a dynamic displacement which implies the possibility of experiment and choice."[8] The play confounds traditions and challenges the audience to participate in the acceptance of choice.

Although the play's challenge appealed to most critics and audiences, it is worth noting that a review in the *New York Times* called the play tasteless and disgusting, focusing on the offensive portrayal of the rabbi. The reviewer did find hilarious the portrayal of a nun by a man on the same bill. It is not surprising that the nun, who is an eccentric because of dress and celibacy, and clearly a subservient female figure in a male-dominated institution, would be accepted as an object of ridicule. To be forced to face a figure of male domination, who begs from the audience for money to buy Torahs, and by implication to be forced to face anti-Semitic attitudes, did, however, unnerve this traditional female reviewer.

While the company is not particularly interested in battling narrow-minded reviewers (Weaver said about the *Times* reaction, "I'd be really worried if they liked us."), there are things about their image, and the interpretations of their performance work that do trouble them. Split Britches does not wish to be labeled into a new marginality. Labels define and then dispense with the thing that they supposedly name. The company demands that the audience know it is feminist and that lesbian desire is part of its performances, but they do not want to be labeled in a way that defines who should be in the audience, who should understand the plays, and what performance vocabulary is appropriate.

> We make strong statements and we like to think that they are non-denominational. Other people would like to just have women [at our performances]. They say "how can you work in front of men? Well, they paid to come and see it, and we have to pay the rent....and I think a man can certainly enjoy these pieces. I would not wish to alienate a man and prevent him from learning something about me and about himself and about the world and having a few laughs and seeing and feeling. I will not be told by men what kind of theatre to do, but any man's welcome to come see my show.[9]

In addition, an exclusive label would specify their theatre as outside the usual, thereby valorizing male and heterosexual theatre by implication because it does not "need" to be labeled.

A second concern is for the autonomy of their productions: writers have brought to their analyses of Split Britches their own agendas which, at times, have obscured the nature of the actual performance. Their plays are political because their lives are political, and while they welcome interpretation and readily acknowledge that theory and technique discussions apply to their work (although they very rarely have them themselves), they do not want such analyses to deny the way in which their theatrically based performance attitude is the source of the actual *stuff* that appears on stage. "The group's gritty, non-compromising sensibility is its sharpest piece of politics" (105) wrote Laurie Stone in a review of *Beauty and the Beast*, and I believe the group would agree.[10]

During interviews, every member of the company stated that, in one way or another, "We just tried to tell our stories the best way we could; and we wanted to be funny and loud and raucous and crazy. And we wanted to reclaim a lot of roles that had been denied us" (Weaver). However, beneath the outrageous comedy, without ever inhibiting it, is a "larger structure; the slapstick, the burlesque, the painful inappropriateness of some of the things some of the characters try to do. We try to love unlovable characters. We try to go from what hurts us" (Margolin, interview).

Upwardly Mobile Home

The basis in pain is very clear in *Upwardly Mobile Home*, the next collective creation. Once again the performances are layered: the company members play a street theatre preparing for a performance of the 1920s revenge tragedy *The Shanghai Gesture*, while living in a van under the Brooklyn Bridge, on which sits a friend who is trying to win them a new recreational vehicle, which is first prize in a bridge sitting marathon. In it, "a bizarre sense of humor combines with a barrage of intersecting ideas to create a complex criticism of American myths. Formally inventive, the piece follows a day in the life of these actresses, with overlapping monologues, songs, and play-within-a-play sequences" (Solomon, "WOW" 99). While the constructedness of identity under the hegemony of these cultural myths is important to the play, more than any other of their pieces *Upwardly Mobile Home* is about presentation and representation: about how human beings relate to each other through performance.

The play opens with an obliquely expository sequence of complaints about the lack of rehearsal time, the lack of milk for coffee, and the sexism and racism of the *Shanghai Gesture* script. Each character, although they are ostensibly a family, has her own accent and seems to be the product of a completely different cultural background. Tammy Whynot (Weaver) is a would-be country singer with a Southern accent, whose first speech of the morning is a description of a dream in which she was picked up by a woman who thought she was Jesus Christ, went to her apartment, and then to Burger King for coffee. Lavine (Margolin) is the director of the troupe's performance, their daily schedule is on her clipboard, and "breadwinner," earning her living by taking surveys about products over the phone. Her accent is New York and her elongation of "yes hon" on the telephone is stereotypical. Peggy Shaw, herself a lesbian mother, plays Mother, who "grandly declaims cliches and aphorisms with the authority of Confucius and the tone of Maria Ouspenskaya, punctuating them with a mirthless laugh" (Cumbow).

The sense of absurdity is as full in this play as in *Beauty and the Beast*, but the humor is much darker and the pace much more cerebral. The daily routine (they have been living under the bridge for six weeks) is punctuated by rehearsals of the play-within-a-play, family arguments, conversations with invisible customers for the used clothes that Tammy tries to peddle, and performances for agents. Most clearly thematic, however, are three monologues about the performer-audience relationship. The pain and desperation of these segments of direct audience address is made particularly disconcerting by the fact that the actors-as-actors, accents and attitudes intact, deliver them.

The development of these monologues is particularly revealing. One of the ideas which arose in the company during discussions concerned the conflicting elements of the individual personality—the pragmatic, the social/conscience, and the physical/sexual/emotional. They decided that the best way to examine them was to embody them in three different characters (Lavine, Mother, and Tammy, respectively). At about the same time, a friend gave the company two old records, one of which was the *Shanghai Gesture*, with which Shaw and Margolin became obsessed. This piece, about the Medea-like revenge of Chinese woman Mother Goddam, who is sold into prostitution by Sir Guy Charteris, her British lover, and which is full of overt racism and serpentine plot twists, was derided by critics when it opened on Broadway in 1926 as "pernicious" and "dreary dirt." It ran for 1,280 performances, and no one ever complained about the problems of representation in the script which are so obvious to audiences now.

In spite of the fact that the company had definite characters and a plot line to connect pieces of *Gesture*, only a week before opening there were no monologues. "Inspired by the pressure of performance" (Shaw, interview), company members sat in the corners of a room and wrote their own monologues. All are about performance, all are in the play, and they are among the most striking individual pieces in the company's repertoire.

The first to be delivered is the "Lesbian mother" speech, which was partially quoted at the beginning of the chapter. "Without dropping her Eastern European character, Shaw directly addresses the spectators. . .She makes the audience aware that it is separate from her fantasy, disrupting the normal theatre convention that requires suspension of disbelief" (Dolan, "Dynamics" 169). In fact, the speech places the audience in the uncomfortable position of having to take responsibility for watching, because Shaw knows she is being watched, Mother knows she is being watched, and the audience knows it is consuming her/their watched performance(s). The monologue begins:

> When I was young I went to a fair. I saw a sign to see a fat lady for twenty-five cents. I paid my twenty-five cents and I walked into the tent. I was alone. It was a big tent....[The fat lady] was alone. I looked at her; she looked at me. She knew I had come to see her being fat. I still remember the daylight seeping through the pin holes in the tent. I ran out of the tent, exhausted. I was that fat lady—she was me. I was tricked. [The sign] promised me entertainment. It gave me much more.[11]

After a brief pause to sing "Real Gone Cat" (the play's leitmotif) in a weak child-voice, the monologue continues through the parts quoted previously and ends with:

> I wear rings for every time I see a fat lady. I wear beads for every time I cry. If I lose my beads and my rings I have my memories. If I sell my beads and my rings I have money to buy food. When I am rich I will buy my mother a house, a car, and a family.

It is a shocking monologue, performed brilliantly, demanding the audience take a new perspective.

The second monologue comes after the funniest moment in the play. Certain that the Yiddish theatre will revive, Lavine has arranged an audition by the family with Mr. Roistitcher, a theatre owner. All three actors climb into one huge skirt to sing "I Like to be in America" from *West Side Story* in Yiddish, chosen, Lavine says "because that ethnicity translates so well." The image of three women singing in an inappropriate language with which only one of them is at all comfortable, moving like a black "girl group" performing a white male's sanitized vision of Puerto Rican life in the big city, provides a collision of falsehoods and stereotypes. There is "something about making this song expatriate from its mother tongue and dragging it into another language where it stands there with its teeth chattering in its underwear that I think is emblematic of the kind of specific sensibility that I bring" said Margolin (interview).

When the agent leaves, Lavine is too depressed to work and interrupts a rehearsal to deliver a monologue that asserts her abilities ("I'm a good actress...and I'm very feminine"), begs for recognition, and finally screams at the audience to leave. "I know what you're thinking." Tammy's monologue, delivered shortly after, begins as a list of all the minor horrors that she is tired of, and resolves itself into a dream (in sequined jacket) of singing "Your Good Girl's Gonna Go Bad," a country western song about a wife who will "cheapen" herself to be what her husband desires. The singing here is purposefully terrible and wildly nonrhythmic, but is followed almost immediately by an a capella performance of "Sentimental Gentleman" in which the three part harmony is strikingly good. (At another point in the show Margolin does a phenomenally awful and emotional performance of "Who Knows" from *West Side Story*, desperately begging the world for an event as if the song was an actual character speech, all the while stripping off her street costume to reveal the strapless red evening gown that she will wear as Sir Guy in *The Shanghai Gesture*.)

The family receives a note via a pail from above that Little Lost Petal (the bridge sitter) has met a woman with a co-op apartment and is leaving the bridge to settle down with her. The company performs *Gesture* anyway, all in fabulous gowns.

The play as they perform it focuses, as does *Beauty*, on the manipulation of women in patriarchal society and on race and class exploitation (exactly the opposite of the blithely sexist and racist attitudes that seem to underlie the script in its original production). The energy with which it is performed and the pretensions of Lavine during her radio-like expository speeches, make the play, infanticide and all, hilarious--yet significant social issues are foregrounded. The internal production ends with Mother's full throated performance of "Real Gone Cat," which is followed by hope-filled plans to drive the van to New Orleans where the troupe will perform *Medea*, although Mother has found the value of the emotionally bitter narrative of Mother Goddam's sale into sexual slavery, which she delivers while the others pack to leave. Their desires are woven into a montage, during which Tammy lip-syncs her country song, Lavine seems in control of decisions, and fears of the characters voiced earlier are apparently confronted. The ending is both upbeat and illusory: think what they will, the van can only be parked someplace else, not someplace better, for such a group.

> The women's activities—fantasizing, bickering, working, rehearsing—overlap to comment, by accretion and collision, on the conditions and possibilities of three apparently downwardly mobile Americans. There is no sentimentalization of poverty here; the actors, white, presumably middle-class, do not pretend to portray real poor people, as so often happens in weepy works about the Downtrodden. Nor do they play themselves, as so often happens in self-serving works about

> Struggling Artists. The characters dreams and obstacles are convincing, while the play itself, through its juxtapositions, criticizes them and the situation that creates them. (Solomon, "Collective" 93)

The characters are all ridiculous and attractive, type-cast because they build on the "invisible" parts (both fantasies and fears) of the company members, while fabulously inappropriate because of the incongruence of the performers and the characters in the interior play.

The piece clearly builds on the cast's ability to make rapid additions of roles and attitudes without dropping the basic characteristics of a focal persona. The acting style, while as presentational as in *Beauty*, is more controlled and more highly textured. Their next piece, *Little Women: The Tragedy*, while using burlesque and play-within-a-play structures, assumes the representational "theory" that *Upwardly Mobile Home* first proposed in its comic assault on a cornerstone of women's and lesbian's oppression: the censoring of vitality and desire.

WORKING WITH OTHERS—1985–1987

Before they could begin new work, however, old pressures had to be released. In 1985, WOW lost its lease and had to move. Since Margolin did not want to tour regularly, Shaw and Weaver focused on reestablishing WOW. For the next two years, the company did tour now and again and spent a little time performing in Europe, but it did not develop any new pieces. The members found that they had to deal with some conflicting needs, but that they did not want to dissolve the company. "One thing that helps us stay together is our ability, at the right moment, to separate and do other work" (Weaver, interview).

Weaver began to direct more for other groups while Shaw designed shows at WOW and performed in several other people's productions, including Holly Hughes's *The Lady Dick*. Margolin was writing and performing with Reno as half of "Coupla Weirdos" and beginning to write solo performance pieces. In 1985 Shaw and Weaver rejoined Spiderwoman for a revival of *Disgusting Songs and Pukey Images*, but this time in a production that made the lesbian attraction between Shaw and Weaver a clear part of the performance. Since their relationship was a significant factor in their split from Spiderwoman in the first place, this production has been seen as an important indicator of the crumbling of walls that ostracized lesbian performance in the past, even from the most astute political and feminist theatres, although Weaver finds this evaluation "a bit overblown."

It is interesting that in the year when the company members were working alone, Split Britches was still together enough to receive the Villager Award for Best Ensemble, and an Obie (award for excellence to Off-Broadway theatre) the next year, both significant honors.

But Weaver and Shaw still wanted to tour and so began a full length project with Holly Hughes, bringing to the collaboration with this playwright-performer many of the collective procedures that they had developed. Work on the play *Dress Suits for Hire* began with lists of images, stories, and much discussion of performance fantasies (both what Shaw and Weaver wanted to do on stage and what Hughes wanted to see them do). They experimented with workshops on physical development (the "transformation" experiments they did have become a part of Weaver's teaching work). The result was a script that combines Hughes' anger, Weaver's and Shaw's protean performance ability, and the predilection for striking theatrical images apparent in the previous work of all three into "more than a tale of two women's symbiotic and consuming desire for each other; [the play] also weaves a larger tale about the construction of female sexuality and sexual preference in a patriarchal society" (Davy, "Reading" 170).

The script uses long passages of highly charged, "poetic" prose to trace the way in which Michigan (Weaver) and Deeluxe (Shaw), living almost as hermits in a used clothing rental shop in New York City, perform for each other a variety of identities, obsessively dressing their desire in old clothes and borrowed stereotypes, "over-constructing the performative dimensions of their piece, to produce a kind of 'radical presence'...[through which] the operations of theatrical representation are over-determined, foregrounded, and made visible, thereby undermining, paradoxically, the construction of *woman as body* [author's emphasis]" (Davy, "Reading" 158).[12]

As the two women sing, talk to Michigan's mechanical dog and "Little Peter," the pimp-like presence in the fingers of Deeluxe's right hand who takes over her body periodically, they run in circles, as did the women in *Split Britches*, unable to escape into a hostile world, unable to escape from it, and unable to create identities for themselves that would give them some stability in a separate reality. Generating fresh controversy among lesbian theoreticians about the appropriateness of certain imagery and performance decision in lesbian representation, the piece is painful and angry. Even in its humor, it is an assault on the audience visually and emotionally.[13]

Shaw's performance as Deeluxe was riveting, enough to earn her an Obie for performance, an award rarely given to performers who so boldly challenge the political and performance standards of the New York theatre community. However, the performances were very draining and, although Weaver had the release of doing some film work in She Must Be Seeing Things, a relatively realistic film about a lesbian love affair, Split Britches wanted to create a new work together again. In the summer of 1987, supported by a small grant from the New York State Council on the Arts, the company began work on what was to become *Little Women: The Tragedy*, which was described in the flier for their London run as a play "about censorship, Louisa May Alcott, Little Women, pornography, morality, burlesque, and sex. Set in the heaven of our dreams...[the characters] examine their differences, desires and demons."

Little Women: The Tragedy

Their work alone and in collaboration with others definitely influenced their collective process, but company members had difficulty articulating just how. It is clear, though, that the content and some staging choices in *Little Women* integrated outside work. The play's opening monologue, which toys with the way in which idioms define, more than just describe, reality, beginning with the difference between one who "*stands* accused" and one who "*sits* in judgement," reveals the same structural approach that Margolin uses in some of her solo work. "The Singing Dictionary," for example, is described in her flier as "a 25-minute love letter to language that includes the monologue in which Ms. Margolin plays a letter in a word, entitled Silent N."[14] Interestingly, Margolin notes the effect of her collective work on her solos more than the other way around. "I'm able to treat myself in a very collective way. I can admit of all different parts of myself because I'm used to reaching out the arms of my imagination to embrace not just myself, but several people....I bring the same kind of tool [to my solo work], but I tap a different source" or the same source more deeply (interview).

The collaboration with Hughes helps account for a different physical sense about *Little Women*. As in *Dress Suits*, there is a certain daring about the expression of sexuality, coupled with a more direct use of dressing (both the body and the stage) to reveal and subvert the ideology behind gender representation. The directness raised some questions, not to mention eyebrows, particularly among feminists who accused company members of displaying themselves to the delight of men in the audience. In fact, Jerry Tallmer, in an astoundingly myopic review of the play in the *New York Post*, focused on his own sexual reaction and what he perceived to be the group's knowledgeable display of their bodies to tantalize.

The discussion raises a serious question for groups who wish to bring any kind of marginalized theatre "out of the closet": What are the dangers of performing in front of an audience that reads the signs of performance in a different social context than the performers? The company believes that "if you put honest ideas in front of them and do it well, the audience is educated by that to accept [a new point of view]" (Shaw, interview). Company members argue that avoiding certain performance possibilities because of the nature of the potential audience gives control to the very forces their theatre wishes to combat. "I am not going to prepare my performance to avoid titillating a voyeur. I trust where my performances come from and that much freedom I will never give up again....As long as it comes from the right place, I know I am doing the right thing" (Margolin, interview).

It can also be argued, in support of Split Britches' decision, that their visual deconstruction of performance forms which objectify women, especially lesbian women, are subversive, not accidentally self-exploitative. "It is when the arbitrary character of the sign is asserted that the significance of its imposition on one group by another stands out most clearly....[The question must be raised about] what constitutes a potentially counterhegemonic appropriation of an image and what merely restates that image" (Auslander, "Toward" 27). The answer seems to be that Split Britches' every moment on stage is indeed a challenge to the ideology that imposes meaning on signs and gender on actions.

Part of that imposition occurs through censorship. During early discussions about what was to become *Little Women*, the group began to focus on the difficulty of being antipornography and anticensorship. At a friend's suggestion they read *Little Women* and were amazed by Alcott's moral absolutism, which they discovered was also characteristic of the "potboilers" she had published under a pseudonym. Alcott's biography suggested to them that this novel, so eagerly embraced as part of the male dominated canon, was hiding as much as it revealed.

Stage fantasies and desires also entered into the development of this play. For one, Weaver became excited by a text about the way in which designers in the Italian Renaissance created heaven on stage. In addition, the company was still examining the hidden aspects of people who have had their identities imposed on them by social expectations or have made choices which (sometimes secretly) defy convention. Although Alcott was a natural subject for such an examination, so were the company members themselves. Margolin is most "dependent on her brain" of the members in the group, while Weaver has always depended on her body for sensuality in performance and for ideas in the development stage: a fact she believes comes from the southerner's acceptance of self as intellectually inferior (Weaver, interview). The character of the writer, who could remain separate from characters she creates (and that can then be seen on stage as the conflicting sides of her own psyche), allowed for those performance habits to be challenged: Weaver is "the person," while Margolin is her "strumpet" side and Shaw her "preacher" side.

From the darkness Margolin enters. She is wearing a red robe under which she is apparently nude. After eyeing the audience for several moments, in a most feisty manner she begins. "Well I don't know what you expect me to say; I really don't."[15] From the outset, it is made clear that the performance will not be for the audience, but will be *with* them, that they are and will be complicit in the choices made. "The question of address, of who produces cultural representations and for whom...and of who receives them and in what contexts," questions about "the notion of spectatorship, which has been central to the feminist critique of representation and the production of different images of difference" (de Lauretis 168) are immediately raised. In this and other aspects, the production is far more cerebral than the company's earlier work. Heidi Blackwell, company manager, noted that "they did what they wanted to in *Little Women* in terms of exploring the audience and in exploring the spectator" (interview).

Margolin is about to take another 90 degree turn (she had already discussed language, her relationship with the audience, and sex in a sleazy hotel in New Jersey) when Weaver enters in a long robe.

> Someone said to us 'you should do *Little Women,*' so we thought we'd give it a try. And then we became interested in the life and work of Louisa May Alcott and the mystery that surrounds that life. And then we became interested in censorship, and pornography, and morality, and how that might be influenced by set design during the Italian Renaissance. And then we became interested in burlesque as a style, and then we became interested in sex. For those of you who fear for your mortal souls...all of you vice crusaders, self-appointed vigilantes, and drama critics—this is not a theatre, it's a hall, and this is not a show, it's a concert, a lecture,...a dissertation,...and we are here for your literary entertainment."

Shaw stamps on, yells "Hit it, maestro," and the play proper begins.

The cast reenters, although all that is visible of them are their feet under a sheet that hangs from a very large umbrella. They have a conversation as Meg (Shaw), Amy (Margolin), and Jo (Weaver) from the novel about writer's block and Jo's "boyishness." Suddenly three pairs of binoculars appear from under the umbrella and the audience is on display. The cast mutters, "oh god," and the like until the umbrella flies up, revealing the nude cast members before a quick blackout. Margolin's voice asks for that to be rolled back again, there is another brief nude tableaux, and she says "Uh huh, just what I thought" in a "superior" tone.

When we again see the cast, they are dressed as angels. During the next scene they discover that they are all dead, that Weaver's character always knows what the others are thinking ("I'm the writer" she states in explanation), and they begin to assume the personae that they will juxtapose with their characters from the novel to create a visual and associational dialectic that is at the core of the action of the play. There is a rather silly routine with suitcases (all the burlesque routines are overstated, making their foolishness both the source of their humor and the basis for their critique). Weaver, covered by sheer fabric with "strategically" placed leaves, does an unstrip—dressing in bloomers, frilly slip, hoop skirted dress, hat and gloves—literally constructing her gender in front of the audience. Margolin soon appears in teddy and stockings and Shaw enters dressed as a revivalist preacher who more-than-vaguely resembles a carnival barker/con artist and clown. (Obie Award winner Susan Young designed costumes for this production.)

In the midst of all of this, the cast is hanging cardboard clouds with drawings of and directions for elements of a Renaissance heaven setting drawn on them. By the time Margolin introduces herself as "what remains of Louisa May Alcott [whose] life is a play of two characters and since I chose to remain unmarried I play both parts," the anchors of the usual theatre experience have been discarded. "The fabric is constantly torn and then restitched into a new pattern.

The act of unmasking itself becomes a masking—most vividly in the creation of a set out of a set designer's manual. It's not just the character's gender that is in flux, but the characters themselves. It is not just stereotypes, but the very mechanisms of perception underlying them that are thrown into question" (Massa 100). Alcott introduces the other characters by describing her life as a drama of two hands, the right, which supported the family, is the voice of reason, "sweet self-denial," and morality, and the left is romance and, somehow, a man's soul in a woman's body.

Shaw, as the rather sensual revivalist preacher, delivers a spiel ("stand back, I spit when I talk") about "the gray area between the heart and the thighs," Margolin does an off-color song, discusses how it led to censorship, and tries to find out if she can still make the audience members "put their hands in their pockets" (masturbate). Suddenly Alcott enters and the second of several dialogues as characters from the novel, mostly about sex role socialization and Jo's gender "confusion," begins.

These monologues are interrupted by (or they are interruptions of) a variety of performer/character interactions that demand the audience examine its own moral dictates and its own apparatus of reception. At one point audience members are brought on stage to have their pictures taken with cast members while each photo is orally "captioned." At another, Margolin suddenly drops a novel-scene, which was being played by having performers shout to each other from places in the audience on opposite sides of the theatre, because she didn't like it, and begins an argument in which she and the preacher try to justify their lives—the strumpet just fulfilled people's "built-in" desires to see other's bodies, and the preacher "believed everything I ever told anybody."

Weaver as "writer" negotiates a settlement by having them play out a seduction scene in an imaginary garden that she began to describe in her initial monologue (the meeting of her left and right hands). It ends as Margolin and Shaw, "costumed in the tradition of the butch-femme couple, make love wildly and theatrically, unsettling the oppositions which burden the authoress and the lesbian" (Keller 241). The scene parodies the actions and exaggerates the trappings of forbidden heterosexuality; it pokes fun at the moral absolutism symbolized by the priest/whore dichotomy which is made even more absurd in a lesbian context. Margolin, reclaiming the costume and identity of the seductive femme from exclusivity to either sexual desire, is hilarious in this scene, alienating (in a Brechtian sense) rather than titillating, and thereby foregrounding the male definition of female desire.[16]

In a final disruption of the audience's passivity, Weaver suddenly turns to the audience to ask if there are any questions. She alternates answering actual questions as Weaver-the-actress with answering questions from imagined audience members as Alcott, mixing the "real" with the "imaginary." She develops the image of wearing her shoe on her nose (which she actually does) as an action that would attract attention by revealing her real, idiosyncratic self, although whether it is the Weaver-self or the Alcott-self we cannot be certain. As Alcott she denies writing potboilers, asks "must I spend my whole life being loved for the parts of myself I despise," and compares the minor pain of the battle wounds of the men she nursed to wounds "of the lies of little women."

As Weaver, she has fielded questions about herself (Do you bleach your hair—yes), the play (Why not *Little Men*—because the costumes are not as interesting), but mostly about the performance. In London several women in the audience used the opportunity to attack the production as pornographic and to accuse the company members of exhibitionism. More important than the nature of the questions is the company's confidence in its own work. They do not allow the audience's style to dictate their production style, and demand *even in the midst of performance* that audience members examine their own reception attitudes. They present themselves as both subject of the play and object of audience query. "The company members forthrightly implicate their own desires and experiences in the interpolation of the figure of Alcott" (Keller 240) and insist that the audience do the same.

The dialogue with the audience implicates, as well, the accepted pattern of relationships in most theatre. The question and answer period is far more real than either the "realism" of Alcott's novel, which has been shown in context to be a deliberate Victorian lie, or the putting on of character that Weaver did during the "unstrip" scene. However, direct audience address is "not realistic," and the call for questions seems to redefine the terms of performance and reception by allowing the audience to modify authorial intent, to set the agenda. One could argue, however, that this is not a redefinition, but a deconstruction, an unmasking of the actual workings of realism, which"supports the dominant ideology by constructing the reader as a subject (or more correctly, an 'individual') within that ideology. It poses an apparently objective or distanced viewpoint from which both the narrator and the reader can assess the action and ultimate meaning of the text, a pose which makes the operations of ideology covert, since the illusion is created for the reader that he or she is the source of meaning or understanding, unfettered by structures of culture" (Forte 115).

The performance ends with a return to the issues and images of the beginning. While Alcott sits on a swing in her Victorian attire, the picture of the myth of woman, as obviously constructed by a sensibility blinded by convention as the heaven with which she is surrounded, her opposing sides demand to be seen and loved. Margolin slips into the opening monologue at the point it was interrupted, Shaw reads a purple passage from a romance novel, and Weaver hides under the umbrella where she giggles until she collapses. They sing "I know you're hopin' when you're dead, you're dead" from under the umbrella and end with an encore song about censorship, "It's not what I say it's the way that I say it."

Reviewers in New York, Boston, London, and Seattle, where the play opened the National Gay and Lesbian Theatre Festival in 1990, were all positive. Though theoretical debates have arisen among analysts, all agree that the sheer theatrical inventiveness and the striking performance intensity and quality, make this production an exciting experience. In spite of Weaver's claim from stage that the audience is about to see a dissertation, the "techniques both expand and clarify the issues of feminism, female sexuality, desire and differences, pornography, and censorship, and add up to a hilarious and sexy evening of lesbian-identified theatre" (Keller 241).

A NEW RELATIONSHIP—1988–PRESENT

Little Women: The Tragedy was given a first reading at WOW in May of 1987, was reworked in New York, and finally presented as a finished product in early 1988 at the Women's Theatre Festival in Boston. But that product had to go on tour and Margolin did not want to go with it.

Before the *Little Women* project began, the company members decided that the finished piece had to be designed so that someone could be replaced if necessary. Even so, when Margolin made the decision not to go, she was terrified and Weaver was angry (Weaver, interview), but they talked through their feelings, deciding that it was better to continue performing in this way than either not perform (not go because one collective member did not want to go), or force an action by one member. The notion of consensus was in this way balanced with personal need to negotiate a separation rather than precipitate a rupture. The decision of this company, whose work is so clearly based in personal experience, to make provisions for new performers stands in sharp contrast to the limited, and ultimately destructive, performance possibilities of the United Mime Workers.

The difficulties of touring and the differing desires of company members are much like those of other collectives. For one, attitudes differ—Margolin is a homebody who says Weaver and Shaw are "like turtles." Weaver notes that one of the things that attracted her to vaudeville was the travel. For another, Shaw and Weaver are a couple. Although they "learned to be a couple but not act as a couple in a group situation" during the year they hid their relationship in Spiderwoman (Weaver, interview), Margolin still feels the pain of separation from significant others and the loss of that support system. Finally, Margolin is interested in exploring themes using heterosexual identified imagery that she feels would not be in keeping with the focus of her work as a company member (e.g., a routine in which she plays the Supreme Court preparing for a date with Russian ambassador Separationov Churchnstate).

Little Women toured Europe with Peg Healy in the role of Alcott's left hand. Weaver describes the experience as "healthy," releasing the worry about resentment, and challenging the onstage habits that she and Shaw had developed. Margolin remained in New York writing solo pieces which she asked Weaver to help direct. The company's most recent show, *Anniversary Waltz*, which is a two person review celebrating Shaw and Weaver's decade-plus together, was partially written by Margolin, who still tours for briefer periods. Their attempt to balance collective connections with individual mobility bode well for the company's continuation, at least as "coconspirators."

A number of projects outside of performance have also occupied the company's time, including Weaver and Shaw's work at WOW. The most radical departure, though, may have been their residency at Hampshire College. Supported by a large grant from the Massachusetts Council for the Arts and Humanities, Split Britches spent several weeks living in Amherst, teaching classes, and adapting the Alcestis myth into "Honey I'm Home" with students. The process used to develop the production resembles the collective creation method the company uses alone. Students are encouraged to open up, tell stories, but mostly to provide images—nearly all of which Margolin worked into the script. The processes of scribing, list making, and impulse work are carried on, even though there is some creative, although subtle and supportive, artistic control assumed by the three collective members. The students were treated with respect. Honest choices from their own experience were encouraged and valorized, while superficial performance choices were gently, but clearly, rejected.

Not surprisingly, the piece bears many resemblances to the company's own work—including the use of music, the inclusion of shocking images, and the offbeat sense of humor in the examination of mainstream modes of representation. When a messenger is asked about Alcestis "Is she dead?" the reply is "She lives, but it would be as true to say the is dead." The chorus claims the same person cannot be alive and dead. "Oh no," replies the messenger, "Did you ever see the Donna Reed Show?"[17] The script examines sex role socialization and challenges stereotypes, but with a jaundiced (or realistic) eye. When Alcestis returns at the end, she is "the woman who missed everything," liberated, but without any sense of why or the battles that had to be fought in the past.

In addition to play development and rehearsals, acting classes were taught to actors and nonactors alike. The classes were based on impulse work, sound and movement exercises, and physical transformations. After warm ups (relaxation and stretching), the classes rapidly moved to their feet, and with commitment and energy truly impressive in a student group, explored their own physicality and, by implication, their reliance on language. Weaver is a truly inspirational classroom teacher, and in the five days that I attended her classes, I observed growth not only in the students' self-awareness and self-confidence, but also in their abilities to express themselves and give life to moments of performance.

It was somewhat surprising to see the company at work after reading descriptions of their personal style. Many critics see Split Britches, because of Shaw and Weaver's butch/femme public personae, as a constant performance that moves on and off stage, but remains a performance. What I saw was a rigorous, constantly driving, and task focused group of theatre workers doing their jobs. Admittedly some of the public perception is fostered by the group. After WOW was founded, "Lois and I [Shaw] pursued the academic community very hard because we realized...that we were being written right out of history" (interview). They have performed at the Women and Theatre conference (held just prior to the Association for Theatre in Higher Education conference and attended by many scholars) and appeared on panels as well. However, they like to "spice up" those appearances. "When we have to be in front of the public, we do tend to dress up to accent stereotypical views of ourselves to cause conflict and discussion" (Shaw, interview). Margolin does not usually attend nonperformance events, and so the image of the company is based on Shaw and Weaver's public sensibility. In addition, much was written when the group was first achieving prominence through their more outrageous WOW-centered performance activity.

Their growing reputation enabled, in January 1988, all of the company members quit their day jobs and depend on performance income since. In spite of the increasing need to tour and perform for financial reasons, the company has not developed the management and advertising procedures one would assume would be necessary for survival. Since early in 1988, Heidi Blackwell has managed the company's touring affairs. She facilitates tours, but "does not function as an agent" (Blackwell), relying instead on word of mouth. In one sense the theatre has developed a circuit—they are very popular in London, where they perform every year, and tour other parts of Europe when possible. In the United States they rely on contacts in New York (especially through Women's Inter Art which provides them with performance space frequently), in Boston, among feminist academicians, and with the gay and lesbian arts community.

Amazingly, the company still functions without a yearly budget. Designers are hired and paid a fee when necessary, but the company members determine their wages according to their performance income. Blackwell receives an hourly wage plus a percentage of take on the road. Although this limits long-term planning, it has freed the company from having to write grants for support--something they will not do unless necessary to safeguard their artistic control--although they have received support from other groups which receive grants (like Hampshire College and WOW).

The 1989 schedule included some performances of *Little Women* on the road, a run in New York, and the residency at Hampshire. Shaw and Weaver finally closed *Dress Suits*, and Margolin continued her duo and single work. *Anniversary Waltz*, billed as a "lounge act" (the New York flier designed to appeal to those who have followed the pair's career noted that it will be performed by "that bitch-in-heat Lois Weaver and that Gary Cooper-eyes like slits, no-smile, violence under the skin Peggy Shaw") opened in the Village, had an extended run at La MaMa in early 1990, and then toured the Midwest.

Anniversary Waltz "reworks highlights from Weaver and Shaw's professional relationship to form a narrative line exploring their personal history in which the conscious performance of gendered desire defines the butch/femme couple as lesbian" (Harris 487). However, even their apparently settled role assignment is deconstructed as Shaw appears in both femme and butch garb and tears off Weaver's butch suit to expose a gown underneath. The concept of gender is overturned as a limitation of freedom and choice—two elements of their work about which Split Britches will not compromise.

Weaver continued to work with WOW as well, directing *Queer Justice*, a piece created in workshops with ten women with varying performance experience. Like Split Britches' own work, this play uses monologues, self-defined fantasy images, and a central grievance—contemporary crime—as structural elements. The cast sits as jury, although each member has individual moments to perform her fantasy and mete out justice. The loosely woven script suggests "a tacit feminist critique of the 'capitalist patriarchy'" (Solomon, *Queer* 366) while it, perhaps more important, provides a collective and communal celebration of the lesbian community for cast and audience alike.

In 1982, Lois Weaver's conservative, religious, Blue Ridge Mountain family came to see *Split Britches*, a play that stages the lives of members of that family who had been marginalized or forgotten because of their eccentricities, their sex, and their sexuality. After the performance the company found Lois Weaver's jubilant father in the lobby bragging about his family—of whom he brought pictures to performances, and about whom other family members added details that were incorporated into the play. Almost eight years later, Weaver said "sometimes we feel marginalized on every level. Peggy and I feel marginalized because we're gay, and our company feels marginalized because it's experimental, and it's experimental and gay so it's marginalized within the gay community because it's not a Broadway musical" (interview). *Anniversary Waltz* examines their own lives, again bringing to the stage the imagery of marginalized women. And yet the company continues to take risks on stage, to be as funny as they know how and as truthful as they can. "The representation of the subject-in-process, practicing resistance, exploding the strait jacket of gender through doing the 'work' of self-inscription on stage, before an audience, is both theoretically and practically a vital, imaginative, political act" (Reinelt 52). They "sing the right songs," as John McGrath might put it, and they sing them well.

NOTES

1. For a full account of the history of WOW see Alisa Solomon, "The WOW Cafe." The entire issue of *The Drama Review* in which this article appears is devoted to examining East Village performance.

2. A number of critics have noted that Peggy Shaw and Lois Weaver seem to be performing the same butch and femme personae on the street that are apparent in much of their onstage work. To Sue Ellen Case, "focusing on the feminist subject, endowed with the agency for political change, located among women, outside the ideology of sexual difference, and thus the social institution of heterosexuality, it would appear that the lesbian roles of butch and femme, as dynamic duo, offer precisely the strong subject position the movement requires" ("Toward" 283). In other words, there is a dialectic tension between the hegemonic assignment of gender and what Janelle Reinelt called "the capacity to choose and shape a variety of subject positions [that] reintroduces agency to the stage" ("Feminist" 54). In their performances, though, even the conventions of butch/femme representation are challenged.

3. It is interesting to note that when this play was adapted for Public Television, a medium that even at its best is designed to respond to the audience's desire for a traditionally structured narrative, the (male) director did not want a close-up of the teacup to be included (Weaver, interview).

4. 74-75. All quotations from *Split Britches* are from the published script in *Women & Performance*, 4, no.2 (1989): 68-95.

5. See Sue Ellen Case, *Feminism and Theatre*, Jill Dolan, *The Feminist Spectator as Critic*, and various essays is Helen Chinoy and Linda Walsh Jenkins, *Women in American Theatre*, among others, for explanations of the distinctions between cultural (or radical), liberal, and materialist feminisms as they operate in the theatre.

6. Particularly confusing to the appreciation of Split Britches work is the view that is all too frequently used to justify "political theatre" by its supporters and vilify it by its detractors (and, unfortunately, has resulted in a number of poor productions). It is the assumption that the *basis* of collaborative (and particularly women's) theatre is rhetorical and political. "All feminist theatres are rhetorical enterprises; their primary aim is action not art," wrote Patti Gillespie, who was quoted by Judith Zivanovic in *Women in Theatre* (210).

7. All quotations from *Beauty and the Beast* are transcribed from a videotape of a performance on June 30, 1986, at WOW.

8. Kritzer (129) was writing about Caryl Churchill, whose work is grounded in collective practice.

9. Margolin interview by the author. The issue arose most dramatically at the University of Michigan when, during a panel discussion following a performance, panelists questioned the male spectators' ability to receive and respond to the production. In an interview with Laurie Stone, Shaw stated: "We defended the men's right. They paid. They stayed for a discussion. And the women on the panel were attacking them—my audience, who I had just worked with an hour and a half. Who I felt very close to." Moreover, the men were admitting to parallels in their own lives.

10. Peggy Shaw pointed to an incident outside the work of the collective to illustrate how much weight incidental staging decisions can be given as "evidence" of the group's intention. During performances of *The Lady Dick*, Holly Hughes was becoming rather violent on stage. On one particular night, Shaw became so incensed that, on the spur of the moment, she turned to the audience and asked someone to call 911. Kate Davy, who was in the audience that night, wrote an analysis of Shaw's place on stage as a "representative of representation" who was asserting that Hughes's presence (as narrator/playwright) was a "crime against representation" to which Shaw's character was objecting, all based on an ad lib, but claimed as central to the production's intended message (Davy, "Constructing" 51).

11. All quotations from *Upwardly Mobile Home* are transcribed from a videotape of a performance on November 17, 1984, at WOW.

12. The script is in *The Drama Review* 33.1 (Spring 1989): 132-52.

13. See, for example, Sue Ellen Case, "A Case Concerning Hughes" and Holly Hughes "Replies."

14. See Deborah Margolin, "N." *Harper's* 276 (April 1988): 47.

15. All quotations from *Little Women* were transcribed from a videotape of a performance on March 25, 1989, at the Women in Theatre Festival in Boston.

16. For a fuller analysis of the A-effect in plays that challenge the ideology of gender, see Elin Diamond, "Brechtian Theory/Feminist Theory: Toward a Gestic Feminist Criticism."

17. All quotations from the Alcestis project were recorded in my notes during rehearsals.

7

Legacies and Futures

> The revolutionary artist should not uncritically accept the existing forces of artistic production, but should develop and revolutionize those forces. In doing so he creates new social relations between artist and audience; he overcomes the contradiction which limits artistic forces potentially available to everyone to the privileged property of a few. . .It is not just a question of pushing a revolutionary "message" through existing media; it is a question of revolutionizing the media themselves.
>
> Walter Benjamin, "The Author as Producer"

The four collectives described in this volume have garnered international respect and produced work that is both theatrically viable and socially responsible. Their organizational strategies, while clearly distinct, are similar to each other in significant ways, the most striking of which are the open communication networks, the equalization of power through access and opportunity to use information, and the development of the *center*.

While the number of collectives in the United States remains small, the phenomenon worldwide is quite different. One could cite any of hundreds of *Madan* theatres in South Korea, Charabanc in Belfast, Philippine Educational Theatre Association (PETA) in the Philippines, Red Ladder and other women's theatres in Great Britain, Teatro Vivo in Guatemala, and many other Latin American companies as proof of this claim. Still, the contributions of collectives in this country, because of their devotion to reinvigorating the theatre through the modification of apparatuses and processes by which theatre is created, is significant. While the future is shaky for individual companies, collective organization will remain a vital choice for activist theatre makers. Problems are certain to beset individual companies, but the benefits that accrue to theatre makers and audiences alike far outweigh the risks.

THE "REVOLUTIONARY" PROCESS

All collective companies that I examined try to develop or maintain a fruitful and collaborative relationship with their audiences. The first step in the process, therefore, is almost always a definition of the community from and for whom the collective will initially create its theatre pieces. Many groups are organized as representatives of a specific community, interest, or ethnic group, such as women, Chicanos, blacks, rural residents, gays and lesbians, or union members. Other groups are more concerned with particular political causes or issues at one time or another, such as nuclear proliferation, rape, sexual abuse, Latin America, or pollution. In any case, a collective usually begins by conducting some research to discover the knowledge or concerns of its community, even if it is only the desultory examination of the collective members' own lives as members of that community. The closer the ties with the community, the less formal this discovery phase need be. For example, the Dakota Theatre Caravan moved into new towns and needed to do significant research, as did Esperanza in Guadalupe, while Split Britches often began knowing that it is subject to the same pressures as those for whom it will perform, as did Esperanza with *La Victima*.

Second, each group subjects the information gained to political, social, aesthetic, and emotional analysis. For some theatres, this is a separate step out of which emerges an understanding of the community's agenda. For others, general political analysis has been agreed on already, and the scrutiny here is to discover a particular issue or concern that the community expresses either explicitly or implicitly. What is developed is an ideational guide by which the needs of the community can be balanced with the needs of the theatre company in the creative process.

Following this, the group works as a unit developing all facets of production. Individual input through open communication channels is mixed in the center and constantly reworked or modified until consensus can be reached about how to proceed, or at least what to attempt. Expertise and personal wisdom are sought, but they too are scrutinized by the vision from the center. This work is, in one way or another, improvisational, even if it only consists of discussion. The free exchange of ideas and responses provides a creative springboard from which combinations of previously dissociated ideas can be launched. The open and supportive structure encourages the exploration of ideas that artists might hesitate to suggest in the more repressive situation of a theatre with a hierarchical structure.

Each collective has discovered that it needs to arrive at a certain level of detail during the improvisational phase. For some, it is a definition of *what* each character, scene, or action needs to accomplish, but not exactly *how*. For others, it is almost a completed script that needs only be polished and staged. It may include a picture of the set or merely a suggestion of the ambiance that the action requires. Costumes may be suggested, actually designed, or merely noted as appropriate to situation and class. Alternately, the work may just be a series of bits and pieces with a tenuous thematic connection at this point.

In any case, the next step for nearly every group is to give individuals with particular training or desire the task of realizing the ideas of the group in a specific medium: set, costume, lights, dialogue, movement, and music. Not only realization, but elaboration, is required. Almost all collectives have discovered that once a member who has participated in the process begins to actualize the group's desire in a particular way, insights into the most productive, communicative, or theatrical means of expressing the creative impulse of the troupe will occur. It is, in fact, in the individual's completion of the group's task that the strength and connectedness of the center reveals itself most clearly, although the process of actualization by individuals is always followed by critical evaluation of the whole and of each part by the entire company.

The process from this point on recycles to various steps, reworking each aspect until consensus is reached on every debatable point. By this time the production has a life of its own and the collective members assume roles that have been determined by the needs of the production rather than a predetermined hierarchy.

The final step occurs *after* the production has been mounted. The company, in alliance with its audience, requests open responses to the production. Many groups conduct more-or-less structured discussions immediately after the performance, while others just make themselves available to audience members. This usually does not indicate that the work was unfinished when it was performed (Split Britches is a notable exception, but so is its relationship to its audience), nor that the theatre group is willing to relegate its responsibility to the public. It is, rather, an acknowledgement that all participants in the theatre-making process shape the form of a theatre piece which, in turn, is a shaping force in the larger social dynamic. That is, theatre is somehow constitutive, and not just reflective. It means that artists in collective people's theatres believe that it is the responsibility of the theatre to reach the people, to serve society as well as art, and that they, therefore, have a responsibility to test the degree of rhetorical success of their work beyond the official mainstream response of theatre critics.

The process, then, is a progressive one in every sense of the word. It is designed to be part of the movement toward social change, and at the same time to provide a place and time in which artists of the theatre can develop their art and craft in a supportive and fresh atmosphere.

> The ultimate vision...is a theatre collective made up of autonomous individuals, struggling to reach consensus. The objective is for each

> member involved to reach full satisfaction in the work, to achieve unity in the production and, in the process, to mirror the possibilities of non-authoritarian organizational structures. In practice, this is no easy task! It is a fine line between compromise and collective responsibility. For us...the research has only begun....But we have seen a glimpse of the human potential and a future (theatre) where all people take action (actors).
>
> A true actors' theatre is a laboratory in human endeavor and never an exercise in self-oppression (Torch 90).

PROBLEMS AND WEAKNESSES

This certainly does not mean that a theatre in which all companies are organized collectively would be a utopia. Collective organization is far from trouble-free. Not only are collectives subject to the task-oriented difficulties of most other small groups, but they seem to have a limited life regardless of operational style. A frequent cause of breakups arises from the desire of the group to maintain itself while, at the same time, fulfilling the needs of (or at least not exploiting) its members. Maxine Klein has gone so far as to advise that from the outset collective theatres should establish some normative obligations even before the nature of their creative process has begun to develop, because

> no matter how in tune with one another people may appear at the start of a venture, as time, poverty, and hard work take their toll, problems can and often do arise....So it is best to be forearmed with a contract agreed to in the calm of careful collective deliberation, the aim of which must be to protect both the individual and the theatre itself. And it is most important to note from the outset that these two sets of needs, though ultimately complimentary, do not always seem one and the same, especially in moments of conflict and particularly because of pressures from the society around us (*98%* 150).

The demands made on members of collective theatres, because of the nature of artistic work and the need for a constantly changing product, are very great indeed.

These pressures, coupled with constant financial struggle, lead to burnout, another problem of collectives. There is rarely time off for collective members, and the demands of the process do not allow for "goofing off." Sometimes an actor can no longer generate the energy to "get up for" performances, and becomes unresponsive, irritable, or even ill. He or she begins to make demands on other members for an unreasonable amount of support, yet tries to flee any disruptions in his or her own normal daily flow. At times, the only cure is separation, and this is particularly disruptive for collectives because of the great difficulty in replacing departing members, especially temporarily.

A third difficulty is that collective working methods can suffer from inefficiency or boredom, because of the need to consider every idea, or from fragmentation, because of conflicts due to either artistic or interpersonal complications. Any of these can disrupt the cohesive unit that is essential to collective creation. Most groups have established, therefore, either formalized or unspecified mechanisms for maintaining cohesiveness, (i.e., for "social control"). For the most part, these mechanisms are designed to prevent either a particular interpersonal difficulty from dominating the affairs of the group, or an individual or coalition from assuming power or increasing its status.

The question of status maintenance so closely relates to both political and practical concerns that it deserves some elaboration. In conventional small groups in the United States, a number of factors that contribute to low status are the result of prejudice. The youngest and oldest citizens (particularly if the eldest are senior citizens) are frequently relegated to low status levels. The same is true of women, people of color, those without money or professional credentials, homosexuals, handicapped persons, and so on. Because ageism, sexism, racism, and elitism prevent full participation for many persons, a great number of creative suggestions are lost to small groups, not to mention to society as a whole. All too often, because conventionally organized groups are tied closely to prevailing societal attitudes, it is impossible for them to modify biases that preclude truly progressive working atmospheres.

Collectives, organized around the principle that everyone must take equal responsibility for getting the work done and for the resulting product, remove these biases as far as possible from their work. This results in increased cohesiveness: something that all experts agree increases productivity and creativity. In spite of their openness in process, though, the manner in which collectives are formed almost always results in a rather homogeneous membership. This unfortunately prevents the collective apparatus from taking full advantage of its own strengths. (In fact, the rarity of racially diverse people's theatre companies is a matter of concern for all progressive theatres.)

There are two other factors that affect cohesiveness: group structure and leadership style. The communication structure in a collective theatre, for example, actually requires participation (some collectives have mechanisms for demanding suggestions from reticent members), thereby increasing not only the flow of ideas, but also each individual's stake in and responsibility for the style and content of productions.

Because there is no designated leader, the organization and effectiveness and of the problem-solving structure become even more important. Most often, the sensitivity of the center recognizes problems quickly and promotes the use of a specific solution process that is unique to the group. However, unlike hierarchies in which the self-perpetuating architecture of the structure demands that each place be filled and that compromises be made to keep a person in his or her slot, the collective can ill afford to compromise basic ideological values in order to maintain structural consistency.[1] The strength of collective organization depends on ideological integrity, and sometimes individuals must leave.

The greatest difficulty for collectives is in replacing those who do leave. Because of the cohesiveness of the groups, and because the collective structure allows for the development of specific processes that reflect the particular needs of group members, the exit of a single member, while not catastrophic, is usually traumatic—so much so that the failure of most collectives can be directly traced to their inability to integrate new people over time.

The reasons for this go beyond process exclusivity. Frequently the people who would like to join a collective bring very different experiential backgrounds into the group. Because collectives, like other organizations, tend to become more rigid over the years, and because so many of the interpersonal processes become traditional but not explicit, it takes some time for new members to become acclimated to the group and for old members to fully trust them. Newer members of collectives often complain that they felt like students when they entered an established group in spite of the group's claim to equality of status and power for every member. Often there is a devaluation of the ideas of the new member at the very time that the group needs new energy and the new member needs to be assimilated into the flow of the process. By the time the group opens up, the new person is frequently gone.

A second reason is that new members are rarely brought in to "fill a slot." A person cannot simply join a collective, read a job description, and begin to work. There is certainly a variety of task-specific organization in most collective theatres, but the structure is so fluid that immersion in the totality of the process is really the only way to participate. The time and energy required of a new member to do this are often excessive.

Finally, the length of commitment necessary is often frightening, especially to theatre makers who are used to task groups that come together for relatively short rehearsal periods and then perform the resulting production for only as long as the public will pay or the actor wishes to stay in the role. Collectives are permanent groups, and while this permanence excludes many, it does allow those who successfully enter collective theatres to engage in a level of exploration into their art through means that are unavailable in any other structure.

The chance for a group to continue to work together for a long period, though, carries its own dangers. The creations of some collectives become repetitive; there is a sense in production that the ideas in the center are inbred or that manifestations of the process in performance are too self-reflexive. The problem arises not because groups run out of stories to tell, but because they do not have the time or knowledge to discover new ways to tell them. It is far more deleterious to a company to stagnate aesthetically than thematically.

However, individual growth and change can be significantly enhanced in a collective. One of the processes that is most disruptive in a conventionally organized small group is that of individual deviance from the group's standards or beliefs. Because a hierarchical structure requires a significant number of normative values to function, it can tolerate relatively little deviation from procedures and almost none from role expectations. In a collective, however, flexibility and independence are increased and great variance of behavior among members is allowed for. Therefore, deviance is much less of a factor, unless it is deviance from a primary belief of the group, and that almost always leads to separation.

Nevertheless, even in a collective, normative social influences and the pressure toward conformity are greatly increased over time. This, it seems, would decrease creative suggestions and minimize the ability of an individual to voice objections, and to resist group pressures that run counter to his or her individual judgment. However, because the functioning of a collective depends on sharing ability and experience, on empowerment through access to and ability to use information, and on full appreciation of the value of each member to the formation of the center, collectives have a tendency in their earlier years to use the pressure to demand "conformity" *not* with a particular set of actions, but with an ideal based on responsibility.

> Normative social influences can be utilized to buttress as well as to undermine individual integrity. In other words, normative social influences can be exerted to help make an individual be an individual and not merely a mirror or puppet of the group. Groups can demand of their members that they have self-respect, that they value their own experience, that they be capable of acting without slavish regard for popularity. Unless groups encourage their members to express their own, independent judgments, group consensus is likely to be an empty achievement. Group process which rests on the distortion of individual experience undermines its own potential for creativity and productiveness. (Deutsch & Gerard 476)

On the other hand, that which rests on the maintenance of a multivoiced center enhances exploration and creative intervention. However, the process of artistic entropy can only be slowed down unless new members bring in new ideas.

Problems arising from struggles for power can also destroy the chance for meaningful consensus and hence prevent the collective from accomplishing any work. In fact, according to Steve Kent, long-time director with the Provisional Theatre collective, "all struggles are power struggles, and...issues concerning power within each group must be dealt with" (Goldbard & Adams 7). We have been taught that the exercise of individual power is the only way to get what we need or to make happen what we think should happen. In collectives, because so many role restrictions have been removed, the temptation is great to resort to "power plays" during periods of frustration in order to get new ideas implemented. In terms of collective organization, the center can be seen as a balance of forces, most of which are aligned toward the accomplishment of certain ends through certain means. When any one member of the group attempts, through the use of individual power rather than the power of a valuable idea, to manipulate the actions of either another individual or the group, disruptions occur in the core of the organization. If the group resists, energies are directed away from the accomplishment of the task. If the group acquiesces without a full consideration of the implications because of a need to "get on," its members feel put upon. In either case, the most basic values of the collective are compromised. At times, coalitions are formed, creating power clusters that destroy the group. For example, the Pageant Players, a highly influential collective theatre of the early 1970s, split over questions of the balance of aesthetic and political concerns and disbanded, in spite of the fact that it had been producing very fine work beforehand. Splits in Esperanza and Spiderwoman were tied to power struggles as well.

Administrative difficulties can also hamper the development or cohesion of a collective. The business needs of an arts collective do not disappear merely because the group refuses to act exploitatively. Financial and administrative affairs can swamp a collective at the time of its most creative spurts. However, when energy or people are diverted to the administrative, and removed from the creative side of the work, then there is the possibility that one side or the other will feel compromised. This accounts for the fact that the business side of collective theatres is frequently so troublesome. Collective members do not want to split the group, nor do they feel it is appropriate to give "outsiders" control of such an important function. What frequently happens is that members of the company take on management roles as additional responsibilities, creating great burdens on themselves and hastening burnout, or that managerial functions are haphazardly performed, exacerbating financial and audience development problems; problems which are particularly acute for theatres with a political commitment to reach audiences, through affordable and relevant productions, who do not normally attend the theatre. Collective members often indicate greater personal satisfaction than in leader-centered groups, though, and this can serve as a reward to offset or balance financial struggles for quite a while.

In spite of their difficulties, most theatres that are organized collectively continue to produce works of high quality and progressive political integrity.

SUCCESSES AND LEGACIES

Although until the recent past, establishment critics rarely reported on their activities (and they were rarely studied in academia), people's theatres in the United States are vital, even though they appear to be under siege at the beginning of the 1990s, while other theatres, in spite of their constant search for the new, still reach only 2 percent of the country. One need only attend the People's Theatre Festival each year in San Francisco, read the announcement of activities by members of Alternate ROOTS (Regional Organization Of Theatres

South) published in that organization's monthly bulletin, hear the discussions at a TENAZ festival, or see the American Festival, to know that there are groups producing theatre that is deeply rooted in the stories and lives of the people and deeply committed to progressive change.

In Europe and, especially, in Latin America and parts of Asia, where the theatre is more closely aligned with the people's struggle (sometimes in support of and sometimes in opposition to a particular government or policy), explorations into theatre outside the ideological repression of hierarchy have been so successful that some theorists in those countries *assume* that a progressive political orientation will generate collective organization. In the United States, as well, the revitalization of interest in collective effort was spurred by the need for a new people's ideology that would spawn images that remained in the public sphere and could replace that of the western, capitalist, archetypical, individual hero, who is supremely successful by material standards, isolated as leaders must be ("It's lonely at the top"), and heroic through actions that validate the system.

It is interesting to note that as people's theatre began to move toward collective creations, avant garde or experimental theatres moved toward individual and idiosyncratic productions. For example, the Wooster Group under the directorship of Elizabeth le Compte produced some autobiographical monologues, while single artists toured the country doing performance art, forms at times so personal that they were inaccessible even to the relatively small audiences who attended. Nonetheless, entire journals were quickly devoted to such productions, while the coverage of people's theatre remained sparse at best.[2] The cult of the individual artist still dominates theatre study, but questions are beginning to be raised about the relationship of the process of creation to the representation of subject in individual, hierarchical, and collective creations.

The companies mentioned in the previous chapters have all achieved a measure of success both in and out of their programmatic realms. Their work has empowered their members, and those people will bring attitudes and expectations to whatever companies they subsequently join or form. It is difficult to speculate on the way in which collective work will affect the activities of members in other realms, but it is easy to see Lois Weaver's collective experience in her teaching, Douglas Paterson's in his organizational work for ATHE, and Roderigo Duarte-Clark's in his efforts to assist new companies. Personally, my own years as a member of the Other Theatre Company have colored my work in the classroom and as a director in academic and even community theatre.

The involvement of the audience in the collective process has empowered theatregoers as well as theatre makers. There are new audiences with new expectations. Some of this is accidental: The small size of companies required actors to play multiple roles. Audiences expecting typecasting and the inhabiting of a role by (or lamination of the role to the physical identity of) the actor were disillusioned. The work of character creation in front of the audience demystified the theatre, and the actor-as-worker—and her or his character—could be seen as choices within the limitations of systemic demands. The demonstrative stance, even during the most emotional moments of work by the Caravan or Esperanza, is essentially Brechtian. The oscillation between the actor and the character (or characters) presents a political and representational position that says, in effect, that "I" as performer am aware of more than the character is and that "you" as audience should try to interpret rather than accept, to become aware of the implications of the representation of character and action.

When successful, this "balancing act" solves the problem of much political theatre in which a character who should not have political awareness suddenly becomes the *raissoneur* (spokesperson for the author), or undergoes an unmotivated and inconsistent shift of political stance. It also denies the so called truth of any presentation, deconstructing the patterns that present the "right" answers and forcing the audience to face the way in which the sign constitutes a reality and embodies an ideology rather than accepting the presentation as a mirror of reality.[3]

Forms of Representation

A second source of empowerment comes from the denial by collectives, both in process and product, of standards of evaluation that are claimed as universal by the dominant power structure. Collectives concentrate on performance, "the place where fiction and reality interpenetrate" (Running-Johnson 179), so collective writing often focuses on the multiple and the transformational. It denies, thereby, the necessity for a unity imposed by psychologically defined character "consistency" and linear narrativity or inevitability, which are the hallmarks of commercial theatre forms.

Collectives also challenge the very concept of form and representation. Historically, form has been considered "a complex unity of at least three elements: it is partly shaped by a 'relatively autonomous' literary history of forms; it crystallizes out of certain dominant ideological structures,...[and] it embodies a specific set of relations between author and audience....The writer finds his choice [of form] already ideologically circumscribed" (Eagleton 26). More recently, forms of representation have been explained as elaborations of forms of perception in the intended audience.

Conspicuously absent from these analyses is a consideration of the embodiment of process in form: of the way in which the form of the performance text represents the author's sensibility (either individual or collective center) as subject and is shaped by the pressure and presence of an ideologically inscribed means of production and its concomitant power structure (hierarchical, collaborative, or collective). Collectively created forms frequently move away from hero worship, rely to a lesser degree on psychology and narrativity, and contain the inescapable ambiguity of humanized and polyvocal political analysis.

Part of this phenomenon can be accounted for by examining the structure of collective theatres. As we have seen, collectives provide a viable, growth-oriented workplace for theatre makers. As traditional roles are questioned and performers are freed from the restrictions of their position in the hierarchy of establishment theatre, each member of the collective is enabled (and perhaps inspired) to contribute more fully than he or she might have in other environments. This feeds the center where unique combinations of ideas are developed.

The dialectic inherent in consensus making is also a tool for motivation and discovery. For some, collective decision making points to the complexity of issues and the usefulness of careful deliberation and analysis. Their search for the resolution of differences almost naturally leads them to a theatre that examines social conflict, and, therefore, episode and history. The Dakota Theatre Caravan's rural epic *Dakota Roads* and the British company Red Ladder's *Strike While the Iron Is Hot* (about the development of a woman's social and sexual political consciousness) are more-or-less typical examples. For others, the process leads to a belief that all voices must be accommodated and that bipolar debates are reductionist, and this often leads them to nonlinear and highly theatrical performances. The layered productions of Split Britches, the segmented plays of Theatre X, and the experiments with systems of composition by UMW serve as illustrations. Both approaches distinguish collective productions from the establishment theatre's concentration on psychology and character in a manner that is nonhistorical and asocial.

This is not to say that collective creations are devoid of character or (a charge that has been made) mired in one-dimensional stereotypes. It only means that the scripts that are developed are concerned with social and political motivations, while the nature of collective work gives the actors the opportunity to then add performance centered "whys" and "wherefores." As Armand Gatti described the process used by his theatre in France: "This attitude allowed us the advantage of expressing or polarizing a character with an idea as a starting point. And because the actors were there on the set, they developed the characters each day through the show."[4]

The goal of such exploration and creation for earlier, more programmatically specific, collectives was a work that powerfully and accurately expressed a political reality through images that could be apprehended more or less directly by the targeted audience. However, fewer people's theatres are targeting audiences as they did in the past. Without abrogating their political stance, a number of collectives have begun the examination of the very medium through which their messages are communicated (the "appropriate forms" debate discussed in Chapter 1 continues). While not every collective process has as one of its goals the creation of new forms or the deconstruction of old modes of representation in performance, collectives are often found challenging the apparatus of performance as well as of creation: the two levels of mediation between subject and reception.

It seems to me that there are currently three developmental trends in the search for counter-hegemonic modes of production in collectives. The first begins with an understanding of what is believed to be the language, and possibly the capability, of the audience. Such beliefs lead to the choice of certain rhetorical strategies and representational modes in performance, choices that have often resulted in widely accepted productions, although they restrict formal experimentation and representational innovativeness. At times they may even obscure the ideology of the company in the interest of cultural respect and accessibility. The works of the Dakota Theatre Caravan and Teatro de la Esperanza are often in this mode. A second trend results from a company's decision to be influenced by an established form, but with an eye to its roots and to the implications of its original historical context. Some of Esperanza's more recent work reflects this decision making attitude, as does the use of commedia dell'arte and melodrama by other companies.

However, because of the nature of the collective center, forms are often deconstructed and reassembled so that their implications are foregrounded and the very nature of the mediation is made translucent revealing (although "through a glass darkly") the unmediated reality of the multipositional subject. This third development, in which the creation process is consciously aligned with the multifaceted and somewhat anarchic possibilities of performance, is apparent in the United Mime Worker's use of mime and montage and in Split Britches' refashioning of vaudeville and burlesque. Both these companies, it might easily be argued, have created modes of representation that embody a process which itself embodies a counter-hegemonic ideology.

THE RECENT PAST AND THE NEAR FUTURE—THE 1980s–1990s

There are reasons to believe that collective practice will have an impact on theatre making and theatre study in the decades to come, especially if we examine the forces that have shaped the recent history of the people's theatre movement in the United States, the arena in which the collective theatre usually functions.

Responding to Change—The 1980s

Disregard for the variety of cultures in the United States was a major concern in the decades between World Wars I and II, as it began to be in the 1980s, but this is only the most obvious parallel between that period and the past decade. For one thing, the early part of the period between the wars was a time of ecstasy. The "war to end all wars" had been fought, the economy was returning to a peacetime level of growth, and the people were concerned with celebrating themselves in a most self-oriented way. The commercial theatre was escapist and reflected a consumer materialism. In many ways, the period since Vietnam has been the same. The seventies were characterized as the time of the "me generation," and the commercial theatre of the time, even when it explored serious matters, no longer examined the "big picture." Instead, it substituted concentration on very small individual or family conflicts for concern with historical analysis, international considerations, or progressive change. The less serious theatre of the period exhibited those who could not fit into society only as comic figures, usually without any implied social criticism. The theatre of the eighties had, then, a background similar to that of the thirties and forties.

However, there were other currents in theatre outside the commercial realm that affected that period, and again there is a parallel. Expressionism and Method acting were the springboards for much of the growth of theatre art then, and the experimental theatre of the sixties provided the same impetus recently. Much of the real innovation between the wars was coming from Europe in response to severe difficulties there. The most lively people's theatre in the eighties was happening in Latin America, and it began to have an effect on people's theatre in the United States. Groups like Teatro Escambray from Cuba, and Teatro Vivo (in exile from Guatemala), both of which have toured extensively in the United States, as well as Teatro Experimental de Cali of Colombia, which has served as a training ground for North American artists and a source of new performance theories for a variety of groups, were very influential here. The "Cultural Brigade" from the United States, which toured Cuba in 1981, brought back a number of exciting ideas, while in the opposite direction, Theatre X's frequent trips to work with the Mickery Theatre in Amsterdam introduced European influences to American audiences and theatre makers. It is important to note that almost every one of these influential theatre companies operates as a collective.

The thirties and forties were very much like the eighties in a number of other ways, each of which provided an impetus toward a vital people's theatre movement. Both were periods of high unemployment, worker dissatisfaction, and a steady reorientation of production facilities toward the military. Over the past few years, as labor's clout declined, there has been a rise of labor and union theatres producing plays that appeal directly to organized labor. As the earlier period had been, the eighties was a time of rapid technological growth, not only in the workplace, but in the home and the theatre as well. Computers have changed the prospects for future employment for many, while they have made possible the development of devices that can make work and leisure more pleasant and productive. In media and entertainment, effects became possible that even a few years ago were unthought of. This kind of rapid change is often disruptive, causing generational conflicts between parents who are used to a different set of tools and children who lose sight of the value of tradition. The demand for innovation causes competition between modes of entertainment, and the theatre has been fighting the same uphill battle against film that it did in the forties. Television has eclipsed both media.

In the political and social arenas, there are many parallels as well. Historical reductionism is a characteristic of both periods, although the devil incarnate was Hitler in the forties, while the source of all evil in the eighties was a either Soviet or Arab leader. Concomitant with such thought, there began a rise in scapegoating and open prejudice, particularly of a racist and sexist nature. The eighties may have been less overt about such things than the forties, but the signs of regression to earlier attitudes are very apparent. Finally, as the direction of any country moves towards protectionism and chauvinism, those with the most to protect in terms of the power structure gather as many signs of their status around them as possible, and the distinctions between the classes, between the haves and have-nots, become clearer. This was also the case in the eighties as it was in the forties.

It is not unreasonable to assume, then, that the arts near the end of the century would respond as they did in the decades between the wars, and there is much evidence to show that this has indeed begun. The commercial theatre has begun to rely ever more heavily on the "carriage trade," raising its prices beyond the means of most people and presenting either sure-shot extravaganzas (e.g., *Cats* and *Dancing*) or resurrections of old chestnuts (e.g., *Brigadoon* and *Death of a Salesman*). Popular music has returned to the safe topics of love and sex, the plastic arts have retreated to museums, and romance novels dominate bookstore shelves. The government, via the NEA, has retreated from public support for the arts, just as it did when it ceased to fund the Federal Theatre Project.

However, also as in the Forties, there is a vibrant world of noncommercial and small producer work that is flourishing. The number of public artists painting murals and helping communities make their surroundings more livable and attractive is on the rise. There are movements in music toward a social consciousness, and there has been a resurgence of interest in folk music and festivals. In the theatre, there are many companies producing theatre that is truly responsive to the needs of the people and is representative of the positive values of their culture and lives. *We Are Strong*, published in 1983 by the Institute for Cultural Policy Studies organized by the Cherry Creek Theatre), listed over one hundred people's art producers, many of which were collectively organized theatres. In spite of the fact that Federal and state supports are decreasing, some of these groups have been able to generate enough of a popular following and, by banding together, enough political clout to remain solvent.

The rising sense of a movement in the eighties led to the formation of a number of support groups for people's theatres and other artists. Alternate ROOTS, "a coalition of community based performing arts organizations and individuals located throughout the Southeast [and] devoted to the nurturing and encouragement of Southern performing artists committed to the creation of an original, indigenous art" (Lerner 16), still provides technical and administrative assistance to its over eighty member artists and groups. Together, the performers reach audiences of over one million each year and constitute a powerful force in the cultural growth of the southern United States.

The People's Theatre Coalition (PTC), composed of ten community-based theatre companies in the San Francisco Bay area, devoted itself to providing performance space for groups and assisting them through financial aid, conferences, and cross-cultural exchange. "No single style of language speaks equally to all Americans—separately, our companies address themselves to different communities. Together, we address the majority. Separately, our companies already serve as focal points of community life for our different audiences. Together, we work to join our audiences, to create a larger community. We look forward to the day when thousands of people will pack theaters, knowing they will see their lives, reflected there" (People's Theatre Coalition flier). PTC sponsored performances by people's theatres on tour in the Coalition's small theatre in the Fort Mason Center in San Francisco, drawing a widely varied audience of nearly 25,000 each year. The group cosponsored events such as the People's Theatre Festival, the Asian American Playwrights Series, and a Performance and Disability Festival. It offers classes and runs a theatre school full-time in the summer.

TENAZ, the organization of Chicano theatres, has remained active through the past decade, giving support to Hispanic theatre makers in the United States and Latin America. It has become a forum for debates on performance theory and political efficacy, a sponsor of festivals, and a liaison with Latin American theatres that tour the United States. TENAZ is particularly supportive of collective creation as a way to touch the pulse of the audience, and is probably more concerned with political or social action as a direct result of theatre performance than any other group.

Other groups, such as the Alliance for Cultural Democracy (ACD, formerly the Neighborhood Arts Programs National Organizing Committee, NAPNOC), provide networking and support for the whole range of cultural workers by focusing on the issues of cultural democracy, artist survival, and governmental cultural policy at the local, regional, and national levels. Even the American Theatre Association (ATA) joined the movement to support a diversity of theatres in the eighties. In its "Position Paper on the Status of a National Theatre in the United States," the ATA's Commission on Theatre Development noted that "there is no real need for an institutionalized national theatre, and we do not believe efforts should be expended to attempt to create one." The commission found "the notion of a national theatre...antithetical to the pluralism that is fundamental to the American way of life" and voiced the opinion that institutionalization runs the risks of lessening quality and invention while inviting "bureaucratic/political intervention." It defined, instead, national theatre as that which already exists and called for a change in policy that would encourage the "flourishment and growth of minority and experimental theatres" and "eliminate governmental funding policies which favor 'well-established' operations" (2). This, of course, is exactly the opposite of the policy undertaken by the Reagan administration's NEA, which has chosen to follow the advice of the conservative Heritage Foundation think tank and the 1965 Rockefeller Panel report, which warned against "popularization" and "democratization" in the arts.

Bolstered by support groups and public response, and given the opportunity to share ideas with other theatres at ongoing festivals and at such special events as the Gathering, people's theatres pursued their goals vigorously, though the results were only mildly encouraging. New audiences have been developed in various parts of the country, and new theatre creators (particularly women, minorities, and rural people who had been excluded from full participation in the theatre for decades) became active contributors to the movement. The theatre did become more accessible as new performance spaces were opened and areas that large commercial theatres avoid were visited by people's theatre troupes. Battles for survival were as often lost as won, and the work of collective theatres remained marginalized and often undocumented, but there are signs of revitalization in the face of ever more vehement challenges from the right.

The Emergent Theatre—The 1990s

According to John McGrath, there are three main elements of artistic production at any period in history: Residual, which draws its sources from previous periods, but still remains vital in the present; Dominant, which "exercises hegemony over the period culturally"; and Emergent, in which "new meanings and values, new practices, new relationships and kinds of relationships are constantly being created" ("Theory" 44). He points to commercial, federally subsidized, and fringe theatre in Great Britain as representatives of the three types, respectively. I believe that it is appropriate to substitute collective theatre for fringe theatre in the Americas.

Assuming that collective theatres, as they develop, continue to produce more progressive work in both aesthetic and political terms, such theatres have the potential to become an ever more influential force in society and in the theatre specifically. As more actors are involved in collective work, more will probably be dissatisfied with the exploitative nature of traditional hierarchies and will demand changes in the structure of theatre making institutions. Collectives have the potential to remain as models of social change, working not only against oppression, but for freedom. As such, they will remain in the vanguard of cultural expression without removing themselves from the people whose culture it is they are reformulating into theatrical statements.

However, in spite of the generally positive picture for socially conscious theatre, there are, and historically have been, a number of problems. The most significant are financial strains, which have been exacerbated in the 1990s by the increasing strength of the political and religious right. In the wake of the recent conservative retrenchment, governmental and foundation monies have become even more concentrated in safe areas, on institutions in the "arts orthodoxy" who claim political neutrality. In the wake of the NEA's punitive actions toward museums exhibiting Robert Maplethorpe's photographs and its reneging on grants to theatre progressives such as Holly Hughes, concerns over censorship have come to the fore. Moreover, in the wake of some highly publicized studies on the relationship between pornography and violence against women, even some of those on the left are calling for limits on what is permissible. The more stridently political theatres of the left and many collectives—whose very process is based on the assumption of freedom of expression—fear the strings attached to outside support. As a result, people's theatres are usually operating on the financial brink, and their members are almost always poorly paid. This is a strain on individuals and the group as a whole, and often leads to self-exploitation or resignation. The Provisional Theatre's Barry Opper, in an open letter, blamed this stress as the most significant factor in that collective's dissolution after fifteen years.

There are a number of possible solutions to the financial problem, but each has drawbacks and some are antithetical to the nature of people's or collective theatres as a whole. For some, grants are essential, but the company must then be certain that it does not alienate the funding organizations. This can amount to self-censorship and lead to a loss of political or artistic integrity. Other groups maintain that merely accepting money from the very organizations that are exploiting the people in the first place is tantamount to selling out. For this reason, many argue that people's theatres need to be self-sufficient. Some answer that grant money is the only way to hold down ticket prices, and that since all capital is tied up in monopoly capital, which was appropriated from the workers in the first place, grants are merely a return of the people's own money to them. The solution that has been used by a number of groups is the creation of umbrella organizations that apply for general artistic grants and then distribute them to people's groups. This puts a buffer between small groups and funding organizations as well as enabling them to participate in competition for the very large foundation sums.

Another possibility is to raise ticket prices. This, of course, would prevent the audiences that the theatre is trying to reach from attending. There is an interesting side effect to this difficulty, however. People tend to assume that things that are inexpensive have little value, and some currently avoid people's theatres just because the cost is low.

The best solution, then, seems to be to attract large audiences at low prices. However, because most collectives perform in communities of limited size and in small houses, "large" has to be defined as "many small" audiences, and this requires frequent performances and much touring. This not only decreases the time available for the creation of new pieces, but it is exhausting and leads to rapid burnout. In addition, it severely inhibits the collective members' other activities and removes them from interaction with the community on which the theatre's existence is premised. Without this connection, the theatre can lose touch with its culture and roots and begin to create in isolation. It is worth remembering that the two collectives studied in this volume that are still thriving return frequently to their community roots: Esperanza moved to San Francisco to have an active community relationship, and Split Britches still develops pieces at WOW with the support of the audiences in front of whom they began.

An inability of collective theatre groups to achieve fuller integration into the activist community is the second major difficulty and has additional causes outside of the financial arena. For one, the theatre is often not taken seriously by those organizations doing other positive community work. It is difficult for theatres to constantly seek out groups to help, yet rarely is a theatre invited to participate in community action otherwise (Polsgrove 51–52). Second, people have been educated away from the theatre as a whole, and political theatre in particular. There is still a remnant of the attitude that theatre people are aloof intellectuals whose concerns are very different than those of regular working people. The theatre itself has been so mystified that people believe that theatre attendance is only for an elite and highly educated cognoscenti. Finally, the alternate life-style and political commitment involved in collectivization lead collective members away from some of the social activities through which they might otherwise come into contact with the community.

What begins to happen is that the theatre loses its ability to act as a positive force in the daily life of its own community. It draws its audiences from those who already agree with its political premise and finds that the same segment of the population is represented while it is on tour. Some, like the Dakota Theatre Caravan and the United Mime Workers, tried to find their solution by performing for audiences in areas where there is not usually theatre, where the people attend and are excited by the concern the productions reveal for their problems and lives. However, when the Caravan felt the need for a home base—for financial and relational stability—it naively ended up as part of a commercial "tourist trap."

Other groups promote spectacles in which the community at large serves as the theatre maker under the guidance (and animation) of the collective members. Some Chicano theatre makers, who believe that the involvement of Latin American theatres with their audiences' daily lives should serve as the American model, feel that contemporary people's theatre "shares fundamental orientations with the dominant profit theatre industry...the performance-centered relationship with the public and therefore, the engagement of the audience in situational, singular and momentary contexts....This is a critical point, since the framework of performance influences the course of communication and ultimately the acceleration or deceleration of social change" (Herrara 4). As a result, everything, including politicization of the audience, must happen during the time of the performance, unless the company becomes involved as an integral tool for problem solving in the community (as Augusto Boal suggests is necessary, but is rare in theatre in the United States).[5]

Most people's theatre makers argue, instead, that one must discover socially responsible and artistically viable methods for manipulating an audience. Herrera examined the Artaudian and Brechtian methods of reaching an audience, concluded that the latter is the frequent model, and then questioned whether *teatros* really take time to find out if their methods work, and if their audiences really understand what is being said (Herrara, "Communicating"). Split Britches, avoiding the Artaudian and the *l'écriture féminine* of cultural feminists,[6] elaborates on the Brechtian model of actor as demonstrator and deconstructs the traditional apparatus of audience manipulation, confronting the audience with the *how* of presentation as the core of its content.

In some ways, the concern here is very much like that of the workers' theatre for a call to action, and also of the experimental sixties theatre for more active audience involvement. The terms of the debate are sometimes even the same. In 1965, R.G. Davis questioned whether Brecht or Artaud should provide a model and concluded that anything that works is acceptable. "But remember," he added, "that they are European sources, and it is America we are confronting: perhaps baseball is the best inspiration" (151).

A theoretical grounding for this debate may be found in the writings of Antonio Gramsci, whose description of the relationship of institutions outside the political structure of the state (like theatres) to that structure, indicates the way in which those institutions (often unintentionally) legitimate dominant ideology and reify its power structure. His explanation points, to me, to the need for a new organization of the productive process to create forms that are *not* the embodiment of hegemonic ideology and do *not* rely on the representational assumptions of that ideology. The search must continue for a way to communicate with and be accepted by audiences. Collectives provide a new route for this search, one that is revolutionary in its dismissal of the hierarchical process, which almost inevitably puts the stamp of its ideology on the product it produces. In this way collectives are more likely to produce interventionist theatre, providing a front for progressive struggle outside existing institutions and practices.[7]

Yet the very structures that can provide a revolutionary break also contain their own exploitative difficulties. As the collective and its members mature, new concerns arise. The difficulty of integrating new members has been discussed earlier, but is worth mentioning again because it is so important, especially in terms of the need for temporary replacements for collective members who wish to assume other obligations or make growth-oriented changes for a period of time. Frequently, the desire to raise a family conflicts with the needs of the group. A pregnant woman must be on leave for a time, and then one parent or the other often needs an additional leave to take care of the child. Touring becomes much more difficult when children are involved, especially as they reach school age. Because most collectives are built around the involvement of

and committed to polyphony" (Keyssar 169).

Even in the best of times this would be difficult, but in the 1990s when it seems there will be increasing repression and diminishing resources, it will be nearly impossible unless new sources of money and energy are found. People's theatre must find new audiences if it is to survive. The carriage trade has no interest in, and in fact is opposed to, theatre that questions the status quo. It, and its financial representatives, cannot be the center of focus for any part of the movement. The assumption must be that the peoples of this country will support theatre if it supports them.

The theme of people's theatre in the nineties, and the decades to follow, must be cultural democracy. This does not mean that issue-oriented theatre is no longer appropriate. Some people may argue that all other concerns pale in relationship to the possibility that we risk planetary destruction. What it does mean, however, is that the theatre of the people must focus even the largest thematic concerns through the lens of the people, and be able to express those concerns through the plurality of peoples who continue to struggle against cultural, as well as economic and territorial, imperialism. "At a time when to invoke the totalizing concept of the political...is to participate in the multinational capitalist enterprise on its own terms, an enterprise which specifically seeks to elide difference and enable everyone quite literally to speak to everyone else, the counterhegemonic interest group is the most plausible locus of radical political action (Auslander, "Debating" 8).

The people need theatres that reflect such pluralism with a sense of the broad society and local community. Collectives like Teatro de la Esperanza, the Dakota Theatre Caravan, the United Mime Workers, and Split Britches, with their multifaceted and interactive centers, provide a structure in which the search for this theatre can be conducted. They provide new models and new perspectives that are free from the constraints of hierarchical structures based on business principles, free from the romanticized competitiveness of individualism, and free from the mystification of genius, process, and art. They are proof that revolutionary change can lead to viable means of creating progressive and quality work in a human and humane manner.

NOTES

1. The ideology here is, in general, commitment to nonexploitative values and the acceptance of political and social responsibility beyond that normally expected in an externally established social system, yet without the rewards or power of individual leadership.

2. The articles in *Theaterwork* and the "Grassroots Theatre" special issue of *The Drama Review* are notable exceptions. Feminist critics have been examining the implications of all varieties of performance in such journals as *Theatre Journal* (the May 1988 issue was on "Feminist Diversions"), *The Drama Review* (Spring 1989), and *Women & Performance*.

3. For an analysis of the representation practices of Brecht, the source of some of the ideas in this paragraph, see Per K. Brask and Helmut-Harry Loewen, "Playing With Distances: a Probing into Brecht's (Re)Presentations."

4. Armand Gatti, "Armand Gatti on Time, Place, and the Theatrical Event," 73. Gatti's play, created in this manner, but based on a book by a Russian dissident, created such a furor that the dissident was released from prison. The ability of the collective process to generate images of great political power has been confirmed frequently in Europe, Latin America, and, to a growing, extent in the struggles for freedom in Asia.

5. The Living Stage Theatre Company, which was founded and directed by Robert Alexander, is not collective, but works as a tool for social change by using theatre as therapy to empower the socially disenfranchised. John Malpede's LAPD (Los Angeles Poverty Department) works with the homeless and poor in L.A. While there are companies for whom animation is central, they are relatively rare and small. Although Augusto Boal's influence is spreading in the United States (he was the keynote speaker at the 1992 ATHE conference and has conducted hundreds of hours of workshops in the United States and Europe), compared to the work of PETA, theatres in the west have just begun to skim the surface of this kind of work.

6. The concept of "feminine writing" was developed by Hélène Cixous in "La Rire de la Médusa" in 1975, in which she presented a theory about the relationship of the female body and the written text.

7. See John McGrath, "The Theory and Practice of Political Theatre," for an examination in this vein of work done mostly by labor theatres in Great Britain.

8. A graduate program with a concentration in People's Theatre was begun by Douglas Paterson at the University of Omaha-Nebraska in the mid-1980s, but could not sustain its funding.

Bibliography

The Bibliography is divided into two major sections. The **Sources Cited** section includes only works which have been specifically referenced in the body of the book or in the endnotes. The **Additional Sources** section includes works which provide additional information about topics or theatres mentioned in the text. Entries are grouped in five subsections: one listing sources related to somewhat broader topics and one on each of the theatres studied in detail. In some cases, entries were included under theatre-specific sections for ease of location, even though the issues they raise may be applicable to the further study of collective process in general (e.g., most works that focus on women's theatre or take a feminist stance are listed in the section on Split Britches, although the concerns they evidence are of broader significance).

In the interest of space, I have chosen not to include in these listings reviews of specific productions unless they were quoted in the text or developed important ideas not found elsewhere.

SOURCES CITED

"An American Festival: A Celebration of Heritage, Community, and the Arts." Program for the festival, September, 17-27, 1989, Cornell University, Ithica, N.Y.

American Theatre Association's Commission on Theatre Development. "An ATA Position Paper on the Status of a National Theatre in the United States." *Theatre News* 15 (March 1985): 2.

Anderson, Jack. "Stage: United Mime Workers Perform." *New York Times* 11 September 1980, sec.3, p.14.

Arnoult, Peter. "The Sixth Theatre in the United States, 1968-1979." Paper presented at the Eighteenth Biennial Conference of the International Theatre Institute, Sofia, Bulgaria, 13 July 1979. Ms. Theatre X archives.

Auslander, Philip, Johannes Birringer, John Bell, and Richard Schechner. "Debating 'Ways of Seeing, Loci of Cognition.'" *The Drama Review* 32,no.2 (Summer 1988): 4-13.

Auslander, Philip. "Toward a Concept of the Political in Postmodern Theatre." *Theatre Journal* 39,no.1 (March 1987): 20-34.

Bales, R. F. "A Set of Categories for the Analysis of Small Group Interaction." *American Sociological Review* 15 (1950): 257-63.

Bavelas, A. "Communication Patterns in Task Oriented Groups." In *Group Dynamics: Research and Theory*. 3d ed. Edited by Dorwin Cartwright and Alvin Zander, pp 503-11. New York: Harper and Row, 1968.

Bechtold, Dan. "Theatre Group Writes Dakota Musicals." *Winner Advocate and Tripp County Journal*, 14 November 1979, sec.2, p.13.

Beck, Julian. *The Life of the Theatre: The Relation of the Artist to the Struggle of the People*. San Francisco: City Lights Books, 1972.

Benedetti, Robert L. *Seeming, Being and Becoming: Acting in Our Century*. New York: Drama Book Specialists, 1976.

Benjamin, Walter. *Reflections: Essays, Aphorisms, Autobiographical Writings*. Edited by Peter Deneto. Translated by Edmund Jephcott. New York: Harcourt Brace Jovanovich, 1978.

Blackwell, Heidi. Interview by author. Urbana, Ill., August, 1982.

Blair, Rhonda. Interview with Peggy Shaw and Lois Weaver. Unpublished transcript, 1986.

Boal, Augusto. *Theatre of the Oppressed*. London: Pluto Press, 1979.

Boston Vocations for Social Change. *No Bosses Here: A Manual on Working Collectively*. Boston: Strongforce Series, 1977.

Brask, Per K. and Helmut-Harry Loewen. "Playing With Distances: A Probing into Brecht's (Re)Presentations." *Journal of Dramatic Theory and Criticism* 2,no.2 (Spring 1988): 69-79.

Brecht, Bertolt. "A Short Organum for the Theatre." In *Brecht on Theatre*, translated by John Willett, pp. 179-205. New York: Hill and Wang, 1964.

Brockett, Oscar. *History of the Theatre*. 3d ed. Boston: Allyn and Bacon, 1977.

Brün, Herbert. "Infraudibles." United Mime Workers archives, photocopy pages numbered 117-21.

Buenaventura, Enrique. "Metaphor and Staging." *Theater Three* 5 (Fall 1988): 47-54.

Case, Sue Ellen. "A Case Concerning Hughes." *The Drama Review* 33,no.4 (Winter 1989): 10-14.

———. *Feminism and Theatre*. New York: Metheun, 1988.

———. "Toward a Butch-Femme Aesthetic." In *Making a Spectacle: Feminist Essays on Contemporary Women's Theatre*, edited by Linda Hart, pp.282-99. Ann Arbor: University of Michigan Press, 1989.

Center for Ecology and Social Justice (part of the Institute for Policy Studies, Washington, D.C.). "Mission Statement." Author's personal files.

Chekhov, Michael. *To The Actor*. New York: Harper, 1991.

Cless, Downing. "Teatro de la Esperanza: 'Actos' of Chicano Culture." *Santa Barbara News & Reviews*, 19 May 1972, p.12.

Chinoy, Helen Krich, and Linda Walsh Jenkins, eds. *Women in American Theatre: Careers, Images, Movements*. Rev.ed. New York: Theatre Communications Group, 1987.

Christon, Lawrence. "Dakota's 'Dusting Off the '30s'." *Los Angeles Times*, 21 May 1980, p.6.

Cixous, Hélène. "La Rire de la Médusa." *L'Arc* 61 (1975): 39-54.

Craig, Edward Gordon. *On the Art of the Theatre*. Boston, 1905.

Crosbie, Paul V., ed. *Interaction in Small Groups*. New York: MacMillan, 1975.

Cumbow, Robert C. "You Won't Forget Mother in 'Upwardly Mobile Home.'" *Seattle Post-Intelligencer*, June 14-20, 1985.

Dakota Theatre Caravan. *Dakota Roads: The Story of a Prairie Family*. Ms., 1980; Revision for performances in Wall, South Dakota, Ms., 1983.Dakota Theatre Caravan archives.

———. "Dakota Theatre Caravan." *Theaterwork* 1,no.2 (January/February 1981): 8-9.

———. *Dusting off the Thirties*. Ms., 1980. Dakota Theatre Caravan archives.

———. "Evaluation of the Kyle Residency." Report for the South Dakota Arts Council. Dakota Theatre Caravan archives.

———. *Welcome Home*. Ms., 1981. Dakota Theatre Caravan archives.

———. "Workshop Offerings." Flier. Dakota Theatre Caravan archives, 1982.

Davis, Ken. "'Playgrounding:' A New Model for Audience Education Part Two." *Theatre News* 15,no.3 (March 1983): 12-13.

Davis, R. G. *The San Francisco Mime Troupe: The First 10 Years*. Palo Alto,Calif: Ramparts Press, 1975.

Davy, Kate. "Constructing the Spectator: Reception, Context, and Address in Lesbian Performance." *Performing Arts Journal* 10,no.2 (1986): 43-52.

———. "Reading Past the Heterosexual Imperative: *Dress Suits to Hire*." *The Drama Review* 33,no.1 (Spring 1989): 153-70.

de Lauretis, Teresa. "Sexual Indifference and Lesbian Representation." *Theatre Journal* 40,no.2 (May 1988): 155-77.

Deutsch, Morton, and Harold B. Gerard. "A Study of Normative and Informational Social Influences Upon Individual Judgement." In *Interaction in Small Groups*, edited by Paul V. Crosbie, pp.463-77. New York: MacMillan, 1975.

Diamond, Betty. "'Brown-Eyed Children of the Sun': The Cultural Politics of El Teatro Campesino." Ph.D. diss., University of Wisconsin, 1977.

Diamond, Elin. "Brechtian Theory/Feminist Theory: Toward a Gestic Feminist Criticism." *The Drama Review* 32,no.1 (Spring 1988): 82-94.

Docken, Midg. "'Dusting Off the Thirties' Offers Depression-era Humor, Music." *St. Pual Sunday Pioneer Press*, 4 May 1980.

Dolan, Jill. "The Dynamics of Desire: Sexuality and Gender in Pornography and Performance." *Theatre Journal* 39,no.2 (May 1987): 156-74.

———. *The Feminist Spectator as Critic*. Ann Arbor: UMI Research Press, 1988.

Duarte-Clark, Rodrigo. *Brujerias*. Original. El Teatro de la Esperanza archives.

———. Interview by author. Santa Barbara, Calif., July, 1982.

Eagleton, Terry. *Marxism and Literary Criticism*. Berkeley: University of California Press, 1976.

El Teatro de la Esperanza. *Guadalupe*. In *Necessary Theatre: Six Plays about the Chicano Experience*, edited by Jorge Huerta, pp.217-57. Houston, Tex.: Arte Publico Press, 1989.

———. *La Victima*. In *Necessary Theatre: Six Plays about the Chicano Experience*, edited by Jorge Huerta, pp.325-65. Houston, Tex.: Arte Publico Press, 1989.

———. Various grant applications, publicity packets, and miscellaneous papers. El Teatro de la Esperanza archives.

———. *We All Have Talent*. Ms., 1976. El Teatro de la Esperanza archives.

———. *Working Together*. Ms., 1976. El Teatro de la Esperanza archives.

Espener, Maida Watson. "Enrique Buenaventura's Theory of the Committed Theatre." *Latin American Theatre Review* 9,no.2 (Spring 1976): 43-47.

Famon, Franz. *The Wretched of the Earth*. New York: Grove, 1968.

Feldman, Bob. Interview by author. Urbana, Ill., August, 1982.

———. "Theatre–Montage." *Left Curve* no. 11 (1986) pp. 57-61.

———. "The Rise and Fall of the CCCCA." *NAPNOC Notes* 5 (October 1980): 3-7.

Forte, Jeanie. "Realism, Narrative and the Feminist Playwright—A Problem of Reception." *Modern Drama* 32,no.1 (March 1989): 115-27.

Friedman, Daniel. "Contemporary Theatre for Working-Class Audiences in the United States." In *Theatre for Working-Class Audiences in the United States, 1830-1980*, edited by Bruce McConachie and Daniel Friedman, pp.197-246. Westport, Conn.: Greenwood Press, 1985.

Gard, Robert Edward, Marston Balch, and Pauline B. Temkin. *Theatre in America: Appraisal and Challenge for the National Theatre*. Madison, Wisc.: Educational Research Services, 1968.

Garson, Barbara. "Short Takes: *Shadows beyond the Benefit of a Doubt: Matters of Fact or Friction*." *Village Voice*, 26 September 1982, p.106.

Gatti, Armand. "Armand Gatti on Time, Place, and the Theatrical Event." Transcribed and edited by Jean-Paul Lenin. Translated by Nancy Oakes. *Modern Drama* 25,no.1 (March 1982): 69-81.

Glasser, D. Scott, for the Dakota Theatre Caravan. Letter of Agreement Proposal to the Actor's Equity Association. 30 August 1979.

——— Interview by author. Wall, S.Dakota, July, 1982.

Glassman, Jeff. *A Buck Apiece*. Ms., 1975. United Mime Workers archives.

———. *Good Piece*. Ms., 1975. United Mime Workers archives.

———. Interview by author. Urbana, Ill., August, 1982.

———. *Just Standing Around*. Ms., 1984. United Mime Workers archives.

———. Letter to Arnau. July 3, 1978. United Mime Workers archives.

Glassman, Jeff. "Notes." United Mime Workers archives.

Goldbard, Arlene, and Don Adams. "Vital Signs: The Gathering & Alternate ROOTS." *NAPNOC Notes* 15 (September 1981): 1-8.

Guerra, Victor. "An Interview with Roderigo Duarte of *El Teatro de la Esperanza*." *Revista Chicano-Riquena* 7,no.1 (Spring 1983): 112-20.

Gussow, Mel. "Comedy: United Mime Workers." *New York Times*, 19 September 1982, p.67.

Halpert, Susanna. "The *Tecolote Visions*: The Dynamics of a Collaboration." *Theaterwork* 3,no.2 (January/February 1983): 23-28.

Hare, Paul A. *Handbook of Small Group Research*. 2d ed. New York: Free Press, 1976.

Harris, Hillary. "Theatre Review: *Anniversary Waltz*." *Theatre Journal* 42,no.2 (December 1990): 484-88.

Herrara, Juan Felipe. "Communicating with *The People* in the 80's: A Critical Review of the 11th TENAZ Teatro Festival." *Revista Literaria de el Tecolote* 2,nos.3 and 4 (December 1981): 1.

Himelstein, Morgan. *Drama Was a Weapon: The Left-Wing Theatre in New York, 1929-1941*. New Brunswick, N. J.: Rutgers University Press, 1963.

Hirsch, Edward. "The Gallous Story and the Dirty Deed: The Two *Playboys*." *Modern Drama* 26, no.1 (March 1983): 84-102.

Hodgson, Moria. "The Art of Mime Has Learned to Talk." *New York Times*, 31 August 1980, sec.K, p.1.

Hoffman, Richard L. "Conditions for Creative Problem Solving." *Journal of Psychology* 52 (1961): 429-44.

Holden, Joan. "Collective Playmaking: the Why and the How." *Theatre Quarterly*, 28-36.

———. "The Melodrama is the Message." *American Theatre* 6,no.7 (October 1989): 42-44.

Huerta, Jorge. *Chicano Theater: Themes and Forms*. Ypsilanti, Mich.: Bilingual Press, 1982.

———. "The Evolution of Chicano Theater." Ph.D. diss., University of California-Davis, 1979.

———. "El Teatro de la Esperanza: Keeping in Touch With the People." *The Drama Review* 21,no.1 (March 1977): 37-46.

———, ed. *Necessary Theatre: Six Plays about the Chicano Experience*. Houston, Tex.: Arte Publico Press, 1989.

———, ed. *El Teatro de la Esperanza: An Anthology of Chicano Drama*. Goleta, Calif.: El Teatro de la Esperanza, Inc., 1973.

Hughes, Holly. *Dress Suits to Hire*. *The Drama Review* 33,no.1 (Spring 1989): 132-52.

———. "Replies." *The Drama Review* 33,no.4 (Winter 1989): 14-17.

Illizaliturri, Ruben Castro. Interview by author. Santa Barbara, Calif., July, 1982.

Institute for Cultural Policy Studies. *We Are Strong: A Guide to the Works of Popular Theatres Across the Americas*. Vol. 1. Manketo, Minn.: Institute for Cultural Policy Studies, 1983.

Jenkins, Linda Walsh. "Split Britches." In *Women in American Theatre*, edited by Helen Krich Chinoy and Linda Walsh Jenkins, pp.310-14. New York: Theatre Communications Group, 1987.

Jenkins, Robert Francis. "A Description of Working Principles and Procedures Employed by Selected Peoples' Theatre Groups in the United States." Ph.D. diss., Florida State University, 1980.

Jones, Welton. "'Tecolote Visions' Lacking in Wisdom, Originality." *San Diego Union*, 25 February 1982.

Jowitt, Deborah. "Can a Doll Drink Water? Can a Man Eat Hats?" *Village Voice*, 17 September 1980, pp.70-71.

Kanellos, Nicholas. "Two Centuries of Hispanic Theatre in the Southwest." *Revista Chicano-Riquena* 11,no.1 (Spring 1983): 17-39.

Keller, Kathryn. "Theatre Review: National Gay and Lesbian Theatre Festival." *Theatre Journal* 43,no.2 (May 1991): 239-44.

Keyssar, Helene. *Feminist Theatre: An Introduction to Plays of Contemporary British and American Women*. London: Macmillan Publishers, 1984.

Kirby, Michael. "Editorial: The Third-World Theatre Festival in Seoul." *The Drama Review* 25,no.2 (Summer 1981): 127-30.

———. "On Political Drama." *The Drama Review* 19,no.2 (June 1965): 129-35.

Klein, Maxine. *Theatre for the 98%*. Boston: South End Press, 1978.

———. *Time, Space, and Designs for Actors*. Boston: Houghton Mifflin, 1975.

Kramer, Mary. "This Troupe Mimes with Satire and a Message." *The Grand Rapids [Michigan] Press*, 24 April 1980, p.83.

Kritzer, Amelia Howe. "Theatricality and Empowerment in the Plays of Caryl Churchill." *Journal of Dramatic Theory and Criticism* 4,no.1 (Fall 1989): 125-31.

Langerman, Deborah. Interview by author. San Francisco, Calif., July, 1982.

———. "Technique as Message." *Theaterwork* 2,no.4 (May/June 1982): 27-29.

———. "Theatre as a Political Tool." *Theaterwork* 1,no.5 (July/August 1981): 30-31.

———. "Towards a Hopeless Theatre." *Theaterwork* 3,no.5 (July/August 1983): 42-44.

———. "United Mime Workers: Champaign, Illinois." *Mime Journal: New Mime in North America* (1982): 175.

Lerner, Ruby. "The Root of ROOTS." *Alternate ROOTS Newsletter*, June, 1982, pp.3-6.

Lewis, Kathy. "Mime at Work—With a Political Twist."*Rochester Patriot*, 4-17 April 1980, p.1.

McConachie, Bruce A. "Reading Context into Performance: Theatrical Formations and Social History." *Journal of Dramatic Theory and Criticism* 3,no.2 (Spring 1989): 229-37.

McCracken, Ellen. "Review of *Guadalupe*." *Educational Theatre Journal* 27,no.4 (December 1975): 554-55.

McDermott, Douglas. "The Workers' Laboratory Theatre: Archetype and Example." In *Theatre for Working-Class Audiences, 1830-1980*, edited by Bruce McConachie and Daniel Friedman, pp.121-42. Westport, Conn.: Greenwood Press, 1985.

McGrath, John. *A Good Night Out: Popular Theatre: Audience, Class and Form.* London: Eyre Methuen, 1981.

——— "The Theory and Practice of Political Theatre." *Theatre Quarterly* 9 (Autumn 1979): 43-54.

Manni, Albert. *The Colonizer and the Colonized.* Boston: Beacon, 1965.

Marak, George E. Jr. "The Evolution of Leadership Structure." In *Interaction in Small Groups*, edited by Paul V. Crosbie, pp.230-37. New York: MacMillan, 1975.

Marcuse, Herbert. "Art in the One-Dimensional Society." In *Radical Perspectives in the Arts*, edited by Lee Baxandall, pp.53-67. Hammondsworth, England: Penguin, 1972.

———. *One-Dimensional Man.* Boston: Beacon Press, 1964.

Margolin, Deborah. Interview by author. Amherst, Mass., October, 1989.

———. "N." *Harper's* 276 (April 1988): 47.

Margolin, Deborah, Peggy Shaw, and Lois Weaver. *Split Britches: A True Story.* In *Women & Performance* 4,no.2 (1988): 68-95.

Margolis, Tina. "Reviews & Resources: *Beauty and the Beast—The One and Only World Famous Vaudeville Review*." *Women & Performance* 1,no.1 (Spring/Summer 1983): 76-78.

Massa, Robert. "Jo's Girls." *The Village Voice*, 27 June 1989, p.100.

Miller, John. "Festival: Teatro Popular." *Other Stages* 5,no.2 (September 1982): 4.

Mincey, Pamela. "Glimpse of the Remarkable World of Mime." *Daily World*, 11 September 1980.

Moreno, Fernando. "Towards a New Latin American Theater." *Theaterwork* 3,no.4 (May/June 1983): 34-39.

Nelson, Joe. Interview by author. Wall, S.Dakota, July, 1982.

———. Letter to the author, 3 September 1985.

Olivara, Anna. Interview by author. Santa Barbara, Calif., July, 1982.

Opper, Barry. "The Provisional Theatre." Paper delivered as part of the panel "Performance Generation: The Director as Composer/Author." American Theatre Association annual Convention, San Diego, August 1980.

———. "A Letter from the Provisional Theatre." *Theaterwork* 1,no.3 (March/April 1981): 13.

Paterson, Douglas. Interview by author. Wall, S. Dakota, July, 1982.

———. "The Living Story." *Theaterwork* 2,no.2 (January/February 1982): 21.

———. "Playmaking with the Dakota Theatre Caravan." *Theaterwork* 2,no.3 (March/April 1982): 7-9.

———. "Popular Theatre and Political Content." *Theaterwork* 1,no.1 (November/December 1980): 12-13.

———. "A Progressive Critique of the Theory of Richard Schechner." *Theaterwork* 4,no.2 (May/June 1981): 13-19.

———. "Some Theoretical Questions of People's Theatre." *Theaterwork* 3,no.2 (January/February 1983): 5-9.

———. "Theatre for a People: The Dakota Theatre Caravan." *The Drama Review* 27,no.2 (Summer 1983): 3-14.

———. "A Working Paper: Towards a People's Theatre." *Theaterwork* 1,no.1 (November/December 1980): 6-9.

Patraka, Vivian M. "Split Britches in *Split Britches*: Performing History, Vaudeville, and the Everyday." *Women & Performance* 4,no.2 (1988): 58-67.

Petrinka, Allen. "El Teatro Begins Eurpoean Tour." *Santa Barbara News and Review*, 14 September 1978.

People's Theatre Coalition. "Flier." Author's personal files.

Polsgrove, Carol. "Curtains or Curtain Call." *The Progressive* 46,no.2 (February 1982): 51-52.

Pottlitzer, Joanne. *Hispanic Theatre in the United States and Puerto Rico*. New York: Ford Foundation, 1988.

Provisional Theatre. "Toward a More Perfect Union—America Piece." *Alternative Theatre* 1,no.1 (September 1975).

Rebitzer, Bob. "Grant Proposal for the Workplace-Oriented-Theatre Groups Project." United Mime Workers archives.

Reinelt, Janelle. "Feminist Theory and the Problem of Performance." *Modern Drama* 32,no.1 (March 1989): 48-57.

———. "The Politics of Form: Realism, Melodrama and Pam Gems' *Camille*." *Women & Performance* 4,no.2 (1988): 96-103.

Reyes, JoAnne. Interview by author. Santa Barbara, Calif., July, 1982.

Reyes, Ruperto. Author's notes on the "Collective Creation Workshop" conducted at the Gathering. St. Peter, Minn., August 1981.

———. Interview by author. Santa Barbara, Calif., July, 1982.

Rezmerski, John. "Small Town Stereotypes Come Tumbling Down in St. Peter." *Theaterwork* 2,no.1 (November/December 1981): 25-30.

Ridgeway, Cecilia. *The Dynamics of Small Groups*. New York: St. Martin's Press, 1983.

Robinson, William. "Festival of American Mime, A Review." *Mime News* 2,no.5 (September/October 1978): 2.

Rockefeller Brothers Fund. *The Performing Arts: Problems and Prospects*. New York: McGraw Hill, 1965.

Running-Johnson, Cynthia. "Feminine writing and its theatrical 'other'" in *Women in Theatre*. Edited by James Redmond, pp.177-84. Cambridge: Cambridge University Press, 1989.

Sainer, Arthur. *Radical Theatre Notebook*. New York: Avon, 1975.

Saucedo, Jose. Interview by author. Santa Barbara, Calif., July, 1982.

Schechner, Richard. *Environmental Theatre*. New York: Hawthorn Books, 1973.

Schmidt, Robyn Sue. Interview by author. Wall, S.Dakota, July, 1982.

Shank, Theodore. *American Alternative Theatre*. New York: Grove Press, 1982.

Shaw, Peggy. Interview by author. Amherst, Mass., October, 1989.

Shaw, M. E. "Some Effects of Problem Complexity upon Problem Solution Efficiency in Different Communication Nets." *Journal of Experimental Psychology* 48 (1954): 211-17.

———. "Some Effects of Unequal Distribution of Information upon Group Performance in Various Communication Nets." *Journal of Abnormal and Social Psychology* 49 (1954): 547-53.

Skloot, Robert. "*We Will Never Die*: The Success and Failure of a Holocaust Pageant." *Theatre Journal* 37,no.2 (May 1985): 167-80.

Solomon, Alisa. "Collective Mobility." *Village Voice*, 13 November 1984, p.93.

———. "The WOW Cafe." *The Drama Review* 29, no.1 (Spring 1985): 92-101.

Split Britches. *Beauty and the Beast*. Videotape of performance at the WOW Cafe, 30 June 1986.

———. *Little Women: The Tragedy*. Videotape of performance at the Women in Theatre Festival: Boston, 25 March 1989.

———. *Split Britches*. Videotape of a performance at the Shanool Theatre, New York City, November 1984. [Script listed under Margolin].

———. *Upwardly Mobile Home*. Videotape of performance at the WOW Cafe, 17 November 1984.

———. Various publicity fliers and bills. Split Britches archives.

Steiner, Ivan D. *Group Practices and Productivity*. New York: Academic Press, 1972.

Steward, Dwight. *Stage Left*. Dover, Del.: Tanager Press, 1970.

Stone, Laurie. "Vixen Fire: *Beauty and the Beast*." *Village Voice*, 19 April 1983, p.105.

———. "Vixen Fire: *Split Britches*." *Village Voice*, 1982.

Suvin, Darko. "Organizational Mediation: The Paris Commune Theatre Law." *The Drama Review* 13,no.4 (Summer 1969): 26-42.

———. "The Mirror and the Dynamo. "In *Radical Perspectives in the Arts*, edited by Lee Baxandall, pp.68-88. Hammondsworth, England: Penguin, 1972.

Swan, Christopher. "A Tiny Masterpiece." *Christian Science Monitor* 28 January 1982.

Tallmer, Jerry. "'Little Women' Just Putting 'Em All On." *New York Post*, 7 July 1989, p.22.

Taylor, Karen Malpede. *People's Theatre in Amerika*. New York: Drama Book Specialists, 1972.

Torch, Chris. "A Letter from Scandanavia about Theatre, Community, and the Future." *The Drama Review* 27,no.4 (Winter 1983): 87-91.

Übersfeld, Anne. "The Pleasure of the Spectator." Translated by Pierre Bouillaguet and Charles Jose. *Modern Drama* 25,no.1 (March 1982): 127-39.

United Mime Workers. "Artistic statement," "Histories," "cover letters," and publicity packets. United Mime Workers archives.

———. *Mime is No Object: The Reproduction of the Working Day*. Photocopy of score, 1978. United Mime Workers archives.

———. Response to author's Questionnaire, p.3.

———. *Shadows beyond the Benefit of a Doubt: Matters of Fact or Friction*. Ms., 1982. United Mime Workers archives.

———. *Shadows Beyond the Benefit of a Doubt: Matters of Fact or Friction*. Videotape of performance and discussion.

Valdez, Luis. "The Actos." In *Guerilla Street Theatre*, edited by Henry Lesnick, pp.195-97. New York: Avon, 1973.

Valenzuela, Jose Luis. Interview by author. Santa Barbara, Calif., July, 1982.

Van Erven, Eugene. *Radical People's Theatre*. Bloomington, Ind.: University Press, 1988.

Vincenti, Claudio. "The American Political Theatre of the Sixties." Ph.D. diss., New York University, 1976.

Voices of Dissent National Network for the Arts of Social Change. "Brochure." Author's personal files.

Walworth, Candace. Interview by author. Urbana, Ill., August, 1982.

———. Letter to author. 26 February 1986.

Wandor, Michelene, ed. "Introduction" to *Strike While the Iron is Hot: Three Plays on Sexual Politics*. London: Journeyman Press, 1980.

Weaver, Lois. Interview by author. Amherst, Mass., October, 1989.

Weinberg, Mark. "Unity in Diversity." *Theaterwork* 2,no.2 (January/February 1982): 6-7.

Weisman, John. *Guerrilla Theatre: Scenarios for the Revolution*. Garden City, N.Y.: Anchor, 1973.

Williams, Jay. *Stage Left*. New York: Scribner's, 1974.

Yarbro-Bejarano, Yvonne. "Chicanas' Experience in Collective Theatre: Ideology and Form." *Women & Performance* 2,no.2 (1985): 45-58.

———. "The Female Subject in Chicano Theatre: Sexuality, Race, and Class." *Theatre Journal* 38,no.4 (December 1986): 389-407.

———. "The Image of the Chicana in Teatro." *Theaterwork* 2,no.4 (May/June 1982): 19-21.

———. "The Role of Women in Chicano Theatre Organizations." *El Tecolote Magazine* 2,nos.3-4 (December 1981).

———. "Teatro Esperanza: Hacia una teoria del teatro chicano." Ms. Translated by Betty Diamond. El Teatro de la Esperanza archives.

Zeck, Jeannie. Interview by author. Wall, S.Dakota, July, 1982.

———. Letter to the author, 2 March 1986.

Zivnaovic, Judith. "The Rhetorical and Political Foundations of Women's Collaborative Theatre" in *Women in Theatre*. Edited by James Redmond, pp.209-19. Cambridge: Cambridge University Press, 1989.

ADDITIONAL SOURCES

Topics

Some useful sources of additional **analysis of small group process** include: Leonard Berkowitz, ed., *Advances in Experimental Social Psychology*, 5 Vols. (New York:

Academic Press, 1964), which includes M. E. Shaw, "Communication Networks," and Ivan D. Steiner, "Perceived Freedom"; Robert S. Cathcart and Larry A. Samovar, eds., *Small Group Communication: A Reader*, 4th ed., (Dubuque, Iowa: William C. Brown, 1984), which includes Ivan D. Steiner, "Collective Action"; Paul V. Crosbie, ed., *Interaction in Small Groups* (New York: MacMillan, 1975), which includes Harold J. Leavitt, "Some Effects of Certain Communication Patterns on Group Performance," and Henry W. Riecken, "The Effect of Talkativeness on Ability to Influence Group Solutions of Problems"; Paul A. Hare, *Creativity in Small Groups: Improving Social Interactions* (Beverly Hills: Sage Publications, 1981); and Paul A. Hare, "A Study of Interaction and Consensus in Different Sized Groups," *American Sociological Review* 17 (June 1952): pp.261-67.

A number of works examine the **history of socially conscious theatre in different periods and/or countries**. Some valuable examples of these are: Peter Ansorge, *Disrupting the Spectacle: Five Years of Experimental and Fringe Theatre in Britain* (London: Pitman Publishing, 1975); David Bradby and John McCormick, *People's Theatre* (London: Croom Helm, 1978); Margaret Croyden, *Lunatics, Lovers, and Poets: The Contemporary Experimental Theatre* (New York: Dell, 1974); Catherine Itzin, *Stages in the Revolution: Political Theatre in Great Britain since 1968* (London: Methuen, 1981); Ross Kidd, "Popular Theatre and Political Action in Canada," *Theaterwork* 1,no.1 (November/December 1981): 11-16; Henry Lesnick, ed., *Guerilla Street Theatre* (New York: Avon, 1973); Ira Levine, *Left Wing Dramatic Theory in the American Theatre* (Ann Arbor: UMI Research Press, 1985); Malone, Diane, "The Small Professional Theatre Movement," *Theatre News* 14 (January 1983): 14; Rockefeller Brothers Fund, *The Performing Arts: Problems and Prospects* (New York: McGraw Hill, 1965); James Roose-Evans, *Experimental Theatre: From Stanislavski to Today* (New York: Avon, 1970); and Arthur Sainer, *The Sleepwalker and the Assassin: A View of the Contemporary Theatre* (New York: Bridgehead Books, 1964).

Many works focus primarily on **one theatre, theatre maker, or theoretician**. Some of the most valuable for background on topics in this book include: Alive and Trucking Theatre Company, *Stage Left* (Minneapolis: Alive and Trucking, 1973); Pierre Biner, *The Living Theatre* (New York: Horizon Press, 1972); Boston Theatre Group, "Statement of Purpose" (Archives, 1981); Bertold Brecht, *Brecht on Theatre: The Development of an Aesthetic*, translated and edited by John Willett (New York: Hill and Wang, 1964); Alastair Davidson, *Antonio Gramsci: The Man, His Ideas* (Australia: Australian Left Review Publications, 1968); Robert Pasolli, *A Book on the Open Theatre* (Indianapolis, Ind.: Bobbs-Merrill, 1970); Edgar Quiles and Georg Schutter, "Theatre for a World in Transition: Excerpts from an Interview with Augusto Boal," *Theaterwork* 3 (July/August 1983): 13-21; Leonardo Salamini, *The Sociology of Political Praxis: An Introduction to Gramsci's Theory*, (London: Routledge and Kegan Paul, 1981); San Francisco Mime Troupe, *By Popular Demand* (San Francisco, 1980); Roger Simon, *Gramsci's Political Thought: An Introduction* (London: Lawrence and Wishart, 1982); Eugene van Erven, *Stages of People Power: The Philippines Educational Theater Association* (The Hague: Center for the Study of Education in Developing Countries, 1989) and the *Educational Theatre Journal* (special issue), "Reunion: A Self Portrait of the Group Theatre" 28,no.4 (December 1976).

Many books and articles discuss or present **theories about art and theatre in general** that were examined in the preparation of this book. Some of these are: Don

Adams and Arlene Goldbard, "Freedom and Diversity: U.S. History & the Challenge of Cultural Democracy," *Theaterwork* 1,no.5 (July/August 1981): 3-6; David Bradby, Louis James, and Bernard Sharratt, eds., *Performance and Politics in Popular Drama: Aspects of Popular Entertainment in Theatre, Film, and Television, 1800-1976* (New York: Cambridge University Press, 1980); Bernard Dort, "The Liberated Performance," *Modern Drama* 25,no.1 (March 1983): 60-68; Josette Feral, "Performance and Theatricality: The Subject Demystified," *Modern Drama* 25,no.1 (March 1982): 170-81; Michael Kirby, *A Formalist Theatre* (Philadelphia: University of Pennsylvania Press, 1987); Dave Laing, *The Marxist Theory of Art* (Atlantic Highlands, N.J. Humanities Press, 1978); T. Murray, "The Theatricality of the Van-Guard: Ideology and Contemporary Theatre," *Performing Arts Journal* 24 (1984): 93-99; William Ray, William, *Literary Meaning: From Phenomenology to Deconstruction* (Oxford: Basil Blackwell, 1984); George Szanto, *Theater and Propaganda* (Austin: University of Texas Press, 1978); Ronald Taylor, ed., *Aesthetics and Politics*, 3rd ed. (New York: Verso, 1988); Adolpho Sancho Vazquez *Art and Society* (New York: Monthly Review Press, 1973); and Edgar Wind, *Art and Anarchy* (New York: Vintage, 1969).

Sources for information about **theatres or theories directly addressing social change** include: Don Adams and Arlene Goldbard, "Special Report: NAPNOC's 5th Annual Conference," *NAPNOC Notes* 13 (June 1981): 1-7; Philip Auslander, "Auslander Wins Last Word," *The Drama Review* 33,no.2 (Summer 1989): 15-18; Roger Hudson, "Towards a Definition of People's Theatre," *Theatre Quarterly* 1,no.4 (October/December 1971): 2; Kees P. Epskamp, *Theatre in Search of Social Change: The Relative Significance of Different Theatrical Approaches* (The Hague: Center for the Study of Education in Developing Countries, 1989); Michael Kirby, "Grassroots Theatre: An Introduction," *The Drama Review* 27,no.2 (Summer 1983): 2; Douglas Paterson, "Popular Theatre and Political Content," *Theaterwork* 1,no.1 (November/December 1980): 12-13; Diane Rothenberg, "Social Art/Social Action," *The Drama Review* 32,no.1 (Spring 1988) 61-70; Richard Schechner, "Ways of Seeing, Loci of Cognition," *The Drama Review* 31,no.3 (Fall 1987): 4-7; Debra Wise, Debra, "Transformation & Communitas," *Theaterwork* 2,no.2 (January/February 1982): 20; and the *Theatre Quarterly* (special issue), "Theatre for Social Change" Issue, 2,no.8 (October/December 1972).

Some additional, but difficult to classify, sources that provided **background** for the book include: "An American Festival: A Celebration of Heritage, Community, and the Arts," Program for the opening of the Cornell University Center for Theatre Arts; Douglas Paterson, "New Emphasis on People's Theatre at University of Nebraska Omaha," *Theaterwork* 3,no.1 (November/December 1982): 54-56; Bernard Reines, "The Collective Method in the Workers Theatre," *Workers Theatre*, May 1931, p.3.

El Teatro de la Esperanza

Additional material about Esperanza or Chicano theatre in general may be found in the following: El Teatro de la Esperanza, "El Teatro de la Esperanza," *Theaterwork* 1,no.2 (January/February 1981): 28-29; Nicolas Kanellos and Jorge A. Huerta, eds., *Nuevos Pasos: Chicano and Puerto Rican Drama* (Gary: Indiana University NW, 1979); Luis Valdez, "Notes on Chicano Theatre," in *Guerrilla Theatre: Scenarios for the Revolution*, John Weisman (Garden City, N.Y.: Anchor, 1973); Adrian Vargas, ed., "TENAZ Festival

IV," in *Chicano Theatre Three: Primavera, 1974* (San Jose, Calif.: El Centro Cultural de la Gente, 1974); and Yvonne Yarbro-Bejarano, "Interview with Jorge Huerta," *Revista Literaria de el Tecolote*, 2,nos.3 and 4 (December 1981): 6.

The Dakota Theatre Caravan

Two other articles that give information about this theatre are Douglas Paterson, "A Call for Regional Histories," *Theaterwork* 2,no.5 (July/August 1982): 50-55; and Douglas Paterson, "Manifesto for a People's Theatre," *The Drama Review* T100 (Winter 1983): 70-73.

United Mime Workers

Articles about mime and composition that are relevant to this theatre include: Susan Block, "America's State of Mime," *Theater* 10,no.1 (Fall 1978): 94-98; Kitty, Cunningham, "Theatre Reports: The New Mime Festival at Dance Theatre Workshop," *The Drama Review* 24,no.4 (Winter 1980): 103-10; Stuart Smith, "A Portrait of Herbert Brün," photocopy UMW archives, (1975); and "United Mime Workers," *Mime News* 2 (May/June 1976): 1.

Split Britches

Much has been written recently that examines theatre from a variety of feminist perspectives. Some of the sources examined in preparation for this chapter include: Judith Butler, Judith, "Performance Acts and Gender Constitution: An Essay in Phenomenology and Feminist Theory," *Theatre Journal* 40,no.4 (December 1988): 519-31; Susan Carlson, "Self and Sexuality: Contemporary British Women Playwrights and the Problem of Sexual Identity," *Journal of Dramatic Theory and Criticism* 3,no.2 (Spring 1989): 157-78; Sue Ellen Case, "A Case Concerning Hughes," *The Drama Review* T124 (Winter 1989): 10-14; Sue Ellen Case, "From Split Subject to Split Britches," in *Feminine Focus: The New American Playwrights*, ed. Enoch Brater (Oxford University Press, 1989); Jill Dolan, "Breaking the Code: Musings on Lesbian Sexuality and the Performer," *Modern Drama* 32,no.1 (March 1989): 146-58; Jill Dolan, "In Defense of Discourse: Materialist Feminism, Postmodernism, Poststructuralism...and Theory," *The Drama Review* 33,no.3 (Fall 1989): 58-71; Jill Dolan, "Gender Impersonation Onstage: Destroying or Maintaining the Mirror of Gender Roles," *Women & Performance* 2,no.2 (1985): 4-11; Maggie Humm, *Feminist Criticism: Women as Contemporary Critics* (Sussex, England: The Harvester Press 1986); Linda Walsh Jenkins, "Locating the Language of Gender Experience," *Women & Performance* 2,no.1 (1984): 5-17; Kathryn Keller, "Theatre Review: National Gay and Lesbian Theater Festival," *Theatre Journal* 43,no.2 (May 1991): 239-44; Dinah Luise Leavitt, *Feminist Theatre Groups* (Jefferson, N.C.: McFarland Company, 1980); Elizabeth J. Natalle, *Feminist Theatre: A Study in Persuasion* (Metuchen, N.J. Scarecrow Press, 1985); James Redmond, ed., *Women in Theatre* (Cambridge: Cambridge University Press, 1989), which includes Jill Dolan, "Feminists, lesbians, and other women in theatre:

thoughts on the politics of performance"; Rebecca Schneider, "Polymorphic Perversity and the Lesbian Scientist," interview with Holly Hughes, *The Drama Review* 33,no.1 (Spring 1989): 171-83; "Sensibility and Survival: The New Gay Arts," *Village Voice*, 28 June 1988, pp.21-39; Michelene Wandor, *Carry On Understudies: Theatre and Sexual Politics* (New York: Rutledge and Kegan Paul, 1986); and Sande Zeig, "The Actor as Activator: Deconstructing Gender through Gesture," *Women & Performance* 2,no.2 (1985): 12-17.

Index

About the Author

MARK S. WEINBERG is Associate Professor in the Communication Arts Department at the University of Wisconsin Center-Rock County. Concentrating on theatre and social change, he articulates the agenda of a focus group on the subject as an active board member of the Association for Theatre in Higher Education. A director as well as a theatre historian, he was a founding member of the Other Theatre Company in Madison, Wisconsin. His articles have appeared in the *Journal of Dramatic Theory and Criticism* and *Theaterwork Magazine*.